THE MOUNTAIN WORLD

SWISS FOUNDATION FOR ALPINE RESEARCH

THE
MOUNTAIN WORLD

1962/63

ENGLISH VERSION EDITED BY

MALCOLM BARNES

LONDON: GEORGE ALLEN AND UNWIN LTD
CHICAGO: RAND McNALLY AND COMPANY

DIRECTED BY HANS RICHARD MÜLLER

ON BEHALF OF THE SWISS FOUNDATION FOR ALPINE RESEARCH, ZÜRICH

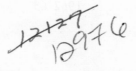

First published in 1964

Library of Congress Catalog Card Number: 53-6419

PRINTED IN GREAT BRITAIN BY
WESTERN PRINTING SERVICES LTD, BRISTOL

ILLUSTRATIONS PRINTED IN SWITZERLAND
BY REGINA-DRUCK, ZÜRICH

PREFACE

In the eleven years of its existence *The Mountain World* has developed into a chronicle of the opening up of the world's mountains, and the volume now before us provides a retrospect over the period from 1960 till the end of 1962, with an occasional overlap in either direction. The material has been arranged in the first place geographically—Europe, Asia, North and South America, Antarctic—and then chronologically within each group. With an eye to continuity, events that have occurred long ago have occasionally been taken into consideration. Finally, outside the sphere of expedition reports will be found a paper on avalanches and a description of a balloon flight over the alpine region.

To publish only authentic reports by members of the expeditions has become for us an obligatory tradition. It ensures the worth and durability of the series over and above the interests of the moment, even if this is achieved at the cost of completeness, which in any case is always doubtful. This has never seemed desirable to us; the careful choice of stories has seemed to us much more significant. That these are unequal in form and content is in the nature of the thing: it is a reflection of the diversity of human temperament, in which there lies a definite attraction. Mountaineers are as different from one another as all other human beings. In the realm of expedition reports we are experiencing the tendency of the time towards increased debunking. Winthrop Young, even in his day, deplored the trend towards describing a climb in the style of an engineer's report. But in the end it is man himself, with his own will, feelings and thoughts, who is responsible for all these adventures. For that reason we have not hesitated to give preference to the live and graphic stories —and in this we believe the reader is with us—even though a wholly factual report regarding a climbing achievement must be important. Such a choice is naturally always more or less subjective; it will be made more difficult through the fact that increasingly in the place of fewer and more important expeditions many are concerned with more modest targets. With regard to the need for objective and impartial information, we offer a *Chronology of Himalayan Expeditions 1960–62* in the form of a completely factual table at the end of the book.

The delay in the appearance of this volume is due in part to the late arrival of some contributions and in part to technical difficulties, especially in the making of the illustrations.

Finally, we would like to remember here our editorial colleague, Marcel Kurz, who has had to lay down his pen owing to serious illness. His many years of valuable co-operation in this series of books deserves our most sincere gratitude.

Zürich, November 1963   *Hans Richard Müller*

CONTENTS

Preface v

The North Face of the Matterhorn. By Hilti von Allmen 1

The Exploration of Hell Hole. By Alfred W. Bögli 6

Ballooning across the Alps. By Fred Dolder 19

Avalanches. By André Roch 28

Masherbrum. By Nicholas B. Clinch 40

The First Indian Attempt on Everest. By Brigadier Gyan Singh 50

Distaghil Sar. By Wolfgang Stefan 60

The Uses of Adversity. By Michael Ward 70

Unexplored West Nepal. By John Tyson 92

Nanga Parbat by the Diamir Flank. By Karl M. Herrligkoffer 102

Pumori—The Daughter Mountain. By Gerhard Lenser 127

Peak of Communism. By Malcolm Slesser 133

Wilfrid Noyce. By A. D. M. Cox 144

Mount McKinley from the Southeast. By Samuel C. Silverstein 149

The Stauning Alps of Eastern Greenland. By Malcolm Slesser 161

The South Stauning Alps in 1961. By James Clarkson 187

The Caullaraju System of the Cordillera Blanca. By Domingo Giobbi 197

The Andes of Venezuela. By Douglas Busk 208

Kerguelen Island. By Albert Bauer 215

Investigations of the Ohio Range, Antarctica. By William E. Long 221

Chronology of Himalayan Expeditions 1960–62. By Anders Bolinder 226

MAPS

Distaghil Sar 65

Western Nepal 100

The Garmo Glacier and Peak of Communism 142

Mount McKinley: SE route 152

Mount McKinley: upper route 158

Diamir Face of Nanga Parbat .... verso plate 34

Cordillera Blanca .... facing plate 52

ILLUSTRATIONS

1 Matterhorn from the north
2 Matterhorn: the north face
3 Summit of the Matterhorn
4 Hell Hole: the Great Pagoda
5 Hell Hole: the Western Solitudes
6 Hell Hole: Bivouac II
7 Hell Hole: (a) Selenite crystal
   (b) Calcite roses
8 Hell Hole: The Altar in Altar Passage
9 Hell Hole: the Arabian Nights Gallery
10 From a balloon above the Alps
11/12 From a balloon above the Jungfrau massif
13 From a balloon above the Aletsch Glacier
14 Avalanche on the Trugberg
15 Avalanche on Rakaposhi
16 Route to Masherbrum
17 Above Camp I on Masherbrum expedition
18 The southeast ridge of Masherbrum
19 Route to Masherbrum
20 (a) View on the ascent of Masherbrum
   (b) Willi Unsoeld at the *bergschrund*
21 View from the summit of Masherbrum towards (a) Gasherbrum, and (b) K2
22 Masherbrum, the southeast flank
23 Gasherbrum group with Hidden Peak
24 Everest and Lhotse
25 Everest: the southwest face
26 Distaghil Sar
27 Ama Dablam: the east flank
28 Ama Dablam from the west
29 Ascent of Ama Dablam
30 View from the west bank of the Khola
31 Satal Prasad
33 Primary school at Sallyana
33 Kanjiroba Himalaya from Jagdula Lekh
34 Nanga Parbat, Diamir flank
35 Pumori, northeast ridge
36 Pumori
37 Pik Kommunisma
38 Mount McKinley: the south face
39 Mount McKinley: the southeast face
40 Icewall on Mount McKinley
41 Tundra landscape, East Greenland
42/43 Stauning Alps: Seitne Glacier
44 Central Stauning Alps
45 Stauning Alps, south ridge of the Sefstrøms Tinde
46/47 Stauning Alps, the Sefstrøm and Gully Glaciers
48 Sefstrøm Glacier: Stauning Alps
49 Caullaraju East
50/51 View from the Nevado Vinci and view from the Nevado Queñuaracra
52 Nevado Queñuaracra
53 Kerguelen, south face of Mount Ross
54 Kerguelen: summit of Mount Ross
55 Kerguelen: Morbihan Bay
56 Kerguelen: King Penguins at Cape Ratmanoff
57 Antarctic, at the foot of the Horlick Range
58 Mount Glossopteris, Horlick Range
59 Fossil sites on Mount Glossopteris
60 Antarctic: the endless ice plain
61 Schulthess Buttress, Ohio Range
62/63 Ascent of Schulthess Buttress
64 Mount Glossopteris: (a) fossil shells, and (b) fossilized tree trunk

1 MATTERHORN (4477.5 m.) FROM THE NORTH. At the extreme left, the Furggen Ridge; in front of it, dividing light and shadow, the Hörnli Ridge; on the right, the Zmutt Ridge; between them, the steep North Face; in the foreground, the Matterhorn Glacier. In the lower left corner, the houses of Stafelalp. (Aerial photograph by Bradford Washburn)

2 MATTERHORN (4477.5 m.). The wintry North Face. It was first climbed in August, 1931, and the first winter ascent succeeded in February, 1962. (Aerial photograph by Bradford Washburn)

3 SUMMIT OF THE MATTERHORN with the upper part of the North Face. In the foreground is the Northeast- or Hörnli Ridge with the Shoulder. The summit is a narrow crest, 250 feet long, and nearly horizontal. The eastern end (at the left), where the Hörnli- and the Furggen Ridges meet, is known as the Swiss Summit. At the western or Italian Summit (at the right) the Zmutt- and Lion Ridges meet. (Aerial photograph by Bradford Washburn)

THE NORTH FACE OF THE MATTERHORN

THE FIRST WINTER ASCENT

By Hilti von Allmen

It was seven o'clock in the evening of February 3, 1962. Beside me Paul Etter had just fired a green rocket flare. It was a signal to our friends in the valley, signifying: "Everything all right." A red rocket, on the other hand. . . . Expectantly, we watched in the direction of Zermatt. The signal had worked! Repeated light flashes meant that we had been understood. And then we saw lights flickering at us from all over the valley.

We were standing at a height of about 13,450 feet in the north face of the Matterhorn and had been cooking soup and tea for almost an hour. Now Paul tried to get into his sleeping bag. This was a tricky problem, for the bulge on which we stood hardly afforded room to sit down. I searched in my overloaded rucksack for the radio and the bivouac equipment. I had to be careful of every movement, because it was very cold and I was afraid I might lose something. In fact, just below this bivouac site my crampons had slipped away. I still felt my dismay when they had first slowly rolled down over the ice and then had suddenly disappeared. Now I hardly dared to make any further movement, and I had not yet told Paul. How I could continue to climb the next day was still a riddle, but I thought that time would perhaps produce an idea, and just now we had time. We would have to sit here for twelve hours.

At last I too managed to squeeze into my sleeping bag. My feet were in rope slings, and I had Paul's shoulder as a prop for my head. And so we sat brooding, without the stones beneath us getting any softer or warmer. A pair of trusty pitons prevented any sliding from the bulge. Our radio was working, and we listened in suspense to the weather report. It prophesied a west wind with snow beginning in the afternoon. And it would become colder.

"That's all we needed," grumbled Paul, but when we discussed the report we grew calmer. For we had observed that this wind would blow the snow from the face, and also that, according to our plans, we should reach the summit by afternoon, or at least have climbed so high that we could traverse out of the top part of the wall to escape onto the Hörnli ridge. How strange it was for us to listen to a news report of our climb. Here we stood in the middle of our adventure, and suddenly we felt like onlookers. What would they now be thinking at home? Surely our families would be

B

worried. Luckily the report was calm and sober. To spare our batteries we turned the radio off.

In the silence and inactivity I became oppressed by worries about the next day: what would happen now that I had lost my crampons? I must tell Paul, and so I asked him casually what he would do if he were at this point without crampons.

"I'd climb on!"

"Really?"

"Well, we have most of the traverses behind us, and on the vertical pitches you could help me with a tight rope from above, and it is not much further to the summit."

Good old Paul! He swallowed hard and became as dumb as a fish when he heard that it would be he who would have to pull me up the next day!

Far down below we heard a hammer pounding. That must be our comrades, three Germans and two Austrians. These two ropes had started with us at three-thirty that morning from the Hörnli hut. The first third of the face proved to be heavily covered with ice, and we had apparently had more practice on ice. As long as possible, we left the belay pitons in the face for their use, but after two hours we agreed to remove them again, for there was too much difference in the speed of the three parties. We did not want to wait. We had to consider the weight we must carry, and the number of our pitons was limited, and the last man had to remove them and pass them back to the leader to use again. So we wished each other luck and climbed ahead by ourselves. That had been well over twelve hours earlier. The hammer blows that now resounded to us through the gloom meant that our comrades were preparing their bivouac below. It would not be a comfortable one. We had climbed 2,600 feet today without seeing a single well-defined ledge. Everything in this face sloped steeply into the enormous depths.

Nevertheless, I was content to be where we were at last, for we were fulfilling a wish which every alpinist has in his head: to be the first to succeed on a route which no one before us had done in winter. We were entirely dependent on our own resources, on our ingenuity, on our strength. In winter this face was virgin territory, and the conditions with which we were faced were correspondingly hard. But I had a feeling of confidence. I thought of the years of careful preparation, the constant practice on ever more difficult rock and ice. From love of the mountains and pleasure in climbing I had given up my profession as a mechanic five years before and had become a guide. In the past two years I had contemplated many a climb which is rated high by modern climbing standards. But as compared with the north face of the Eiger, for instance, where one must follow well-worn traces, I regarded this face as my real master's examination. Here I would show whether I was competent, beyond a mastery of technical difficulties, to lead a great alpine undertaking with a multiple challenge.

2

For the nth time Paul poked me in the ribs: "Don't fall asleep!"

"I'm thinking."

"But you're so quiet."

"I don't usually make a noise when I'm thinking!" But Paul remained dissatisfied until I accompanied his song. It was a duet of yawns and teeth rattling. We estimated the temperature to be at least 30° below zero Centigrade. The village lights of Zermatt shimmered up through the night frost. We thought of warm beds and shivered on, hour after hour. I have never enjoyed bivouacing. I have always preferred seeing the starry sky through a window to viewing it through the visor of a parka hood. Our consolation was to be the first to climb the north face of one of the most famous mountains of the world in winter.

A light wind arose, bringing snow. But the snow did not stick—just as we had observed and reckoned on in our plans. Making plans had become practically a hobby with me: I have never yet undertaken a climb without one, and until now I have always been able to stick to them. I have even let my feelings have their say before any big undertaking. For instance, on the day before my proposed start up the north face of the Eiger, I had just completed our final preparations when the news came of the fall of a solo climber. Shaken, we considered this way and that, and drew comparisons to road accidents where one stops, helps and drives on. It was primarily my feelings which told me that in the mountains it is different; so we put off the start of our ascent.

Also, I have always been fortunate in the choice of my companions on the rope. They have shared my wish to think out every detail of a trip in advance and integrate them into the general plan. They have also shared my respect for feelings which have tipped the scales for or against a climb. I have never deliberately exposed myself to danger, and I have always had a prior conviction of the success of an undertaking. To draw another comparison with the road, I must say that I have never regarded mountaineering as any more dangerous than driving a car. We climbers love life just as much as anyone else: we do not toy with death nor are we weary of living. But to quote Erich Kästner: "Let us be honest. Life is always dangerous!"

I cannot imagine a more vexing penance for any sinner than to creep out of a warm sleeping bag in the early morning. Paul creaked like an old stable door. Then came the first steps, without crampons. . . . I noticed at once that henceforward I would have to climb mainly with my hands. I was not used to this, but it worked, for the distance between us and the parties below continued to increase. We climbed and climbed. When I followed, Paul always held the rope taut, so that at the most I only occasionally slipped from a foothold.

The wind increased, but that was no longer important, for we could see already the cross on the summit of the mountain. At 15.30 the hardly believable had become a

3

reality. We were actually standing on the summit. It was February 4, 1962. Shivering with excitement and cold, I tried to get out my camera. Alas, the zipper was frozen shut—naturally! What's more, my fingers were all stiff and refused to move. But at last I was able to click the shutter.

"You'll need a plastic surgeon if you don't massage your nose at once," said Paul. We rubbed and rubbed, but my fingers remained stiff and without feeling. "We'll take care of both face and fingers in the Solvay Hut." Time was pressing, for the weather was worsening. A little earlier we could still see down to Zermatt. Now we stood in driving snow. Inch-long beards of frozen snow grew all over our faces.

I slid down more than I climbed, but Paul belayed. He would never lose his nerve. I knew that my fingers were no longer working and I climbed badly. I could not even grasp effectively the fixed ropes above the shoulder on the ridge. Here and there we stopped to shout to our comrades, who must be somewhere in the summit wall, for we could discover no traces of their having climbed out onto the shoulder. There was nothing to be seen. We shouted in vain. The storm tore the clouds to pieces on the ridge and thundered between the gendarmes and through the notches. It was as though express trains were constantly roaring past. "Go ahead, let yourself go, I'll hold you!" shouted Paul. Despite all our haste, there was no sign of the hut. I was tired and feared for my fingers, and I knew that we would have to bivouac once more.

It would be a forced bivouac. The new snow on the rock, which was not very steep at this point, was already deep enough to dig a hole. Here we waited. Even Paul remained silent. He must not sleep. I was kept awake by the pain that began to bite at my fingers. Paul swallowed some egg cognac which his mother had brewed: it was his pride and our only luxury, for apart from that we had only brought our essential equipment. I pushed my hands up into my armpits. It was a bit warmer there.

Suddenly snow broke in on us and buried us. We struggled free. Apparently we were lying in the middle of a chute. The same thing was repeated at regular intervals all through the night: digging ourselves in, then a snowslide, then digging ourselves out to get some air, and then digging ourselves in again. It was just as well, for in this way we avoided becoming apathetic and we were protected at least a little from the storm.

At 9.30 a.m. on February 5th I stood at last before the Solvay Hut. Paul pulled the ropes down from the last rapelle piton, and I tried to get into the hut. It was snowed up both outside and in to the level of the windows. The snow had forced its way in through every crack. I broke a window pane in order to enter; the room was four yards square, and the table and benches were buried in snow. Yet we knew for the first time that we were again close to human beings, and we felt that the true and only life is in the valleys at home, and that all summit conquering has meaning only in relation to that.

4

But where were our comrades? What had happened? The storm thundered without pause, and the hut groaned in its moorings. We ate, waited, slept. My fingers looked bad: they were hugely swollen and became blue. The afternoon passed, then the evening. The darkness grew, and still our comrades were missing. Several times Paul stepped out of the hut and shouted in the direction of the shoulder. We looked at each other and said nothing, for we shared the same thoughts.

Suddenly there came a knocking. One man reeled in upon us. A gust of wind pushed four others in after him. Our comrades! How wonderful it is when the worst is feared and the best happens. Encrusted in ice they lay or crouched on the floor, but they were safe.

Only towards noon on the following day did the storm relent a little. Together we began the descent which was made easier by friends who climbed up to meet us. In the twilight we reached the Hörnli hut. Champagne is wonderful, but perhaps it was not the right thing for Paul, for he had never touched it before. He thought it was apple cider and was perplexed at his intoxication. Shortly before midnight the cable-car slid down from Schwarzsee. What a lot of questions the people in Zermatt had!

A year has passed since then and my fingers have healed. We received many honours and were celebrated as "heroes" and "victors" who had won a "battle". These military expressions are badly suited to mountaineering. In the face of the huge indifference of the mountains they seem ridiculous to me. It was ourselves, not the mountain, that we had overcome. During those two days we had succeeded in realizing all the possibilities with which we were endowed, and in contemplating this fact, we feel a great inner peace and satisfaction.

THE EXPLORATION OF HELL HOLE

By Alfred W. Bögli

In the heart of Switzerland, in the Muotatal and its surroundings, lies a karst region of 100 square miles, the largest in the country. Its core of forty square miles is between the Pragel Pass and the Clausen Pass. Of these, eight square miles are drained through Hell Hole. Through each square yard about 500 gallons of water seep into the ground yearly, dissolving the limestone, partly from the surface, partly inside the earth. An exact measurement is only obtainable for the naked boulder fields of which four square miles lie above Hell Hole. Every litre of water which seeps in there carries away 50 mg of lime from the interior of the earth. Therefore Hell Hole grows each year by 13,057 cubic feet. Over longer periods of observation the regional hydrographic conditions change noticeably.

Hell Hole comprises several levels corresponding to the different depth phases of the neighbouring Muotatal. The highest known systems of passages, such as the *Himmelsgang* (Heaven's Passage), with an average height of about 3,200 feet, were formed, at the latest, in pre-glacial times.[1] The deepest parts, below 2,300 feet, originated during the great interglacial period or later.

The limestone water level today lies at 2,100 feet at the front, and at 2,180 feet at the rear of the caves. The water therefore has a slight drop, and it flows at about 100 feet per hour. The high water level, by contrast, lies at 2,400 feet at the front and 2,700 feet at the rear. Above these lie the dry passages into which we retreat during periods of high water. At the *Schleichender Brunnen* (Creeping Spring), a stream source at 2,100 feet, the water appears at the surface again.

Cave exploration includes geology, geomorphology, hydrology, chemistry, pedology, meteorology and biology, and occasionally pre-history. It is therefore, like geography, a synthesizing science. It describes the subterranean landscape which is an integral part of the limestone region. Speleology is therefore a geographical science. Because of its vast extent, Hell Hole is an unsurpassable subject for study.

Eighteen years ago, in the Association for the Geomorphological Exploration of the Swiss Mountains (the parent of today's Swiss Geomorphological Society), several individuals volunteered to work on assigned regions. Mine was the drainage area of the Muota, a region with much bare rock. With its length of four miles, Hell Hole

[1] Bögli, *Das Hölloch*. Aarau, 1963.

6

promised an important insight into the effects of the subterranean waters which are the main feature of that limestone region. In 1946 I entered the cave for the first time with research as my purpose.

The history of the cave begins in 1875. Alois Ulrich is said to be the first man to have entered it. The first public mention of it was in the *Bote der Urschweiz* in 1888. Encouraged by Professor Albert Heim, Paul Egli in 1900 began an investigation of Hell Hole and published his findings in 1904 in a dissertation in Zurich: *Beitrag zur Kenntnis der Höhlen in der Schweiz* ("A Contribution to the Knowledge of the Caves of Switzerland"). He measured 14,040 feet of passages. The last record of a prolonged visit dates from March 3, 1907, when three men reached the *Salle Anglaise*. Then Hell Hole seems to have been forgotten. There was an attempt by a Belgian-Swiss company, with management in Brussels, to exploit Hell Hole touristi-cally. In 1905 they laid out 10,500 feet of paths and stairs and installed electric lighting. But the expected stream of visitors did not appear. High waters destroyed the electric lighting, and the copper wires were torn out in 1917. Until a few years ago, Father Betschardt looked after the cave, and with a carbide lantern he showed the rare visi-tors the bizarre shapes, the Chinese Hat, the Knights' Hall, and the Evil Corner.

In 1946 I began my investigations in the part of the cave then known, where, for the time being, I found all the data I needed concerning the activity of subterranean waters. Moreover, I had such confidence in Egli that I regarded his work as having essentially covered the entire cavern.

The impulse to further exploration came from another direction. O. Oranges, a member of the Société Suisse de Spéléologie (SSS), during a study of cave literature came upon a description of Hell Hole by E. A. Martel.[1] In May 1948 he visited the cave for the first time. The results of this induced his friend, A. Grobet, in August 1949, to test the possibility of a subterranean bivouac. This was carried out from September 10th to 17th and was the starting point for many advances into the un-known. The only telephone line left in the caves was one set up by a military unit, for all later bivouacs were too distant from the entrance. During the following years the SSS mapped the entire area described by Egli as well as the entire Himmels-gang area.

Two months later, on November 6, 1949, the Giant Hall was visited by H. Schluchter and the leader of the subsequent Swiss Dhaulagiri Expedition, Max Eiselin, accompanied by F. Fries, H. Nünlist and B. Baur. They ascertained that Hell Hole must extend beyond the region described by Egli. On November 11th I delivered a lecture to the Naturforschende Gesellschaft of Luzern, in which I spoke about Hell Hole. By chance B. Baur was in the room. He immediately contacted me and told me about their discovery. Naturally I offered to assist them with advice.

[1] *Nature*, Paris 1903.

7

A group of cave explorers collected around Nünlist and Baur, and during thirteen weekends, until autumn 1951, this group made one advance after another into the cave. During the summer of that year I concluded my studies on the surface, and was thereafter free for a more intensive exploration of the cave's interior. So began the Arbeitsgemeinschaft SAC-Höllochforschung (Association of the Swiss Alpin Club for Hell Hole Exploration), the ASACH, under the technical leadership of H. Nünlist, while I assumed the scientific leadership.

On December 26, 1951, we occupied the first SAC bivouac, and on February 21st the second. The number of new passages was so great that the chart of the caves soon became a confusing web. In the same winter the SSS also went to work. Consequently the total length of Hell Hole grew to sixteen miles, whereby it was promoted into the front rank of the world's giant caverns.

Two results are especially worth mentioning. The marks chart which I had drawn up was tested, and we still make use of it without change. It was published as the first of its kind.[1] The second result had consequences which we did not suspect. There proved to be an error of 600 feet in the polygonal line: *Riesensaal—Titanengang— Trait d'Union—Himmelsgang—Riesensaal* (Giant Hall—Titan Passage—*Trait d'Union*—Heaven's Passage—Giant Hall). Judging by our measurements, this error must lie in the *Couloir Granges*, which we had not measured ourselves.

W. Burkhalter, J. Gygax, L. Kaiser and I entered the cave on August 15, 1952, for twenty-four hours, to measure the stretch from the *Pilatusstollen* to the *Pas de l'Echelle*. In contrast to the old map, we found that directions changed in a wild zigzag. Obviously our predecessors had been hindered in their measurements by the low passages, only twenty to thirty inches high. It was necessary to measure sixty-three stretches. The error of 600 feet was reduced to sixty feet, which is little in view of the many hundreds of measurements in the entire polygonal series.

As we were returning we noticed the more rapid cadence of the dripping in the *Salle Anglais.* An hour later we heard in the distance a deep rumbling. At the *Todesschlund* (Maw of Death), where usually the silence is only broken by a quiet dripping, there was now a waterfall thundering into the depths. We climbed down beside it, somewhat exposed, for ten feet, and then traversed on a downward-sloping ledge, sprayed with water, to a passage leading to the *Regenhalle* (Rain Hall). But here, in the *Hexenkessel* (Witches' Cauldron), plunging water was resounding on the stones, and beside it a jet as thick as a thigh exploded against a gigantic rock. We came through relatively dry. Then we moved through the absolute silence of the Labyrinth and the Catacombs, westwards to the *Domgang* (Cathedral Passage). From below we heard the noise of a waterfall in the *Wasserdom* (Water Cathedral). By the sound of its splashing we could tell that the cavern was rapidly being filled. We hur-

[1] Bögli, *Im Banne der Höhle.* 1953.

8

4 HELL HOLE. The Great Pagoda in the Pagoda Passage. If one is not carrying bivouac gear, one may reach it after a hike of 18 hours. (Photograph by A. Bögli)

5 HELL HOLE. Descent through the rubble of the Western Solitude. (Photograph by A. Bögli)

6 HELL HOLE. The base camp for the big advances.

7 following page top: AN IDEALLY FORMED SELENITE CRYSTAL from the clay of the Heaven Passage. This form could only be found in a few places in Hell Hole.
   bottom: Calciteroses, a crystallization from the calm, calcium-rich water. (Photograph by A.Bögli)

ried, for our return route led for some distance through the overflow passages. Hardly were we through when water shot into the passage and filled it. At 7.40, seventeen hours after our entrance into the cave, we stood to the west of the *Fuchsloch* (Foxhole) before an uncrossable, wildly swirling stretch of water beyond which the *Kleine Höllbach* (Little Hell Brook) raged. But behind us we were threatened by the *Grosser Höllbach* (Great Hell Brook). If that should now break into our passages, then we would be trapped between two siphons and drowned. The inexorableness of this prospect compelled us to retreat as quickly as possible out of the deadly zone. We now heard the thunder of wild torrents from all sides, where before there had only been small brooks or absolute silence.

In the *Riesensaal* (Giant Hall) we reached our headquarters, which were dry but surrounded by the uproar of the unbridled waters. Here we took stock of our situation. The prospects looked bad. Hardly anything was yet known about the behaviour of high waters. We reckoned we would be imprisoned for three weeks. The state of our provisions was even worse. In our rucksacks were only one day's rations. In the SSS camp and in Bivouac I there were small supplies. Our bivouac equipment was worst of all. Apart from a petrol burner there was nothing. And this at 5° Centigrade and 95 per cent humidity! The rocks were damp. We decided on the severest rationing and meals at twelve-hour intervals.

Twelve hours later Burkhalter and I reached the SSS camp. We found three candles, two pounds of carbide and twelve meals. On the following day Burkhalter and Gygax went off on a long journey to Bivouac I. The *Pas de l'Echelle*, with its smooth, vertical wall, was the biggest obstacle. They mastered it, and after sixteen hours they returned with twenty pounds of carbide, gasoline and a little food. On their way they had eaten only a can of sardines and an Ovosport. Discipline and comradeship! We divided the food into twenty days' rations. They sufficed for 300 to 400 calories, twice daily. But that was better than starving. One can get used to a grumbling stomach.

We improved our bivouac site, and on the sandy side of the *Riesensaal* (Giant Hall) we built a passably horizontal sleeping place. We observed how the water broke into new passages. Thus we gained a unique insight into the behaviour of the high waters, especially those of the *Grosser Höllbach* (Great Hell Brook) which, during the end phase, swallows its own waters with groans and roars. On August 23rd we moved to the *Fuchsloch* (Foxhole) so as to be ready for an attempt to break out, for the water level had sunk considerably. On Sunday, at 9.20, the Cellar Siphon opened with remarkable noises.

At six in the evening we started. The remaining half of our provisions was left behind. An hour and a half later we stood, wet up to our necks, behind the locked entrance to the cave. Outside a violet twilight glowed, and it smelled invitingly of ozone and rain. We broke open the gate and emerged to freedom after 224 hours of imprisonment and deprivation.

We were frightened to learn that we had become the centre of a great hubbub created by the newspapers. Amid all the confusion we only gradually became aware of the rescue team's generous readiness to help and of the people's deep participation in our adventure. Still later, we realized that by our unvoluntary stay we had made unique scientific observations of the behaviour of subterranean waters. These observations would bear fruit in our work for years to come and also provide an important basis for the security of coming expeditions.

The following winter was a great success, despite early appearances to the contrary. At first we met obstacles at every turn. Our explorations seemed to have come to a dead end between the *Riesensaal* and the *Tuffrosensee*. We had set up two bivouacs. I was in the *Glitzertor* (Glitter Gateway) with five comrades. One of the four new-comers, A. Haenggi, was able to transfer to the research team where he became for years my right hand man. The Nünlist group stayed at Bivouac I. From there Baur, Burkhalter and Gygax probed beyond the Burkhalter Lake into an enormous new corridor, the SAC Passage, of which they measured a mile on their first try. During the winter they and their comrades reached the SAC Siphon after an advance of 14,190 feet. Including side-passages, we covered seven and a half new miles during this winter, so that by March, 1953, Hell Hole had been charted for twenty-three miles.

During the winter 1953–54 we moved into our new Bivouac II behind the Burk-halter Lake in a branch of the SAC Passage. From there we systematically explored the side-passages. By analysing our records of the passages I concluded that there must be, in the chamber by the *Kiesburg* (Gravel Castle), a large off-branch that we had hitherto overlooked. There the Nünlist group hit upon a shaft which had caved in after the first few yards. A spirally ascending pressure pipe went around the caved-in area and descended to the old passage beyond it. An abyss of 130 feet led to a low passage which ended in the SAC Passage. We named it the *Verturzgang* (Cave-in Passage).

After the New Year Steffen and I searched for a continuation of the *Rabengang* (Raven Passage) behind the *Ratssaal* (Council Hall). Soon we stood before a pit sixty-five feet deep. Behind a bulging rock I discovered an easily negotiable oblique shaft which led us down to the bottom. Thence we followed a big tunnel, the *Schlundgang* (Pit Passage) eastwards. In places it is thirty feet high. Finally it follows a cleft and ends beyond a lake in two shafts at least 100 feet deep. These have not been explored to this day. The Pit Passage is a part of the great high-water course which at times conducts 530 cubic feet of water per second. In one place, boulders the size of a head had been hurled upwards for twenty-one feet, through a hole thirty-three square feet in cross section, into an upper chamber.

10

In the many ponds of this passage live various types of animals. Among them are planarias, cave isopods, and collemboles. Up to now, thirty-six species of animals have been discovered in the entire Hell Hole. These include two endemites.

The following winter also had a good start. Analysis of the passages led to another success: in a recess not far from Bivouac II, A. Haenggi and I found a hole in the wall and a thirty-foot-high cleft up which we chimneyed to discover access to a complicated system of passages several miles in length. It is connected with the *Jaegerstollen* (Hunter's Tunnel) by various shafts. In our advance we crossed above the lonely caves we had already measured, and came to a passage that was from twenty to forty feet wide, but only from fifteen to thirty inches high. We named it the *Rollgang* (Roll Passage). It ended in a crevice, the *Himmelsleiter* (Heaven's Ladder), which led vertically upward. We climbed it by an easy chimney technique and reached a horizontal "sandwich shaft", that is, a shaft through which one can barely push oneself, lying down. It terminated at the lovely *Weiss-See* (White Lake) which was full of calcite rocks. Beyond this the passage was barred by stalactites, except for an opening of four inches through which the cave wind whistled sharply.

On New Year's Day, 1955, we followed the SAC Passage and the *Hoffnungsgang* (Hope Passage) to the east. At the *Trughalle* (Deception Hall) we split up. The Nünlist group missed the big passage downwards, and in the *Pagodengang* (Pagoda Passage) they found the biggest stalagmites of Hell Hole. Baur, Haenggi, Henseler and I went against the wind and discovered a low tangle of passages which led to a siphon place. There we were met by the gurgle of a brook, and it was obvious that only a slight rising of the water would suffice to seal off the tunnel. A little later we found, somewhat higher, a steep, holdless branch which in an emergency would connect us with the *Pagodengang* (Pagoda Passage) above us. Still higher there followed a gorge-like stretch of passage which led on over several vertical steps. The *Schluchtgang* (Gorge Passage) ends with a width of twenty-three feet and a height of thirteen feet in a confusion of boulders through which the wind whistles. After 202 hours we returned to the surface. Hell Hole had now grown to thirty-four miles, a figure which would have further interesting consequences.

The winter of 1955–56 brought unfavourable weather conditions. An unexpected föhn storm developed during December 3rd and 4th, while we were moving up provisions. An eruption of high waters delayed the return of our comrades for sixteen hours. The second transport group of thirty men moved under the same threat, for it rained up to 3,000 feet. But they returned without incident.

After Christmas the weather was uncertain. The winter was of an Atlantic mild-oceanic type. One of our comrades, who was participating in an exploratory trip for the first time, had a fit of cave-craziness on his second day. He was sitting with a friend in a gloomy, low side-passage of the *Schuttunnel* (Rubble Tunnel), listening to

11

the water dripping from the walls and awaiting the return of a reconnoitring party. Suddenly, without a word, he grabbed his rucksack and fled like a weasel in the direction of the *Schuttunnel* (Rubble Tunnel). There his friend overtook him and found him sitting apathetically on a rock, not knowing how he had got there. Suspecting nothing, the others regarded the whole incident as an amusing occurrence—and then forgot about him.

On the following day began the big journey into the region of the *Pagodengang* (Pagoda Passage). After the first rest stop our newcomer complained of head and body aches. This could be something serious, so I decided with two companions to take him out of the cave. Meanwhile, Nünlist and five other men continued their journey. At Bivouac II it became plain to me that the patient was suffering from claustrophobia. Then Ulrich recalled the occurrence of the previous day. Happily it was nothing more serious, for we could not reach the exit. The siphon in the Styx was closed; once again there was high water! We therefore retreated to Bivouac II and uneasily awaited the others.

In the meantime the advance party had gone to work in the Pagoda System. Suddenly and quite unexpectedly water thundered out of a funnel into the main passage. Nünlist and his two companions fled in the direction of the *Trughalle* (Deception Hall) and were able to warn the three other men who were somewhat further ahead. Water broke in from all sides. They withdrew through the *Hoffnungs-stollen* (Hope Tunnel) into the SAC Passage. However, at the *Dreiecksee* (Three Corner Lake) this passage was filled with water up to the ceiling and had become a siphon. To avoid it, they moved into the *Versturzgang* (Cave-in Passage) which had been discovered two years previously. There Baur pitoned his way up the 130-foot vertical chimney wall. Thus they got around the siphon and arrived exhausted at Bivouac II after nine and a half hours. On New Year's Eve two weather reporters, thoroughly wet, arrived with the news that a thaw had set in up to 6,500 feet. They had been delayed by the high waters of the Styx. We broke camp at once and reached the exit after only 129 hours of exploration.

As we entered the Hell Hole Restaurant, Frau Suter, our "cave mother", approached us waving a newspaper. In it we read that Hell Hole was no longer the most extensive cavern in the world; the thirty-four-mile Flint Ridge Cave in Kentucky claimed precedence. We were surprised, for right beside Flint Ridge Cave lies Mammoth Cave, which, according to the encyclopedia, is supposed to extend for between 100 and 220 miles. Later I received a communication from the head of the National Speleological Society that to date only twelve miles of Mammoth Cave had been measured and that the US Geological Survey estimated that at most it extended to twenty-six miles. But at this time thirty-six miles of the Hell Hole had already been measured, so that, to our surprise and joy, it had become the longest cave in the world.

12

In the winter of 1956–57 we brought the expeditionary baggage to Bivouac II by two preparatory transport trips. On December 26th we carried part of it to Bivouac IV in the *Umbradom* (Umbra Cathedral), our advanced base. On the following days, R. Theiler and I performed several colouring experiments with fluorescine, of which we used ten pounds. In winter conditions the water takes twenty-four hours to travel from the steep part of the "Stich" at the ascent to the *Trughalle* (Deception Hall) to the *Donnertal* (Thunder Valley), and to the outflow at the *Schleichender Brunnen* (Creeping Spring) it even takes 196 hours. The Muota Stream, which receives the water from this spring, was coloured grass green for a considerable time.

At the same time we prepared to make an advance in the *Schluchtgang* (Gorge Passage). The clay-plastered, holdless wall in the *Lehmdom* (Clay Cathedral) was an obstacle which we could only surmount with great effort. Beyond it we entered a big passage which developed above into vertical shafts in which big loose boulders waited to topple. A pronounced updraft hinted at big continuations of the cave above. Our only help here would be a climbing pole. We were in the most remote and most difficult part of the Hell Hole and were in danger of being shut in by any high water. We knew nothing about the behaviour of the *Schluchtgang Siphon* (Gorge Passage Siphon). Nünlist stayed below at the brook and watched the water. It seemed to him as though the noise of the water was growing louder and so he gave the alarm. Hardly had the news reached us when we received another report that the water was not rising. Our experiences in the previous year had made us nervous. We discontinued our advance.

On the next day we returned to Bivouac II. Here Gygax was experimenting with a home-made radio receiver. The results promised much but did not satisfy him. The explorations that now followed were held up by rope breakages, luckily without injury to anyone. Our chief of supplies and technical leader, Nünlist, found that these were due to the ropes rotting in the damp cave air.

During our march back the cave wind suddenly changed direction. That is a sign of a greater incursion of warm air. In cold weather the wind blows downward. If it grows warmer, the wind slackens noticeably. If the temperature in the valley rises above 6° C., or if the föhn is blowing, then the air in the caves moves upward towards the entrance. After 240 hours of exploration we walked out into a world which had a springtime dampness and warmth, although it was only January.

Several weeks later, during safe weather conditions, my comrades and I pushed for twenty-five hours deep into the region of the cave water level. We measured 3,800 feet of new passages and connected the *Rabengang* (Raven Passage) with the *Anubisgang* (Anubis Passage). At the same time the Hegnauer group worked in the equally deep Orkus, one of the worst complexes of passages next to the cave water level.

13

We carried our material out on February 17, 1957. On the same day we had a foretaste of the consequences of an accident. I was leading a club tour of the SAC to the *Wasserdom* (Water Cathedral). At a quite undangerous point, one of the older members stumbled and tore his knee cap, a rare accident. I immediately left the cave and alerted two men of the rescue team from the Mythen Section of the SAC. They came with two 165-foot ropes and a mountain stretcher. My companions, who were transporting our baggage from the caves, also hurried to help. Although the distance to the entrance was only 6,000 feet, it took us sixteen hours to carry our patient out.

But that was not all. A week later five men of an excursion were trapped by high waters, and they had to wait five days behind the *Kellersiphon* (Cellar Siphon) before members of the ASACH could rescue them.

Rope breakages, high waters, and the exploratory work, which became ever more difficult, began to wear our nerves, although, thanks to great caution, our explorations had as yet been free of accidents.

In December 1957 ninety-two porters carried the expedition's baggage to Bivouac II. Included were 1,540 feet of new impregnated hemp rope (most of which became unusable after two years) and one climbing pole. At the same time Gubser tried out radio reception in the caves. With a 600-foot antenna, the transistor apparatus functioned quite well, even when under a ceiling of 2,950 feet of stone. We could receive only the long-medium wave-lengths from Beromünster and the long waves. But we could now hear weather reports and thus guard against unpleasant surprises of high water.

We advanced once more from Bivouac IV into the *Schluchtgang* (Gorge Passage). In the *Lehmdom* (Clay Cathedral) the climbing pole proved very useful. It consisted of five two-meter sections of anticorodal pipe connected by socket joints. From the end hung a rope ladder on which one ascended. Since Nünlist, as a climber, did not entirely trust this device, he did not commit it fully in the chimney and so did not obtain the desired success. Meanwhile Theiler and I squeezed through a sandwich passage. At last we called on Gubser for assistance. Together we reached a passage five yards wide and four high. On one side it passes into a climbable shaft, which Ulrich and Gubser ascended, and on the other side it drops away into the depths. We named it the *Gubsergang* (Gubser Passage). It is the most remote point in the cave. Perhaps there is a continuation from there, but we still do not know because since then the weather has prevented every advance into such distant passages.

During the same winter the members of the SSS made considerable progress in the region of the *Himmelsgang* (Heaven Passage), where they measured 5,085 feet of new passages. Thereby the length of Hell Hole rose to forty-two miles.

After the great difficulties in the remotest part of Hell Hole we felt a need for another attempt in that region. With R. Burger I charted numerous promising shafts and measured three caves. At the same time T. Bucher, W. Burkhalter and J. Gygax were working on the same problem in the deeper layers of the *Bödmerenwald* (Bödmeren Forest). Our younger co-workers became increasingly independent, but their results kept flowing in to me, so that the scientific leadership could only rejoice at this development.

The tendency towards a mild oceanic winter, which began in the fall of 1955, continued—dangerous weather for Hell Hole exploration. In the night before December 28th, Gubser, Kuhn, and Nünlist were at Bivouac IV, while Theiler and I were approaching from Bivouac II. Scarcely was the *Dreiecksee* (Three Corner Lake) behind us when we began to hear rumbling and grumbling from that direction. It was the first sign of a new incursion of high waters. We hurried to get out of the deeper-lying parts of the passages. At midnight we arrived at Bivouac IV, where Gubser told us the weather report: rain and thaw up to 6,500 feet.

A little later we were shut in. Nünlist wanted to begin severe rationing at once with twelve-hour intervals between meals, after the pattern of 1952. The majority, however, wished to stay on the normal meal routine, because we had enough provisions for at least three weeks. Besides, the water rose or sank as much as one centimetre per minute, so that with luck we might be free within twelve hours. So Gubser, Theiler and I continued our explorations. By some exposed climbing up a crumbly clay wall in the *Umbradom* (Umbra Cathedral), Gubser reached a shaft. We followed him much more safely and comfortably up a rope ladder. Now even Nünlist could not withstand the temptation to come along. Kuhn had to remain at Bivouac II with an attack of furunculosis. Afer a long ascent, we crept through a narrow hole into a big passage through which the *Bodmerenwaldbach* (Bodmeren Forest Brook) surges downwards. Water was squirting from every crevice. High water! Gubser and I reconnoitred for possible continuations, but we had to turn back because of the wetness and smoothness of the steps in the wall. After seven hours we were back at our bivouac. There Kuhn told us that the water had risen still further and had already penetrated the *Hoffnungsgang* (Hope Passage). That was bad news. But the weather report told of an improvement and within twenty-four hours the water level sank so far that on New Year's Eve our escape route through the *Versturzgang* (Cave-in Passage) opened up. The siphon at the *Dreiecksee* (Three Corner Lake), however, remained closed, as it had three years previously. We began our retreat with our heavy bivouac gear. Gubser easily climbed the Forty-Metre shaft and hung up a rope ladder so that we could quickly follow. After nine and a half hours, an hour after the beginning of the New Year, we reached Bivouac II. Because of a further bad weather report we started again after a brief sleep. The Styx was full of water. The walls dripped, and in the Cellar we had to wade through the water. But outside it was sunny and warm and the Heuberge were free of snow up to their ridges.

While we were sitting at our traditional dinner, pleased at the results of our week of exploration, Nünlist surprised us with an announcement that this was his last trip into Hell Hole. Despite our protests he stood firm by his decision. But I said that a cat never stops chasing mice.

In the summer of 1959 my friends Bucher, Burkhalter and Gygax proposed that we should form an exploration team for special tasks, including an examination of the shafts above Hell Hole. We went at this task together, and during eight weekends we cleared out a hole into which a brook disappeared in the *Roggenloch* (Rye Hole). At a depth of twenty-three feet, the crevice narrowed to a width of eight inches in sound rock. This was for us an impassable obstacle. Our considerable outlay on explosives, on barbed wire to fence off the area, and of time, was nevertheless rewarded, for we had learned something, and the pronounced draft through the opening proved that this brook was connected with Hell Hole. We also explored the neighbouring *Burgerschact* (Burger Shaft) which had been discovered the previous year. It drops vertically for 184 feet and then widens in the shape of a bell.

Once again a warm winter began. For that reason our exploring party used the entrance as a base for its operations. With explosives we opened a boulder-choked side-passage, the *Holzgang* (Wood Passage), and then, partly by delightful climbing, partly through sandwich passages, we reached the cave water level. Nünlist tried to force an advance during hopeless weather, but had to break off without success. During February we used Bivouac I as our base and made some gains in the *Osirisgang* (Osiris Passage) and the *Bogengang* (Bow Passage). Our gain in measured length was, at 2,500 feet, much less than in other years.

The winter 1960–61 was again mild. Gubser gathered a group of expert climbers and made good progress in the rear third of Hell Hole. In the vicinity of the *Dreiecksee* (Three Corner Lake) they climbed a shaft and reached a system of passages that were a mile in length, another part of the high-water course. Nünlist tried his luck for a last time with Steffen and Melliger, but had to retreat because of threatening high water. With my comrades of the exploratory party I got ahead surprisingly well through the high water zone, although the tunnels were usually less than a yard high and were often hopelessly muddy. P. Berg sprained a foot during the approach march and had to limp all the way out.

Our best assistants came more and more from among Boy Scouts. In the summer of 1961, H. Scherz, a Rover, gathered a measuring party and began the theodolitic measuring of the main passage by means of a Wild-Boussoletheolodite TO 400, which had been lent to them. Setting up this instrument occasionally produced exciting situations, especially when both the instrument and its user had to be belayed. G. Bärtsche offered us a group of porters from the Rovers of Schwyz. These became, so to speak, our "Sherpas". Because of this the number of SAC members declined so

8 THE ALTAR IN ALTAR PASSAGE. These stalactites of great purity form translucent veils. Their purity
is typical of the stalactites in Hell Hole. The orange colouration is caused by a minute iron content.
(Photograph by A. Bögli)

9 THE ARABIAN NIGHTS GALLERY. The macaroni stalactites are tubes through which the water drains from the ceiling. On the floor, calcite debris, welded together by calcium precipitations, compose an exceptionally rare form of stalagmites. (Photograph by A. Bögli)

much that we now simply called ourselves the *Arbeitsgemeinschaft Höllochforschung* (Work Team for Hell Hole Exploration), but still retained the title ASACH.

The winter that followed was worthy of its predecessors. It began with higher water than we had ever experienced. It surpassed the hitherto highest level by sixty-five feet. On December 26th our winter expedition began as usual. The transport party strongly supported our advance to Bivouac III. There we found unexpected traces of high water, and at the same time we found that a siphon barred our access to the rear regions. Therefore we retreated to Bivouac II, and further, to Bivouac I. Thereby we lost three days. From there, using a new climbing pole, we climbed the *Blankstollendom* (Smooth Shaft Cathedral). First we reached a point thirty-six feet up a vertical, holdless slot, and there we cemented in two pitons. By means of a pulley, we lifted the pole higher and thereby gained a way into an interesting maze of tunnels of the *Wassergang* (Water Passage). At the same time we continued work on the high water region which had still not been completely examined. One place gave our nerves an exemplary trial. It had two siphon holes and a spring with a quickly-changing outflow. After 175 hours we returned to the surface. Hell Hole had now attained a measured length of forty-one miles.

After our experiences of the previous winters, we desisted during the winter of 1962–63 from an advance into the rear regions. We were quite wrong, as the weather drastically proved. The *Wassergang* (Water Passage) which we had begun to explore in great hope, proved a disappointment. A little further on it broke off into countless tiny holes. However, the Berg group reached an altitude of 3,495 feet, and the altitude difference in Hell Hole thereby grew to 1,395 feet. A brief, transitional period of warm air caused the brooks to swell slightly, and so we retreated from the high water zone in which we had meanwhile resumed explorations. So we began working in the region between the *Altarstollen* (Altar Tunnel) and the *Galerie des 1001 nuits* (Arabian Nights Gallery). Besides new passages, we found some that had been explored but not yet measured.

A group of divers began working with us, in order to follow up the continuations where the siphons of the cave water level had blocked us. These frog-men have already obtained gratifying results.

At the close of the present winter we are confronted by the realization that new tasks of measurement have been added to the old ones, and that the number of our problems is greater than it was at the beginning. The scientific work has years ahead of it. Knowledge of the forms of the caves, the development of the cave in its different phases, and the biology of the caves—all demand further thorough examination.

During the fifteen years from May 1948 to March 1963 a total of forty-seven and a half miles of passages were measured, and of these forty-five were measured by the *Arbeitsgemeinschaft Höllochforschung* (Work Team for Hell Hole Exploration). The remainder will also be measured by ASACH. The SSS also charted a large part, approximately seven and a half miles, most of which they were the first to measure. The explorations of the *Arbeitsgemeinschaft Höllochforschung* (Work Team for Hell Hole Exploration) continue and will be intensified in the coming years.

18

BALLOONING ACROSS THE ALPS

THE FIRST INTERNATIONAL ALPINE BALLOON SPORT WEEK AT MÜRREN, AUGUST 19–26, 1962

By Fred Dolder

The free balloon has passed through several metamorphoses since its invention 180 years ago. There was a long period of utopian hope, experiment and fantastic speculation, during which the balloon was the vehicle of daring exhibitionism, until in the middle of the nineteenth century even the military became interested. Before the Battle of Solferino and during the American Civil War, balloons were used to reconnoitre enemy positions and manoeuvres; soon balloonists became part of the intelligence service, and this first took place in France in 1874.

On the periphery of military application, which was really unsuited to the nature of the free balloon, a civilian interest developed too, which expressed itself in the foundation of aero-clubs and dirigible associations and in the F.A.I. (Féderation Aeronautique Internationale). These associations received considerable financial and organizational assistance from the military, but they made possible the participation of a number of balloonists, without military background, in ballooning competitions. Each year from 1906 to 1938, with an interruption during World War I, a sort of aerostatic world championship was held in the form of Gordon Bennett Air Races, during which some important information was got together concerning the major air currents.

The free balloon had disappeared from the army establishment before World War II, and the spectacular air races, too, belong irrevocably to the past. It was gradually realized that the balloon was entirely unsuited to competitions that are conducted according to measurable values of distance, endurance or height. The only criterion for the skill and reliability of a balloonist is the landing: whether his landings are earlier or later, whether his landing site is in a remote place, a forest, a sheet of water, or a sports field, is of less importance than that the landing is accomplished without damage or injury.

On the other hand, the balloon has become a well-loved source of pleasure, a wonderful experience and a high sporting adventure. The good piloting of an aerostat requires courage and boldness, self-discipline and an ability to make quick decisions. Every trip brings new, often unexpected, experiences, together with an adventurous uncertainty as to direction, height, endurance and the distance covered. But ballooning had always demanded a considerable sacrifice of time and much patience.

From earliest times, moreover, the free balloon has served a scientific purpose. At first this purpose was quite elementary. Experiments were directed at gaining knowledge about unknown phenomena in the third dimension. Physicists, meteorologists, physiologists and researchers interested in ballistics and aviation carried out experiments with the help of the free balloon and acquired knowledge that led to many technological advances.

The first planned traverse of the Alps was prompted by science. On October 3, 1898, the geologist, Professor Albert Heim, the meteorologist, Dr Jule Maurer, and Dr Biedermann started up from Sitten in the free balloon *Wega* (3,268 cubic metres) under the leadership of the already world-renowned Captain Eduard Spelterini. It was the first traverse of the Alps in a balloon.

These promising attempts came to an abrupt end with the first World War. When in September 1926, after a long pause, the seventy-four-year-old Spelterini sailed again toward the Alps in the balloon *Zürich*, his eagle wings failed him. His proud career ended, without accident, but involuntarily, against the rock walls of the Hohe Oferl in Vorarlberg. Five years later the physicist, Professor Auguste Piccard, reached the stratosphere in an ascent above the Alps in the free balloon *F.N.R.S.* (14,000 cubic metres), and in the following year broke his own pioneering record. Thereby he began a chain of scientific ascents to great heights which still continues today, the results of which are disclosing unsuspected possibilities. Said Piccard: "A stratospheric aircraft could easily carry us up to 20,000 feet, but that is a bit too noisy for our taste. Besides, the aeroplane cannot remain long at great heights. Therefore we take to the classic vehicle of the high atmosphere, the stratosphere-balloon. The charm of the trip is only increased by the fact that one starts without knowing where one will land."

ALPINE BALLOONING

It may be in the nature of things that during a period of sixty years, from 1898 to 1957, all planned Alpine crossings by balloon were carried out by Swiss balloonists. The record Italian trip in November 1912, which carried the balloon *Basiliola* in a fifty-four-hour flight from Milan over the Julian Alps to Malé (Trentino), was piloted by a Swiss from Tessin, the twenty-nine-year-old Flori. Captain Spelterini came from a mountainous region in eastern Switzerland. He had piloted balloons all over the world professionally, but he was obviously so impressed by his first traverse of the Alps for scientific purposes that he led nine more high Alpine flights and considered these the greatest achievement of his 570 balloon ascents.

In June 1908 R. O. Müller made a sensational ascent from the Eigergletscher Station, followed by a dramatic twenty-one-hour flight. He was accompanied by

Victor de Beauclair, Fräulein Marie Löbenberg, and the writer, Konrad Falke. R. O. Müller was a keen mountaineer. He not only flew over the four-thousanders in a free balloon, but also climbed them on foot. In Switzerland civilian balloon sport was obviously strongly influenced by mountaineering from the start.

Up to August 1962 alpine crossings by balloon had only occurred individually. The ascents started from different places at different seasons, and showed the greatest technical differences. Spelterini used five different balloons for his first five high-alpine flights, and Interlaken is the only place from which he ascended twice.

In general one can say that what the English call "ballooning" consists of individual achievements. Ascents are usually sporadic, and the data gained by such trips can only rarely be used for the development of either ballooning or other activities. Comparative data is almost entirely lacking, and often the material which is brought home does not even suffice to reconstruct an exact tour. There is an additional obstacle: the flight patterns of commercial air routes are becoming even thicker, and they allow less and less room for the free balloon. Perhaps some day there will be room only above alpine regions. Luckily, alpine flights by balloon give one a grandiose experience of nature, and they can at the same time be of service to scientific research.

When Professor Piccard undertook his ascent into the stratosphere he did not know what he would find there or to what results his ventures would lead. At first he wanted simply to prove that man could actually venture to such heights, and when we made our plans for the first International Alpine Balloon Sport Week we knew just as little about the sort of results this aeronautic event would produce. In the foreground was our desire to arrange a unique experience for a few enthusiastic mountaineers and balloonists, though at the same time we sought to demonstrate that simultaneous ascents in the high Alps were possible. For only through the simultaneous ascents of several balloons can reliable comparative data be obtained which can be of service to aerostatics and science. Further, we wished to build up the material foundation which would help us to finance such ascents in the future.

On August 12, 1910, Captain Spelterini made his first ascent from Mürren. It was his eighth high-alpine flight. He landed near Lanzo, north of Turin. On August 30, 1957, a second balloon left Mürren to make physiological tests at high altitude with the Everest climbers, Dölf Reist and Jürg Marmet; Fred Dolder was pilot. They landed near to San Nazzaro on Lake Maggiore. On August 13, 1961, a third aerostat rose from Mürren, the balloon *Bernina*, with Fred Dolder as pilot, E. A. Sautter and Phil Walker. After a flight of seven hours they made a landing by Besnate-Vergiate in the north Italian plains. With three ascents and as many successful alpine traverses from north to south, Mürren had proved an excellent starting point for balloon trips in the Alps.

A new advance was planned for 1962: a "frontal assault" against the myth that high-alpine flights by balloon were dangerous. Because balloon ascents are only rarely made in the Alps and the published accounts of them have given an impression of extreme dangerousness, pilots and passengers were surrounded with the glamorous aura of pioneers of aviation. Yet, to this day no high alpine flight has ended in an accident. Naturally ballooning in the Alps must be just as carefully aware of all the dangerous factors as must every other high-alpine sport, and it is true that in the mountains ballooning has the added danger of a forced landing on unsuitable terrain. To meet this danger, modern meteorological information and alpine rescue techniques have made things much easier. What is needed above all is a systematic study of thermal air currents in the Alpine valleys, a study to which the free balloon can itself contribute. Otherwise, I do not see why it should be more dangerous to fly across the Alps in a wicker basket between 13,000 and 16,000 feet than to fly across the Lake of Constance between 6,500 and 10,000 feet, something which during the season is done every week. The factors that are decisive for a good result are the air currents, that is, the right wind. The practice of free ballooning in the Alps therefore demands a thorough adjustment to the weather conditions.

The International Balloon Sport Week in Mürren has already opened the door. With a carefully planned organization, expert advice, and reliable weather reports, six balloon pilots went up in two groups of three within four days, and they not only accomplished their mission but declared that they would be ready at any time to take off from Mürren again. Among them were two ladies who took off in a free balloon in the Alps for the first time. Thereby the surprising realization was reached that even today ballooning can be of valuable service to scientific research (topographic, meteorological, physiological), not to mention the rich returns in the form of photographs.

On August 18 and 19, 1962, participants from Belgium, Germany, France, Netherlands, Switzerland and the United States met for the First International Alpine Balloon Sport Week at the village of Mürren, which lies on a cliff terrace at 5,400 feet. Four hundred steel containers with a total content of 84,720 cubic feet of hydrogen, had been brought up on the cable railway and set up on the level lawn in front of the Palace Hotel. These were replaced within three days after the take-off of the first party of three. 1.2 miles from the launching site, and across the Lauterbrunnen Valley, which lies 2,600 feet below Mürren, rises the huge and vertical face of the Schwarz Mönch. And about 4.4 miles away gleam the mighty, ice-covered summits of the Oberland trinity, the Eiger, Mönch, and Jungfrau. The range continues to the east and south with the well-known giants of the Bernese and Valaisian Alps. In whatever direction the wind may blow, a balloon ascent from Mürren will always lead over high mountains.

The Swiss Central Aviation Weather Station had set up an auxiliary post in Mürren.

22

Their forecast for August 20th was so promising that the organizers decided to send up the first three balloons two days ahead of schedule. The lots fell to the US balloon *N 10 W* (33,258 cubic feet) with the pilot Mrs Conny Wolf, the Swiss balloon *Circus Knie—Stadt Rapperswil* (35,300 cubic feet) with pilot Fred Dolder, and the Belgian balloon *OO-BGD* (33,258 cubic feet) with pilot Albert Van den Bemden. *N 10 W* started at 10.35, *HB-BIW* at 10.43, and *OO-BGD* at 10.50 o'clock. The first two had to fight against strong down-drafts during take-off, as a result of which *HB-BIW* lost half its flight ballast, and was soon climbing at thirteen feet per second and later at ten feet per second, so that within twenty minutes it had reached a height of 15,400 feet. Above the Great Aletsch Glacier at 11.15 a.m. it reached a height of 18,370 feet, whereupon the pilot decided to prevent further ascent by opening the valve. The balloon was drifting at eight knots on a south-easterly course in the direction of Märjelensee-Eggishorn. Balloon *OO-BGD* landed at 1.25 p.m. on the south slope of the Pizzo Martello in the Italian Valle Antigorio. Balloon *HB-BIW* landed at 1.40 p.m. on the northern slope of the Pizzo Gelato, in the Italian Valle di Campo, and *N 10 W* came down on the south slope of the Pizzo Leone near Corte on Lake Maggiore.

The flights lasted between two hours thirty-five minutes and five hours five minutes. The distance covered was between twenty-eight and forty-eight miles. Thus the times and distances were those of average tourist flights. Not so the altitudes reached: 15,400, 17,100 and 18,400 feet. Between the height at which the pressure was equalized and the beginning of the descent each balloon used up only two sacks of ballast (about 100 pounds). The balloons *HB-BIW* and *N 10 W* followed classic examples and were only filled to 65% of their volumes, so that they should fill out tightly and reach an equalization of pressure between 12,500 and 13,500 feet. By comparison *OO-BGD* was filled to 80% of its volume, which permitted it to fly for a longer time at a considerably lower level than the others. It was a notable fact that the directions of the balloons fanned out only very little so long as they remained above 10,000 feet.

It was the same with the second group which took off within five minutes on August 23rd: at 1.05 p.m. the *Utrecht* (22,945 cubic feet) with the pilot Nini Boesman (Netherlands), at 1.07 p.m. the *OO-BAA* (33,859 cubic feet) piloted by Habib Eskenazi (Turkey), and at 1.10 p.m. the *Bernina* (44,478 cubic feet) with the pilot Jo Scheer (Germany). Unfortunately, no comparative evaluation can be made from the flight reports of this group. On the basis of the experience gained on August 20th, all the balloons of the second group were filled up to 80% of capacity and their take off was set for the early afternoon. It was hoped thereby to evade the vertical thermal air buffets which had hindered the earlier group in starting, and to miss the thermal updrafts which had hindered them in descending into the valleys in order to land. These expectations were not fulfilled. The entire affair from the first take off on

August 20th to the last landing on August 24th showed that a much more thorough study was needed concerning the phenomenon of the thermally conditioned up-drafts and down-drafts which, in the mountain valleys, can gather into extremely strong winds.

The ascent of the second group had some especially attractive moments. The well-known Dutch balloonist, Nini Boesman, brilliantly piloted the smallest balloon which has yet crossed the Alps. The traditional view that one can only carry out such trips with a big balloon was thereby refuted. This seems important because a smaller balloon can be much more easily retrieved after a landing in difficult terrain. Pilot Scheer made an intermediate landing at sundown on the 7,900-foot Cresta del Colonello. He spent the night in his gondola, and took off again at eight in the morning. An hour later, with clear visibility and free of thermal influences, he drifted down into the valley, where he landed in style in the Italian province of Bergamo. His two companions left at the intermediate stop and descended on foot.

All six balloons landed without mishap, with the exception of a mild ankle sprain suffered by a photo-reporter during the landing of *OO-BGD*. On the other hand, retrieving four of the balloons was arduous. Communications technicians from the Swiss Army had equipped one of the balloons of the second group with a radio transmitter. They said that they were well satisfied with the tests they made, which they could only have carried out in this manner. Thereby they also rendered a valuable service to the organizers of the event. It remains to be seen whether in the future a system of homing pigeons might be of use. Such flying couriers might be of great help in finding balloons landing in remote places.

Words can scarcely be found to describe the overwhelming experience of a balloon journey over the high alps. Once in 1957 we had crossed a sea of ice-covered summits at 21,500 feet and were gliding along without a sound over a high blanket of vapour, when one of my two companions, who had climbed the summit of Everest the previous year, exclaimed: "This experience is quite as fantastic as an ascent in the Himalayas." Another companion who had flown around the world in an aeroplane confessed that nothing had impressed nearly so deeply and enchanted him so much as the flight by a balloon over the high mountains. The pilots who had come to Mürren in a mood of scepticism became enthusiastic proponents of alpine ballooning by the end of the week. "I have learned much in this week, more than I thought I would," said the experienced old doyen of international balloon pilots, Charles Dollfus of Paris, and the German aeronaut Wilhelm Debus ardently quoted Goethe: "A new century has dawned, and I am glad to have participated."

An experienced balloonist from Germany wrote about the Mürren event: "The first alpine balloon sport week in Mürren was a hopeful sign. New meaning was given to Piccard's words: 'Every balloon pilot has but one wish: to cross the Alps.' A virtue

24

10 IN A FREE BALLOON OVER THE ALPS. A view of the Bernese and Valaisian Alps. In the centre, the Jungfrau (4158 m); in the left foreground, the Mönch (4099 m). (Photograph by Erwin Sautter)

11/12 overleaf: OVER THE JUNGFRAU MASSIF ARE TWO OF THE FREE BALLOONS THAT STARTED IN MÜRREN. In the left foreground, the Silberhorn (3695 m.), above it, the West Flank of the Jungfrau; below the balloon to the left, the Kranzberg (3664 m.), to the right, the Gletscherhorn (3983 m.) with the precipice into the Rottal. (Aerial photograph Giegel svz)

13 the third following page: IN A FREE BALLOON above the region of the Aletsch Glacier. (Self-photograph by Heggemann)

has been made of necessity. One has realized in time that here was still every opportunity to prove navigational skill in spite of the general handicaps, and that the free balloon has not been degraded into a step-child of aviation. On the contrary, here the balloon has found its way back to its first and proper purpose: to reveal to man the most grandiose creations of nature, and to help man to regain his awe of the infinite".

FLIGHT REPORTS OF THE PILOTS

Balloons in order of take-offs	Volumes in feet	Pilot	Duration of Flight hours	Air Distance miles	Greatest Altitude	Number of Occupants
N 10 W	33,258	Conny Wolf	5.05	47.8	15,400	2
HB-BIW	35,300	Fred Dolder	2.57	32.5	18,400	2
OO-BGD	33,258	Albt. van dem Bemden	2.35	28.1	17,100	2
OO-BAA	22,945	Nini Boesman	3.20	58.1	14,100	2
OO-BOB	33,859	Habib Eskenazi	3.02	54.7	17,100	2
Bernina	44,478	H. J. Scheer	5.15	93.8	15,000	3

A PASSENGER'S REPORT BY ERWIN S. SAUTTER

"A shovel full! Another half a shovel! Good—we're climbing at three feet a second. Get into the shade!" Orders pour forth from the pilot. It was just as I had thought: balloon passengers are part of the crew. They start before dawn, spreading out the balloon-envelope. They climb into the ridiculously small basket for a flight over an unknown distance and into unknown heights. They all stand on tip-toe for the landing, and once they are back on the ground they become a team of hard-labourers who must retrieve a deflated balloon that weighs half a ton.

"Erwin, get into the shade!" ordered Pilot Fred Dolder from Thalwil, sixty-four years of age, who had taken off from Mürren on his 177th balloon flight. He was sending me to the side of the basket which was away from the sun. Phil Walker, forty-four, a documentary film producer from San Francisco, stared over the opposite side into the green depths of the Lauterbrunnen Valley. We were drifting in a southwesterly direction. The *Bernina*, with 33,200 cubic feet of hydrogen in its gradually rounding belly, flew. It flew with the north wind. "Airborne!" At 11,800 feet we crossed the Wetterlücke between the Breithorn in the east, freshly covered with snow, and the humped Tschingelhorn in the west. Below, ahead and behind us were glaciers, sprinkled with the fresh snow that had fallen during the night. The silence was perfect. "A shovel full!" The silver ballast sand which had been dried over a fire, poured onto the Alps from a height of 12,500 feet above the Lötschental. Silence. The wind did not sing in the "rigging". The free balloon belongs to the winds.

Fred, Phil and I were not professional adventurers. We each had left a wife and

25

child down below. Naturally we were well insured. So why should we be anxious to be in a balloon driven by the breeze over the peaks and glaciers at 13,000 feet? There was no rubber raft nor were there parachutes in case of a fall. But as soon as the basket takes to the air the fear that the balloon might burst is discarded. What it takes is nerves and humour, comradeship and freedom from dizziness, a good eye and a power of decision just as quick as the wind. The balloon pilot is in intimate contact with the winds. The "crew", as Phil called us sand-shovellers and balloon-shadow-seekers, experienced its air baptism above the Valaisian village of Mund. There, at 12.50 on August 13th, a champagne cork popped at 13,300 feet above sea level. From Besnate (Varese) where we landed, Phil wrote a report to his President, John F. Kennedy, in the White House in Washington.

Later I wanted to sign up as a Driver Trainee (one does not *fly* a balloon; one *drives* it). Within five days after a tour, a "Tour Report for Balloon Pilots" should be filled in and sent to the appropriate government department. In our case, the needed forms "D 75 L-A. VIII 56 37918" were missing from the balloon basket. It is a consolation for aspiring balloonists that the wind routes are still free of rowdies, and that collisions do not lie in the nature of aerostats which obey the winds and not human beings.

Balloonists are physicists in their spare time. What Archimedes taught about static buoyancy 2,200 years ago in Syracuse the friends of ballooning practice today in their flights above hills, woods, cities, glaciers and 13,000-foot peaks. Physics dominates the thinking of balloonists. All their conversation is about ballast and pressure equalization, radiation and meteorological inversion (air layers in which the temperature rises as one ascends), atmospheric pressure and the elasticity of hydrogen, that not entirely danger-free element. According to the books, planetary mists and the youngest stars (several hundred thousand years old) consist mainly of hydrogen and helium, so one might regard the balloonist who rides with "super-hydrogen" as a pilot of a young star....

In ballooning the take-off is a science but landing is an art. The decision to descend from an altitude of 14,000 feet to the ground at 800 feet above sea level was made by Fred Dolder at 3.20 p.m. between the Lago d'Orta and the Lago Maggiore, which was glittering festively in the depths. He underlined his decision with several regular pulls on a red cord. With a hiss the colourless and odourless hydrogen escaped into the blue sky above the "Province of the Seven Lakes". The variometer, which indicates the rate of climb or drop in metres per second, is, next to the altimeter, the most important instrument aboard a balloon. A loss of altitude of 200 feet per minute or 12,000 feet per hour proceeds with imperceptible rapidity.

Hastily we sought the shadow of the balloon in order to determine our direction above Gallarate and Busto Arsizio. Aeroplanes climbed up from the private airfield of the SIAI-Marchetti at Vergiate to identify the balloon which had German markings

26

and was flying a Swiss flag. The balloon had been lent to us by the German Pestalozzi Children's Village of Wahlwies for the Spelterini Memorial Flight. We waved with scarves from the basket. The aeroplanes waved back with their wings. They were welcoming us to Italy. Valve!—Sand!—Valve! Fred Dolder held the thick rope which would bring our landing manoeuvres to an end. Phil Walker and I each held a sand bag on the rail of the basket, ready to jettison it if we should need to hop over any obstacle that might appear at the last minute. Our nerves were tensed to the utmost. The heavy tow-line rattled overboard beside me and the basket swayed. People were running below us and we saw that we were between a railway line and a high tension line near a cross-roads on the highway from Milan to Sesto Calende. To the right of the highway there appeared to be some sort of open air festival. Dance music greeted our balloon. Southern heat penetrated our winter clothes. Then we heard the high clear voices of the Lombardy children who caught the tow-line and held it fast, and then, hand over hand, pulled us to earth. The basket settled on a meadow amid noise, heat and earthlings.

"Landed in style with a tow-line", is what we finally wrote in the Tour Report for Balloon Pilots which had to be sent to the Air Ministry. But Phil and I had no time to shake Fred's hand, for after the landing the work begins, that work of retrieval without which ballooning would only be half a sport.

"*A Balloon over the Alps*" (*Wood engraving of* 1869)

27

AVALANCHES

By André Roch

The first men to settle in the snow-covered winter mountains observed that this snow sometimes roared down into the valleys in the form of avalanches, a phenomenon which terrorized certain areas and was long regarded as mysterious. It was often interpreted fancifully, and even today what happens is not always easy to explain. Great progress has recently been made concerning the mechanics of avalanche release, while the phenomena of avalanche movement and its thrust against an obstacle are under study.

THE RELEASE OF AN AVALANCHE

In order to understand the mechanics of avalanche release, a few ideas about friction and resistance are needed. Snow is a powdery material composed of ice crystals of different forms with variable cohesion between themselves. The form and condition of these crystals, as well as their cohesion, change continuously, a fact which constitutes the great difference between the mechanics of soils and that of snow.

(a) Avalanche of non-cohering snow, or snow slide ("coulée")

Let us imagine a powdery mass without cohesion, like dry sand for example. It lies in equilibrium along a slope called its natural talus, which depends on the shape of the crystals, on the mixture of crystals of different sizes and on the compactness of the crystals amongst themselves.

If it were sand instead of snow that fell upon the Alps, this sand would slide progressively to the foot of the slopes that are steeper than its natural talus and would accumulate at the bottom of these slopes along its natural talus. Let us moisten a heap of sand. This dampness gives a certain cohesion to the material and it can now rest in equilibrium on a much steeper slope. Let us cut a vertical slice of small depth from one heap. The vertical slice remains in equilibrium, but as the sand dries its cohesion, due to dampness, decreases. Little collapses take place and once the heap is completely dry it will have resumed its natural talus except for a few structures which remain in precarious equilibrium. When this sand slides it has an internal movement friction (kinetic friction) the angle of which may be equal to its natural talus. On the other

28

hand, in getting it moving a starting friction is set up (static friction) which is greater than the movement friction.

When snow falls, the crystal which is deposited has the shape of a star, a needle, a little column, a hexagonal flake, or a combination of these forms, according to the conditions of its formation in the atmosphere. The stars often possess a quantity of fine branches which become entangled and form a mass containing a great deal of air, able to maintain itself in vertical equilibrium, thanks to the matting together of the needles. The fine branches tend to disappear. Water vapour escapes from the points and is deposited in the hollows, so that a star changes from what is at first a fine dentritic crystal to an increasingly rounded grain. The matting disappears and the grain, if it has not been thrust against its neighbour (by wind-pressure for example or by the weight of a thick layer) only coheres to its neighbour to a minute degree. This transformation is called *destructive metamorphosis*. It causes settling, because the grains take up less space than the original star.

The original crystals form what we call new snow. After the disappearance of the fine branches of the stars, the snow becomes powdery. Becoming increasingly rounded, the grains form granular snow, called old snow, fine or coarse according to whether the grains are smaller or larger than 2 mm.

At the beginning of winter the first layer of snow is often thin. At the soil level its temperature is about 0°C. At the surface it possesses the average seasonal and altitude temperature, let us say − 10°C. in December. There is therefore a great temperature difference between the bottom and the surface and a steep gradient in the case of a thin layer. An air circulation is then set up within the layer. The warm air of the bottom, lighter than the colder air, rises. It cools, becomes heavier and descends again. This air is saturated with moisture. In cooling it becomes supersaturated, for at saturation cold air cannot contain as much moisture as warmer air. This water vapour sublimes on certain conveniently orientated grains, which expand into hexagonal flakes and then into cup crystals with the opening directed towards the cooling current of air. This is *constructive metamorphosis*. The more or less spherical grains or the cup crystals, called depth hoar, form a very weak structure known as loose snow. In movement, these crystals roll one against the other, recalling the flow of a stream.

We should observe that fine granular snow has a greater angle of natural talus than has snow with coarser grains. Big grains are the result of a more advanced metamorphosis and are generally more rounded than the fine grains which recall the original shape.

These snow crystals can be more or less frozen together at their points of contact. Then the snow has a certain *contact cohesion*, stronger when the contacts are greater and the temperature lower. If the temperature rises, the strength of the contacts diminishes and above 0° C. the links between the crystals melt and contact cohesion

29

disappears. It is replaced by a capillary cohesion due to the water in the pores. Thus the snow crystal takes on all sorts of shapes which influence the angles of starting friction and movement friction.

If the cohesion is small in a potential avalanche area, then the retaining forces at the edges of the area are of little importance and we shall ignore them for the moment. We shall now examine how weakly-cohering snows are released, which is in two ways:

1. *Spontaneous releases*, which take place when the resistance to shearing diminishes and becomes smaller than the shear stress, or when that stress becomes greater than the resistance.

2. *Accidental releases*, due to momentary increase of stress caused by the fall of a quantity of snow, or of a rock, or the passing of a skier, etc., or as we shall see, the shock of a rupture other than that of shearing at the bottom.

SPONTANEOUS RELEASES

(a) Due to the lessening of resistance to shearing

Contrary to dry sand, new snow, above all if the crystals are of the star type, can accumulate on the steepest slopes. After a snowfall one often notices vertical walls completely plastered. Then the stars lose their branches and become grains. As stars take up more room than grains, the snow is very slack and contact cohesion is almost non-existent. Resistance to shearing has diminished and becomes less than the shear stress. One grain overturns against its neighbour, which loses equilibrium in its turn, and a snow slide results. Then, the metamorphosis following its course, the avalanches slide over slopes of decreasing inclination. The sun, shining on slopes covered with fresh snow, quickens the metamorphosis and weakens or eliminates the contacts by warming the snow. It is then that numerous avalanches start moving spontaneously.

Generally, snow slides are released during two or three days after snowfall and mainly on slopes exposed to the sun. Then a period of quiet seems to settle in. The stars have partially disappeared, giving place to powdery snow. The very fine grains are angular and after warming by the sun they have refrozen together lightly, which keeps them in equilibrium on the slopes where snow slides have not taken place.

In a low temperature it is only at the end of a fortnight that slides are released spontaneously on the shaded slopes. The grains have enlarged and have become rounded, and although they are still in slight contact, their equilibrium becomes unstable.

It is the lessening of resistance to shearing which is the cause of these spontaneous releases. First of all the matting cohesion of the fresh snow has been eliminated, then the angle of starting friction, due to the fact that the crystals have passed from the angular form to that of more or less spherical grains, has decreased.

For these slides to occur spontaneously, the angle of starting friction of snow without cohesion must become less than the angle of the slope. Once in movement, the angle of kinetic friction being less than that of starting friction, the movement will spread on slopes less steep than the inclination of static friction, so far as the kinetic energy of the mass in movement is big enough to release the layer of snow downhill.

(b) Spontaneous releases due to an increase of shear stress

Other cases of spontaneous release are due to an increase of shear stress. This increase, if it does not happen as a result of external accident, can only be due to the overburden of a new snowfall, or to rainfall on the snow. The mistake is often made of imagining that a layer of snow becomes heavier in melting. Its specific weight has certainly increased, but the proper weight of this layer has remained the same. If it rains, on the other hand, the bed becomes heavier by all the water which it can hold.

It is clear that the shape of the original crystal plays a direct part in the mechanical properties of the snow. Flat or spherical stars take up a lot of room and constitute a very slack and very compressible snow. Little flakes, on the contrary, like those that generally fall at high altitude in winter, settle closely together and form much more compact layers. During snowfall these little flakes cannot keep their equilibrium on steep slopes as can the stars; they roll down to the bottom of the slopes and collect below in a very compact mass. Thus avalanches are rare in the high mountains in winter.

ACCIDENTAL RELEASES

It is possible for some external force to increase the shear stress momentarily to the point at which it exceeds resistance to shearing. Then a release takes place. A rock or a quantity of snow falls from a rock face or a tree, or a skier passes by, or a break in the snow layer is caused by traction, and agitation results. These shocks can break the cohesion and the starting traction (that is to say, resistance to shearing), and the snow

31

starts to move at that spot. So that the initial movement may spread, the thrust of the freed mass against the snow downhill must be big enough to release it in its turn, and so on.

As we have seen, as soon as the snow is in movement its cohesion has disappeared and its static friction has given place to a lesser movement friction. If the slope is sufficiently steeper than the angle of this kinetic friction the sliding spreads. To illustrate this phenomenon the following experiment can be made. While traversing on ski a very steep slope covered with snow *without cohesion*, one can try to push this snow downwards with the lower ski. Nothing happens. When pushing a bigger piece of snow downwards one sees that this piece continues its movement and carries away the snow on the slope as it passes. This experiment shows that it is possible to spread the slide if the initial mass of snow is big enough to overcome the resistance to shearing of the layer situated downhill.

After a snowfall only spontaneous releases take place, but everywhere where a quantity of snow falls down from a wall of rock a snow slide is released. In reality the snow slides one sees when fine weather returns after snowfall are for the most part due to some external event. Spontaneous slides generally take place during heavy snowfalls on steep slopes, which discharge themselves progressively as the snow accumulates.

The type of the snow also plays a part in the spread of a movement. For example, new snow, in which one cannot dissociate matting cohesion from starting friction, has the greatest angle of static friction of 50° to 90° and the smallest angle of movement friction of 17°. In the same way, fine-grained old snow shows a greater difference between these two frictions than does coarse-grained old snow. The values of these frictions are given in the following table:

Type of snow	Static friction (starting friction)	Kinetic friction (movement friction)
Fresh	50° to 90°	17°
Old, fine-grained	53°	32° to 23°
Old, coarse-grained .... }	36° to 40°	23°
Loose, spherically-grained		
Loose, cup-shaped, depth hoar [1]	43°	37° to 32°

[1] The name "depth hoar" is generally reserved for cup-shaped crystals. Spherical crystals of old snow are much more dangerous, since in movement their angle of kinetic friction is only 23°.

The differences between these two frictions have a complex effect upon the spread of movement. With equal cohesion, old coarse-grained snow in movement will more easily release the snow masses downhill of which the angle of starting friction is

14 AVALANCHE ON THE TRUGBERG in the region of the Jungfrau. In the background is the brow of a hanging glacier. (Photograph by André Roch)

15 AVALANCHE ON RAKAPOSHI, Karakorum Himalaya. (Photograph by R. Kappeler)

smaller than that of old fine-grained snow. New snow in a thin layer is relatively stable. It has a matting cohesion and a large angle of starting friction. But in movement its angle of kinetic friction is the smallest in existence (17°). Thus on a slope of the same inclination it will slide more quickly than old snow and its kinetic energy, proportional to the square of the speed, will eventually have a greater chance of releasing the mass further down. The layer on which this new snow lies also plays an important role. If it is hard and smooth the new snow slides easily, but if it is rough the start of the movement is more problematical and a greater initial mass in movement will be needed if the slide is to continue.

On steep slopes the slides channel themselves into couloirs, carrying away any new snow that may be there. The gigantic organ-pipe grooves on the snow faces in the Himalayas are formed in this way. In some parts of these mountains snow falls every afternoon. This snow sticks to the steepest faces, but the first rays of the sun loosen sections of snow which then swept down the couloirs. On the ridges the snow, touched by the sun's rays, melts slightly and afterwards refreezes, then solidifies. Thus the channels and couloirs are regularly swept, while the ridges and ribs increase in volume.

When snow falls until the shear stress is equal to the resistance, the avalanches which then begin to move are the most rapid. In fact, the snow which covers the whole mountainside is in a state of unstable equilibrium. If a rupture develops at any point on the slope it spreads like lightning and the whole slope is in movement at the same time.

This is what happens in those catastrophic situations which occur after consecutive snowfalls exceeding four feet in depth. During such snowfalls the slopes steeper than 40° are less dangerous than those of 30° to 40°, for they discharge themselves progressively as the snow falls. On the other hand, the mountainsides of 30° to 35° become extremely deadly because an enormous thickness of snow is required before they become unstable. For a short period avalanches must be expected everywhere. It is possible that normally dangerous couloirs are not set in movement, while avalanches slip down beside them. That will depend on the chance of an external accident like the fall of a block of snow, or of a cornice, and so on, which starts the layer moving.

If this heavy fall of snow accumulates on a layer of spherically-grained snow of poor cohesion (loose snow), the conditions for a slide are even more favourable. This loose snow can break away at one spot and bring about the release; then its collapse at the passing of an avalanche adds to the movement and makes it possible for the avalanche to travel faster and farther. Let us suppose that new snow has been accumulated by the wind in sufficient quantity to provoke the collapse of the underlying layer of loose snow. The shock of this collapse can eventually spread to a steep section of the slope and cause it to start moving.

D

When new snow accumulates in great quantity the thicker the layer the more it settles. At the end of two days the snow crystals begin to freeze together. On the third day the snow has acquired such cohesion by settlement that the release of catastrophic avalanches is no longer to be feared, though localized ruptures of snow slabs can still take place. The more catastrophic the situation, the quicker it stabilizes itself, because for one thing the slopes discharge themselves, and for another, the thicker the layer the better it settles.

SNOW-SLAB AVALANCHES

When the layers of snow have acquired a certain compactness, when their cohesion is great, the mechanics of release is complicated by the spreading effects of shocks and influences at the edges of the avalanche area. A snow slab is a compact layer of snow, usually of windblown snow, but it is sufficient that in the mantle of snow a layer should have more cohesion than any underlying stratum for the mechanism of snow-slab release to take effect.

Let us consider a snow slab on an infinitely long and wide slope. The force which tends to draw this slab downwards is the component parallel to the slope of the weight of the layers situated above the weakest stratum. For a unit of surface this force sets up a shear stress. The force which holds the slab back is the resistance to shearing of the weakest stratum. Equilibrium depends on the ratio of the resistance to shearing to the shear stress, which we call stability and which we denote by the letter s. When resistance is greater than stress there is equilibrium, and the ratio s is greater than 1. If the shear stress becomes greater than the resistance, the ratio is less than 1 and equilibrium is broken.

This can happen, as we have seen, following either an increase in stress as a result of the overload of new snow, or a lessening of resistance by a metamorphosis of the crystals, or by a rise in temperature.

There can also be a momentary increase of stress following an incident such as the fall of a mass of snow or of a rock, the passing of a skier or a break at the edges, which we shall examine later. It is the possibility of these shocks spreading in the compact

34

snow slab and the greater mass of snow in the slab, which starts to move generally, which constitute the main differences from the avalanches of weakly cohering snow.

With the aim of eliminating the influences at the edges, we have assumed that the slopes are infinitely long and wide, which is never the case in nature. Let us examine the conditions of equilibrium of a snow slab of limited dimension and let us imagine this slab to be anchored on all sides.

The slab which is drawn downwards by the component of its weight in relation to the slope is held back by the resistance to shearing of the weakest stratum on its foundation, by lateral resistance to shearing, by the resistance to compression of the slab downhill, and by resistance to traction uphill. For the slab to start moving all these resistances must be broken, which would appear impossible. But it is amusing to note that the very existence of these resistances constitutes just so many possibilities of release. In fact, the breakage of one of these resistances eventually provokes all the others to break. The first break to develop is known as the primary rupture, and the others are known as secondary ruptures. We shall now consider the conditions of stability on the bottom, that is to say the relation of the resistance to shearing to the shear stress, as the principal criterion of release, and the lateral ruptures, above and below, as internal accidents comparable to external accidents such as the fall of a mass of snow.

We have seen that the rupture takes place when stress surpasses resistance, that is to say when the ratio is less than 1. But when one measures this ratio at the fracture points of avalanches one perceives that releases have taken place for s values of 2, 3 and up to 4. That is to say, the slab has been released with a resistance to shearing at the bottom two, three or even four times greater than the shear stress. This would appear impossible, but here is the explanation: following a shock or a momentary overload, the stress on the base has surpassed the resistance to shearing, which has been broken. This resistance to shearing is composed of cohesion and starting friction. At the break the cohesion is eliminated and when the snow begins to slip the starting friction changes instantly into a lesser movement friction.

So that movement should continue on the slope, it is first necessary that the slope be sufficiently steeper than the angle of kinetic friction and that the original slab be so big that the shock to the slabs downhill sets these in movement, and so on.

If the s ratio is near 1, that is to say the resistance to shearing is not much greater than the stress, the problem of the spread of the movement does not arise. In fact, one sometimes sees snow slabs in which the shearing resistance on the bottom runs instantly over the whole length of the slope. When the stability is great it happens, on the contrary, that traction ruptures develop without any avalanche being released. In fact, one often notices that after a fall of snow all the slopes have split without slipping. There is a relation between the stability s and the possibility of the movement spreading. The greater the ratio s, the more compact should be the slab originally set in movement if the movement is to continue; which is logical, for the shock of a compact slab will be more effective than that of a soft slab.

It now remains for us to study the internal accidents which can provoke a shearing rupture at the base of a slab and release it.

On a slope the snow creeps continually downwards. It creeps more quickly when the layer is thicker and the slope steeper. These differences in speed exert a pull upon the convex parts of slopes, compressions on the concave parts and shear stresses when the speed varies laterally. When the stress exceeds the resistance a rupture develops. The most frequent ruptures are those of traction, but in nature others also develop. It is likewise with the traction ruptures which are most likely to cause the release of an avalanche. Let us imagine a slab on a convex slope. It rests above on a horizontal part and settles. But the more the slope inclines the greater the creep. If this compact slab rests on a thick bed of snow, the creep of this bed increases the traction stress in the slab. The slab is stretched to the limit of its elasticity, small in the snow, but greater when the snow is more compact. Presumably, on rupture, that part of the slab downhill from the fracture line is launched downwards with greater force the greater its elasticity. The stronger the shock the more chance there is that the movement will spread.

The weakest layer in a superposition of strata on which the slab is released is called the lubricating layer, for once their cohesion is broken the crystals act as a lubricant. The best lubricant is new snow (17°), then comes spherically-grained snow (23°) and finally cup crystals (32°). Generally, the lubricating layers are thin layers of new snow which have remained for a certain time on the surface. In their metamorphosis they lose their compressibility and remain in weak cohesion even under the pressure of a further fall of snow. If a layer of hoar-frost forms during the night on a surface crust and a layer of windblown snow accumulates on top, the conditions for a snow-slab avalanche are ideal.

The thickness of the lubricating layer plays a part in the slide. It cannot function satisfactorily if it is too thin. In this case the slide depends also on the cohesion of the sliding layers. If these two layers are very compact, the crystals, clinging strongly together, cannot free themselves and the moving layer slides with difficulty, without being able to acquire speed, as if it were one block of granite rubbing against another. This is what is called the influence of the structure of materials.

A good example of these effects was given to me during an excursion with my twelve-year-old son and some friends. We wanted to descend from the Fondeier Fürkli to Küblis by way of the Strahlegg. So as not to go too far down into the Maladerser Bach we passed along the top of some very steep slopes on the right. At one point we had to traverse a sort of open couloir, overlooked by slopes of at least 45°.

36

One of us entered the couloir and the snow in it started to move. The extremely hard snow slab split into blocks which slipped away slowly, taking our comrade with them. The unfortunate man was unable to get clear, and he slid gently to the middle of the blocks. Two hundred metres lower the whole thing stopped quietly. Our friend got to his feet, brushed his trousers and had to climb up the side in order to rejoin our track, which continued to run along the mountainside. We did not even go down to help him. My son had been very impressed. Had there been a lubricating layer I am convinced that the avalanche would have been deadly. But the compact blocks did not break up into small pieces, which would have rolled over one another, and the hard rubbing of the layers in contact did not allow the blocks to gain speed.

Knowing the mechanics of snow-slab release one can apply this knowledge to practical cases. Thus, for example, if one tries to release an avalanche artificially with detonators or mortars, there appears to be more chances of success if one provokes the traction rupture in the convex part of the slope rather than lower down.

When a tourist has to cross a slope which is presumed dangerous, he will be less likely to start off an avalanche if he passes across the middle of the slope in the neutral zone than if he passes across higher up in the traction zone. But if the avalanche gets moving he will be more surely buried if he is caught in the middle of the slope than if he is higher up. My advice is that it is better to traverse the slope high up and to try to release the avalanche by jumping, for once it is down it is no longer dangerous.

As to forecasting avalanches, one should be able, in theory, to state that for a stability s of up to 2 a layer of a certain compactness will only start moving on a slope of more than so many degrees; for s up to 3 and a certain compactness, the movement will only begin on a slope steeper than so many degrees; and so on. In practice this method is hard to apply, since the thickness of the snow varies from place to place and its strength varies constantly from one day to another. Besides, mere observation of nature is very often sufficient to show the danger. To facilitate the calculation of the danger, one can class avalanches under four principal situations which combine among themselves and which are caused by meteorological or snow conditions favourable to their release. When one knows the predominating situation one should know what kind of avalanche to expect. These situations are: snowfall, wind, unstable internal layers and a rise of temperature.

1. *A snowfall* constitutes an overload. On the one hand it increases the shear stress on the base and in the layers. On the other hand it also causes settling and an increase in cohesion, but this cohesion becomes stronger only after about two days, so that the overload is a danger. It increases also the stresses at the edges of the snow slab and generally provokes a warming up of the base layers, lessening their cohesion. When there is more than 30 to 40 cm (*c.* one foot) of new snow, the danger to the tourist

begins. When 60 cm (*c.* two feet) or more of new snow have fallen the danger becomes general and threatens communications; 1.20 m (*c.* 4 feet) or more constitutes the beginning of a catastrophic situation, threatening villages, isolated houses, etc. This danger is easy to detect. One can only make a mistake about its extent. In intense cold it persists.

2. *Wind* plays a part. If a region is covered with snow that is not windblown and a strong wind rises, it displaces the snow, clears certain slopes and creates a danger in sheltered spots by forming slabs, snowdrifts and snowshields. If wind blows during snowfall it acts the same way and localizes the danger to sheltered slopes. The danger caused by violent wind is easily recognizable by the tourist, but that which is brought about by a moderate wind is much more difficult to detect.

3. If there is a weak *lubricating stratum* inside a snow mantle, it is a cause of instability which can persist for a month or two. This situation is one of the most dangerous for the tourist. In reality, avalanches of this kind are not extremely numerous, but they are practically unforeseeable and are often spaced out over a long period. After a heavy snowfall, the first avalanches generally slide on this new snow. Meanwhile, the new layer can also slide on a weak internal layer of old snow or of frost. Such a situation ends only after a considerable rise in temperature or a heavy snowfall which brings about releases almost everywhere, or a settling of the dangerous layer resulting in its consolidation.

This situation is also one of the most difficult to recognize at the start. It is only after a week that one gradually becomes aware that the avalanches are continuing to run over the inner lubricating layers, one day here, the next day over there, and so on. These weak layers arise from a layer of loose snow, shut in at the beginning of the winter for example, or from a thin layer of new snow which has rested on the surface for a long time and has been transformed into loose grains. It has lost the great compressibility of new snows, it resists the pressure of new layers, settles only a little and remains friable. A layer of surface frost covered by a new stratum constitutes an excellent lubricating layer.

4. *A rise of temperature* always involves danger at the start by lessening the contact cohesion of the layers, thus facilitating ruptures, or by eliminating the matting of fresh snow through activating destructive metamorphosis. But a rise of temperature also provokes settling and stabilization. In the mountains the first considerable rise of temperature in the spring is generally the most dangerous, for it can eventually bring about the release of whole mountainsides in huge avalanches of heavy snow. A strong and rapid rise of temperature on a layer of fresh and soft snow tends to bring about the release of numerous balls of snow. The warmed up surface settles and forms a surface layer of great specific weight, comparable to a soft and heavy crust lying on a still cold, very plastic and poorly cohering layer. The surface stratum has a tendency

38

to flow downwards and the lower part of the layer of fresh snow is deformed by the effect of this slow flow. A slight irregularity allows a lump of sodden snow to escape, which rolls away, gathering up snow as it passes in proportion to the extent of its humidity.

When in the spring the melted and refrozen surface of the snow takes the form of a quantity of pointed humps and rounded hollows, releases due to humidity are no longer to be feared.

A layer, lying on a convex slope and under traction stress, due to its creeping movement, can be fractured following a rise in temperature which weakens its cohesion. But this rise of temperature also renders the snow more plastic and this diminishes the stress. When the cold returns with evening the snow layer resumes a certain rigidity, the stresses increase and fractures sometimes occur at that moment.

In conclusion, although what happens in nature can mostly be explained, it is impossible to predict with certainty where or when an avalanche will start to slide. In principal, the friction angle of the snow lessens with destructive metamorphosis and increases a little with constructive metamorphosis. The cohesion of the snow varies continually. It is strengthened as a result of an increase in pressure (new fall of snow) and weakened by metamorphosis. Thus every avalanche has its hour, depending on the play of stresses and resistances, and also on external events, so that it is always difficult to act with an adequate margin of safety.

Our best way of judging consists of knowing the influences provoking an avalanche situation and observing nature which usually shows its tricks in a generous fashion.

MASHERBRUM

By Nicholas B. Clinch

We stood in the afternoon shadows at the edge of the little Balti village looking at the gleaming mass that blocked the end of the valley. A small cloud drifting across the southeast face emphasized the tremendous scale of the mountain still twenty miles distant. Finally, someone quietly said, "If I had seen a picture of it I wouldn't have come".

It was a poor excuse. We had studied the photographs. Some of us had seen the mountain itself on our earlier trips to the Karakorum range of northwestern Pakistan. We were not deceived. Masherbrum is a 25,660-foot giant that towers above its neighbours and from the Baltoro glacier to the Hushe valley there is no camera angle that reassures you otherwise.

The record of man on Masherbrum was equally unequivocal. It had been attempted three times by mountaineers whose competence matched their courage. In 1938, an era when mountaineers were developing the art of Himalayan route-finding the hard way, a British party led by Major James Waller painstakingly discovered the best route up the mountain and climbed to within a thousand feet of the summit. Then, beset by storm and avalanche, their assault team badly frostbitten, they were purged. The retreat to Srinigar with Robin Hodgkin and Jock Harrison being carried on litters between amputations without anesthetic was a mountaineering epic that has disappeared in the pages of British understatement.

The New Zealanders were next in April 1955. It was a capable party, but they were on the mountain too early in the season; their efforts were slowed, and then stopped, by the deep winter's snow before they reached 23,000 feet.

The British returned in 1957. In an expression of human determination which proved that on high mountains fortune does not favour the brave, they pushed to within 300 feet of the summit. At that point Don Whillans and Joe Walmsley, the leader of the party, after struggling for seven hours on the icy rocks besides the couloir leading to the col between the mountain's twin peaks, placed a piton, attached their reserve rope to it and retreated. It was the climax of several months' effort, during which one of their best climbers, Bob Downes, succumbed to pulmonary edema at camp six.

As we slogged up the flank of Hidden Peak in 1958, Captain S. T. H. Rizvi, a member of that 1957 Masherbrum party, told many unpleasant bedtime stories about

Scaly Alley, the Dome, the great southeast face, and the summit couloir. Masherbrum sounded terrible. But in the evening sunset, for it dominated our view toward the west, Masherbrum was a climber's dream.

Only the completeness of our success on Hidden Peak, a legacy of the cumulative experience of mountaineers in the Himalaya, could explain the faint thought that lay hidden beneath the fatigue as we hiked down the Baltoro glacier. "What's next?" We knew the answer. That pillar in the western sky.

Two years later that faint thought had expanded to the ten climbers, the six HAPs (high altitude porters) and the army of porters travelling under the name of the 1960 American Pakistan Karakorum Expedition that occupied the small Balti village. We were sponsored by the American Alpine Club, together with the Sports Control Committee of the Pakistan Army, and our shiny equipment and immaculate crates of food stamped with the emblem of the Swiss Foundation of Alpine Research were the product of the industry and the mountaineering world of three continents. The demons of permission and finance which consume most embryonic expeditions had been defeated, their scars repressed into the depths of the records and the subconscious of the expedition's organizer.

As we approached our objective we had an heretical feeling of confidence, which even that view from the Balti village did not completely dissipate. Part of it may have been attributable to the knowledge we had gained from our predecessors, for Waller and Walmsley had practically given us a road map to within a few hundred feet of the summit. But most of our confidence was due to the close bond of comradeship among the members of the expedition, the seven Americans, the three Pakistanis and the six Balti HAPs. We were friends when the trip began. We were a mutual admiration society when it was over.

The leader of this blistered assembly of boisterous humorists was George Bell, a 34-year-old nuclear physicist, who managed, against all obstacles, to give the affair just the precise amount of order needed to accomplish the task at hand. Like George, the other Americans, Willi Unsoeld, Dick Emerson, Dick McGowan, Tom Hornbein, the climbing doctor, Tom McCormack, and myself, had been climbing for years, lost in many ranges. We averaged two college degrees and three mountaineering expeditions per man, a startling illustration of the affinity of the mountaineering passion for the academic vacation.

Only Jawed Akhter of the three Pakistani members, all Captains in the Pakistan Army, had any previous mountaineering experience. The year before Jawed had made the first ascent of 23,500 foot Malubiting East, with a British-Pakistan Armed Forces expedition. Imtiaz Azim and Mohd Akram Qureshi overcame their lack of training by a rapid and hard apprenticeship as we pressed up the mountain and they soon carried more than their share of the team effort.

The six HAPs were old and proven companions. Ghulam Razul, the Sirdar and the only man I know who can keep a hundred porters in lock step for thirty-two miles, Abdul Rahim, Rahim Khan, and Quasim had been on Hidden Peak, where they had done an outstanding job. Mohammed Hussain had carried George Bell out from K-2 in 1953 when George had his feet frostbitten. Hussain had been with Jawed on Malubiting.

On May 30, 1960, after a brutal twelve-mile carry from the village of Hushe, over loose moraine and soft snow, the expedition arrived at its base camp site, 13,500 feet, on the snow-covered Masherbrum glacier. The summit of Masherbrum was now 12,000 foreshortened vertical feet and a few miles away.

We spent the next day trying to find everything, or "getting organized" as it is more formally called. The weather was perfect and we were impatient. On June 1st, McGowan, Emerson, Hornbein and Jawed pushed their way through the centre of the first two icefalls on the Serac Glacier and located a site for Camp I at 15,500 feet. The Serac Glacier was the usual labyrinth of seracs and crevasses that makes the climber wonder which will happen first: the bottom fall out or the top fall in.

The route through the middle of the second icefall was impractical for laden men and we were reluctantly forced to use Scaly Alley, a relatively uncrevassed avalanche chute beneath the cliffs at the right edge of the icefall. Although it stimulated the adrenalin of the more timid among us, we were never present when the chute was preempted by falling debris. Indeed, the entire lower part of Masherbrum, the Serac Glacier, Scaly Alley, the basin below Serac Peak, and the slopes leading up the Dome had one aspect in common. They appear dangerous and only the knowledge that our predecessors had trod these glaciers and slopes with relative impunity justified our presence on them. Nothing ever happened to us, and after the first trip over a new section of the route, our minds settled into a weary obliviousness which was occasionally punctuated by flashes of fear at a sharp crack of activity on the mountain above us.

During the first ten days of June there was an unprecedented spell of good weather in the Karakorum, which spurred us to frenzied activity. Imtiaz and Qureshi doubled our carrying capacity by persuading fifteen tough Hushe-wallahs that hauling loads to Camp I would be the easiest rupees they would ever earn in their lives. Dick McGowan, a geography teacher who spends his summers hauling tourists up Mt Rainier as Chief Guide, was in charge of this exercise in mass mountaineering. One blast on the whistle and we all moved forward—with varying degrees of success. When the morning sun reached the Serac Glacier we sank into the snow so deeply that the memory of the first late start was sufficient to enable us to endure the pre-dawn cold thereafter. The whistle was soon lost.

Ghulam Razul kept singing and laughing; sahibs, HAPs and Hushe-wallahs kept picking up their loads and moving through that frozen witch's cauldron; and in five days we hauled over 3,000 pounds of supplies to Camp I. We hired Abdul Rahim's younger brother as a watchman and abandoned base camp, except for occasional forays to discharge porters or pick up the mail.

Meanwhile, Willi Unsoeld and Tom McCormack found a route through the third icefall and across the basin below Serac Peak, a land of large and wandering crevasses, to the base of the slope leading to the top of the dome. After spending a couple of nights under the ice cliffs of Serac Peak, listening to sounds in the dark, the first occupants of Camp II moved it another 500 feet up the Dome to an altitude of 19,500 feet. It was an unreasonably long way from Camp I to a reasonably safe camp site.

From Camp II Unsoeld, McGowan, Emerson and Jawed broke a track up the steep unconsolidated snow of the Dome to establish the route to Camp III. Aluminium ladders were thrown over a couple of dubious snow-bridges on the way to Camp II; fixed lines were draped on the side of the Dome; dark green bamboo wands with flags were placed every rope length; and then the highway was ready for heavy travel. Six Hushe men, who were the fortunate possessors of boots from previous expeditions, were pressed into service for the run to Camp II and the unremitting relaying of supplies continued. (The other Hushe men, who carried from base camp to Camp I, just had home-made mukluks.)

The carry up the Dome was the epitome of Himalayan mountaineering. It was a monotonous never-ending slog up an avalanche slope. Every few hundred feet we collapsed into the bottomless snow and wondered why it never slid and buried Camp II. After a few days of this our wonder almost turned to disappointment.

Now the weather changed and after June 10th it snowed every day for twenty-four days, sometimes lightly, sometimes a blizzard, but snow nevertheless. Every night the snow covered our tracks; every day we rebroke the trail. Thus Camp III, our advance base at 21,000 feet on top of the Dome, became full of men and supplies.

Onward. Bell, McCormack and Emerson slogged a mile and a half across the plateau from advance base and located a site for Camp IV at 22,000 feet. From Camp IV Unsoeld and McGowan groped their way through snow and cloud to find a spot below the edge of the east ridge at 23,000 feet and that was suitable for Camp V. When they returned from this reconnaissance they met George Bell, Tom Hornbein and myself, who had come up to Camp IV with the HAPs on the morning relay. As we were quietly talking, the mist suddenly blew away and we got a discouraging view of the route. Before us the southeast face swept 3,000 feet upward at an angle of about 30° to the twin summits of Masherbrum. On it were many overhanging ice cliffs; the largest, which was more than 200 feet high, extended further across the face than was shown in the photographs taken by the previous expeditions. We would have to take a long detour around it on very steep slopes to reach the snow couloir between the two summits. The cliff menaced the route below it and would penalize any mistakes made above it. However, there was little sign of activity and, as George Bell said reassuringly, "If that thing comes down, it will be an Act of God".

On June 22nd, Willi Unsoeld and Dick McGowan, the first summit team, left Camp V and led up across the face. I followed, escorting Ghulam Razul, Abdul Rahim, Rahim Khan and Qasim. The snow was waist deep, visibility was poor, and we could not find a safe place for Camp VI. Finally, after many hours Unsoeld yelled out of the blowing whiteness that he had found a spot. It was a small platform, restricted by partially concealed crevasses, beneath a thirty-foot serac at 24,000 feet. With hard work and imagination it would hold two tents.

The next day Unsoeld and McGowan climbed 400 feet above Camp VI on slopes steeper than any previously encountered. They placed fixed ropes and returned to Camp VI, which was now occupied by George Bell and Tom Hornbein, the second assault team, who had climbed up from Camp V while the indomitable HAPs, escorted by Jawed, continued to relay loads.

On June 24th Unsoeld and McGowan started for the summit using oxygen. They mounted the fixed lines and then started a delicate traverse across the slope. Their steps threatened to collapse and the ferrules of their ice-axes penetrated the snow only a few inches before striking the unyielding ice beneath. After leading a full rope length, Willi tried to get a belay. He packed snow around the shaft of his axe, shouted for McGowan to join him, and the "patted shaft" belay was born. When McGowan reached Unsoeld he took one look at the stance and the "patted shaft" was replaced by an ice screw. Meanwhile, George Bell and Tom Hornbein attached fixed rope behind the summit pair to safeguard the retreat.

After the "patted shaft" traverse, Willi and Dick struggled upward through deep soft snow to the bergschrund that cut across the face underneath the twin summits at 25,000 feet. They were having trouble with the oxygen equipment, it was 2.30 in the afternoon and the weather was getting worse. We would need another camp. They cached their spare climbing equipment, including the pitons, expansion bolts, and stirrups we had brought for the summit rocks and retreated. During the descent they could see only a few feet through the blowing clouds as small slides of powder snow swirled past their feet. Once McGowan was covered by a slide as he clung to the fixed rope. Later—as snow, slope and air blended into a single blur of white—he stepped over an ice cliff and was held by Unsoeld's belay.

The weather deteriorated. On the morning of June 27th, when they stuck their heads out of the tents at Camp VI, they saw ominous multiple layers of clouds gathering over Chogolisa and the Gasherbrum group. By the time they had packed their equipment for the retreat to Camp V a Karakorum blizzard was raging. They groped their way from wand to wand until a wand was missing. As they stood on the slope trying to determine the proper start for the traverse into Camp V the powder snow

44

swishing around their ankles suddenly rushed over their heads and they were swept down the face. Tumbling head over heels, Hornbein thought, "We really haven't done too well on this mountain". McGowan, his arms pinned by the rope, went under, breathing large quantities of snow. On his third flip, Unsoeld, who was at the edge of the avalanche, managed to drive in his axe, George Bell managed to do a self-arrest, and the four men were deposited on the slope as the powder snow went over an ice cliff just below them. McGowan, who was in poor condition from the large quantities of snow that he had inhaled, got up and promptly collapsed. Just then there was a break in the storm and they could see the tents of Camp V. When Jawed and I heard their shouts we desperately tried to break a track uphill to them, but we could barely move. Fortunately, after Hornbein gave him some codeine, McGowan was able to stumble into Camp V unaided. Our first attempt had ended in the whine of the wind and the hiss of the avalanche.

From the furnace of defeat came a new alloy of determination mixed with caution. The southeast face was no place to be in a storm, but some day the weather would have to clear and when it did. . . . Six of us, Bell, Unsoeld, McCormack, Emerson, Jawed, and I sat in Camp V sharing half rations and poor jokes. Our food supply dwindled as the snow continued to pile up the sides of the tents. Finally Emerson, McCormack, Jawed and I descended to Camp IV. The next day Unsoeld and Bell, the new assault team, would have to follow. But the next day, July 4th, it cleared.

Now! The mountain came alive with climbers and HAPs, Lilliputians determined to bind their Gulliver before he awoke again. Bell and Unsoeld returned to Camp VI, which was completely buried in snow. They dug out one tent and then hastily dug out the second, when they saw that Emerson and Jawed were climbing all the way from Camp IV to join them. Hornbein, McGowan and I returned to Camp V while the HAPs made a double carry from Camp III to Camp V. Below, McCormack, Imtiaz and Qureshi kept the supply line open.

On July 5th Unsoeld, Bell, Emerson and Jawed climbed to the bergschrund at 25,000 feet. The cache of equipment left by McGowan and Unsoeld was gone, either swept away or buried by a slide. Now the only equipment available was a few rappel pickets and ice screws. By packing snow in the schrund and levelling the edge they managed to pitch one tent which tilted slightly to the outside over the face. Jawed and Emerson returned to Camp VI while Bell and Unsoeld crawled into the tent to spend a restless night listening to ice pellets from the west peak strike the tent cloth.

The next day, July 6th, George and Willi left Camp VII at 5.00 a.m. They traversed along the bergschrund until they were directly under the couloir that led to the summit ridge. Cautiously they climbed for several hundred feet toward the throat of the gully and across a snow-covered band of rocks, upon which their crampons and nerves grated, to enter the couloir itself. There was not a breath of wind and they

45

stifled in the heat. On the right the green ice was exposed, on the left it was covered with fluffy snow. Between the ice and the fluff they kicked a fragile ladder of steps, using an ice-axe and an aluminium shovel as support, while they consolidated their gain.

Six hours later they reached the razor-sharp col between the twin peaks and turned toward the East Peak. They were blocked by the first rock step, a shattered mass of friable rock held together by ice and frozen snow. Willi pounded an ice screw, the only available iron, into a crack and delicately traversed the step on the Baltoro Glacier side. Again they balanced along the thin snow edge until they came to the second step, a snout of rock that was cut in the lower section by a twenty-foot chimney. They struggled up the chimney and after a brief stop for lunch they climbed the last part of the step to reach the ridge. Slowly, mechanically, they plodded through the soft snow until the ridge slanted downward. They were up.

It was a stupendous view. The peaks of the lower Baltoro, Paiju, the Trango Towers, the Muztagh Tower, were dwarfed beneath them, while to the north rose the eight-thousanders of the Baltoro — Hidden Peak, Gasherbrum II, Broad Peak and, above all, K-2.

Bell and Unsoeld reached the summit at 3.15 p.m. and spent an hour on top before starting their descent. After climbing and rappelling down the second step, they traversed the ridge and rappelled from the top of the first step into the couloir. Then, using aluminium pickets, they rappelled down the gully and reached Camp VII at 8.00 p.m. where they spent another fitful night.

George Bell and Willi Unsoeld were not the only climbers who had an exciting afternoon. Jawed Akhter, Dick McGowan and Tom Hornbein were moving up the fixed ropes towards Camp VII when McGowan, who had never fully recovered from the avalanche, became ill. They had to retreat. Jawed, in the lead, turned around on the "patted shaft" traverse. His step broke, and he came toppling down the slope. There was no time to get a belay. Hornbein grabbed the fixed rope with his left hand and the climbing rope with his right. The only give in the belay was the stretch in Tom's shoulders, but he held, as Javee plunged into the snow headfirst. It was 160 feet from drop to stop. They returned to Camp VI, where Emerson and I were waiting. McGowan was still feeling weak so Hornbein escorted him down to Camp V through the gathering dusk.

The following day Dick Emerson, Jawed Akhter, and I climbed to Camp VII to make the next assault. On the way we met Unsoeld and Bell coming down. George looked in good shape although we learned later that he had spent the night in a minor delirium, humming nonsense tunes while Unsoeld emptied the contents of the emergency medical kit into him.

When we reached Camp VII we tried to widen the tent platform, but it did not help

46

much. The tent still sagged over the face. Extremely tired, we crawled inside one by one and went to sleep in our cramped quarters without fixing dinner.

At 1 a.m. on July 8th Jawed and I lighted a stove and began melting snow for water. We punctured another can of gas to start a second stove. The valve was defective. The escaping stream of gas hit the flame of the first stove and exploded. Instantly, a fountain of fire shot to the top of the tent and set the inner lining ablaze. I threw the pot of water on it, but it did no good. A few moments of smoky confusion followed; we could not thrash around too violently or we would knock ourselves off the mountain. I was working with a jammed zipper, and Emerson was hunting for his knife when Jawed quietly said, "the fire is out". He had smothered the flames with a pair of down pants. Dick and I were impressed by Jawed's quick thinking. The pants belonged to George Bell.

This attempt to cook ourselves for breakfast was an appropriate beginning to the day's activities. Dick Emerson, our strongest man, was ill from a lack of food and dysentery, but he gallantly insisted that Jawed and I try for the summit while he cleaned up the mess. The two of us left at 7.30 in the morning.

It was a perfect day. The silent grandeur of the surrounding mountains imposed their isolation upon us; the almost obliterated tracks made by Unsoeld and Bell were more than a guide, they were the symbol of strong friends below. We were not alone.

Slowly we climbed upward. Each step had to be rekicked or recut because of the frozen powder that covered it, but eventually we crossed the band of rocks and entered the couloir where we reached a fixed line that had been left by Willi and George. The line made us feel more secure, for we were never certain the next step would hold.

If the step failed, the belay might hold; then again, we were not too certain about that either.

The struggle continued. To our left we could see the rope placed by Don Whillans and Joe Walmsley hanging over steep ice-coated rocks, a reminder to stick to the snow and be thankful. We reached the col, only to be disappointed by its knife-edge. But we could sit down, something that we could not do in the couloir unless we expended precious energy chopping out a stance. Below, Willi Unsoeld and George Bell were going down the traverse between Camps VI and V. We reminded ourselves not to drop the empty oxygen bottle. Meanwhile, beyond our sight and knowledge, Tom McCormack and Abdul Rahim were making the first ascent of impressive Serac Peak, 22,000 feet, which dominated the route to the Dome.

The first rock step on the ridge looked frightening, its rottenness sheathed in ice. The main inspiration for climbing it was not the nearby summit; it was the rappel sling on the top of the step. As we had no equipment except for one ice screw we were condemned to follow the tracks of Unsoeld and Bell every foot of the way. Forty feet out on the traverse over the Baltoro Glacier I looked at the next long stride onto

47

crumbling icy rock; then I looked back at Jawed's axe sunk to the blade in rotten snow with the rope hitched around it. I was slowly gathering my courage as well as my breath when I saw an iron ring in front of me. Unsoeld's ice screw! I clipped in and made the stride with ease. The rest of the traverse was a joy; I knew we would reach the summit.

After several rope-lengths along the ridge we arrived at the second step. Jawed led the chimney and hauled up the pack. Then we slowly trudged the last few hundred feet along the ridge; it was 6.15 p.m. and the mountains were putting on their robes of purple for the night. In a few more steps the expedition would achieve one of its cherished goals, a Pakistani mountaineer would reach the summit of Masherbrum. Yet, as the track ended, my main thought was that we must be careful on the descent. After such an incredible experience it would be a shame to get killed on the way down.

Sunset over the Karakorum filled us with awe and regret. It was unbelievably magnificent and we could not linger to enjoy it. We took a few pictures, made several last glances around us, hoping to capture the scene forever, and then started the descent.

On the short overhanging rappel off the second rock step Jawed lost a down mitten while I got hung up temporarily on my ice-axe. The rappel from the first rock step was worse. Standing in the dark shadows of the couloir, Jawed and I pulled on the doubled ropes. The first one came. The second one cleared the sling and started to drop, but suddenly it stuck. We put all our weight on it, but it refused to budge. We did not dare climb down the couloir and now we could not reach the next picket placed by Unsoeld and Bell. We roped down halfway and then made a bollard out of the loose powder to anchor the next short rappel. In the high cold this took forever. Fortunately there was a full moon and no wind, but the chill still penetrated reindeer boots and down clothing. As we intently worked our way down the couloir we noticed that it was getting light. The sun was coming up! We reached Dick Emerson and our scorched tent at 7.30 in the morning, twenty-four hours after we had left.

Dick, who had recovered from his illness of the day before, plied us with liquid. Then at 3.00 p.m. we packed Camp VII and began the retreat. Skilfully, patiently, Emerson kept his two exhausted companions on a firm belay as we tumbled down the fixed rope to Camp VI.

The next day a storm broke. By the time we had packed Camp VI we could not see more than 100 feet through the blowing snow. Suddenly two figures loomed ahead and we heard the strains of a harmonica. Willi Unsoeld and Tom Hornbein had come up from Camp V to assist us, thereby exposing themselves twice to the danger that had previously engulfed them. They took our packs and guided us down through the swirling snow. Measuring distances by rope-lengths, Unsoeld and Hornbein brilliantly

48

16 ON THE ROUTE TO MASHERBRUM. Camp I of the American-Pakistani Expedition, 1960. (Photograph by George Bell)

17 PORTERS of the Masherbrum Expedition above Camp I. (Photograph by George Bell)
18 following page: THE AMERICANS on the Southeast Ridge of Masherbrum on the approach to Camp III.
     (Photograph by George Bell)
19 the next following page: ON THE ROUTE TO MASHERBRUM. The view from Camp VI (about 23,950 ft.)
     toward the Gasherbrum Group and Hidden Peak. (Photograph by Nick Clinch)

located the traverse into Camp V. An hour later we were safe in the tents. Behind us the newly fallen snow began to avalanche.

Razul and the HAPs were waiting. They picked up Camp V and we continued the descent. Each step was a mechanical victory. We slogged past Camp IV. Every few hundred yards I lay down in the snow while Unsoeld and Hornbein waited at a discreet distance. My thoughts were simple and dull. We had done it. The human tide towards which each of us had contributed and in which each of us was swept forward had reached the summit. If only the entire party could have stood on that final snow ridge as an outward sign of the unity that made success possible! Close friends whose contributions were indispensable had not trod the last final yards because of mere chance. But they knew that this was their triumph. Later, when Whillans, Waller, Walmsley and our other gallant predecessors heard the news they would know that this was their triumph also.

At last there was a ghostly orange glow through the snow ahead. It was the light in the cook tent at Camp III. I reached it and crawled inside.

THE FIRST INDIAN ATTEMPT ON EVEREST (1960)

By Brigadier Gyan Singh

The Himalayas have been for centuries a region of pilgrimage and worship for millions of devout Indians. Equally, traders and missionaries have for generations braved the Himalayan hazards to enter Tibet over some of the highest mountain passes in the world. Among the early explorers and surveyors of this rugged mountainous terrain were some Indians, who, though ill-equipped and untrained in climbing techniques, performed some incredible feats of mountaineering in the execution of their tasks.

Till about ten years ago there were scarcely any Indians who went to the Himalayas for sport. The real impetus to mountaineering in India came from the ascent of Everest in 1953 when, teamed with Sir Edmund Hillary, Tenzing Norgay stood on the roof of the world. The spark of enthusiasm ignited by Tenzing's feat has already developed into a torch to light the path of those who seek adventure and excitement among the Himalayan heights. Indian youth's response to the call of the mountains is yet another sign of national awakening.

Thus, the Himalayan Mountaineering Institute came into being in 1954 to commemorate Tenzing's great achievement. With Tenzing himself as the director of field training, the Institute has trained young men on basic and advanced courses and has also helped in organizing expeditions to lesser peaks in the Himalayas. The sport, however, grew fast and barely four years after the Himalayan Mountaineering Institute was started, an Indian team successfully climbed Cho Oyu, the sixth highest mountain in the world. Encouraged by this success, the sponsoring committee booked Everest for 1960, and also for 1962 in case it was not possible to make an attempt in 1960.

By all standards, an attempt on a mountain of the magnitude of Everest is an ambitious project requiring thorough planning and preparation over a long period. For one reason or another very little work was done in 1958 and, in fact, the first half of 1959 also went by without achieving much in the way of preparation.

During July and August 1959 I had gone to Europe on the invitations of the French Mountaineering Federation and the Swiss Foundation for Alpine Research to attend some international mountaineers' meetings. When I returned to India in September, I was surprised to find that the sponsoring committee offered me the leadership of the expedition. It was a pleasant surprise, and indeed an honour, but I was diffident about accepting the task. However, after some thought I found it impossible to decline.

Once the decision had been made, two immediate tasks confronted us; first the selection of a team, and second the procuring of equipment. The selection of the team was not difficult because at the Himalayan Mountaineering Institute we were able to organize a special pre-Everest course in the Kabru region of western Sikkim in October and November 1959. Twenty-five mountaineers responded to the invitation, and after the course, on Tenzing's recommendation and mine, the sponsoring committee finalized the team. We were happy to find that there were more qualified aspirants than places in the expedition, so several worthy men were unfortunately turned down.

In the end we selected thirteen men, all with considerable Himalayan experience. First there were the three Sherpa instructors from the Mountaineering Institute: Da-Namgyal, Ang Temba and Gombu, all of whom had been on Everest before. Then Keki Bunshah, Captain Narinder Kumar of the Kumaon Regiment, Sonam Gyatsho (who was one of the two who reached the summit of Cho-Oyu in 1958), Flight-Lieutenant Chaudhury, Rajendra Vikram Singh, B. D. Misra, C. P. Vohra, Captain Jungalwalla of the Gorkha Rifles, Instructor-Lieutenant M. S. Kohli of the Indian Navy, and myself. In addition, we had two doctors, Flight-Lieutenant N. S. Bhagwanani and Captain S. K. Das of the Army Medical Corps; a Films Division camera man C. V. Gopal; and a transport officer, Flight-Lieutenant A. J. S. Grewal. Our small signals detachment was led by Captain S. G. Nanda. Meteorologist K. U. Shankar Rao, and the Secretary of the Indian Mountaineering Federation, Sohan Singh, also accompanied us.

The second problem was far more difficult because it had been decided that as much of our equipment as possible should be manufactured in India, and imports should be restricted to specialized items only. In the past most expeditions to Himalayan peaks, including Indian expeditions, had to use European equipment. But we knew that we could rely on the skill and ingenuity of our own countrymen. In nearly all cases the indigenous equipment stood the severe test very well indeed. This in itself is perhaps one of the expedition's major achievements. It will perhaps be possible in the near future for Himalayan expeditions to obtain reliable equipment and stores in India, thus reducing expenditure on transportation, and delays and irritations at arrival ports.

While we knew that India could make the equipment, the time factor was against us. We had barely five months in which to train and select the team, obtain prototypes of equipment and test them, place final orders for stores and equipment, and ensure delivery in time for us to start packing on February 20, 1960.

The attempt on a major Himalayan peak is, to a large extent, a logistical problem of great magnitude, the planning and preparation for which must begin the day the project is conceived. If success on a mountain like Everest is to be assured, a team of ten to twelve climbers and over forty Sherpas must first be properly equipped and transported with adequate supplies to the base of the mountain. To achieve this, many of the resources of modern technology must be mobilized. It was very gratifying to find that Indian industry and ordnance factories co-operated in a magnificent manner. Under Tenzing's personal supervision, Sherpas and Nepali women of Darjeeling worked long hours knitting excellent woollen wear for the expedition. The Swiss Foundation for Alpine Research in Zurich gave us unstinted support and handled the supply of oxygen apparatus and other essential imported items. For three months the members of the team and many friends, as well as our sponsors, worked almost round the clock collecting the nineteen tons of equipment and stores which began to arrive at the Central Vista Mess in New Delhi towards the middle of February 1960. Now everyone worked eagerly sorting out the gear, classifying it, and packing it in sixty-pound loads. Finally, on February 27th, we passed our first big hurdle. We laid out the packages on the lawns of the mess ready for transportation by road to Lucknow on the first lap of our journey to Everest.

When we arrived in Jayanagar on March 4th, most of our Sherpas and over 700 porters were already waiting for us. We had only one day in which to register the porters, pay them advances, allot them loads and divide them into two parties, as it was not convenient for so many to march in one train. Here Tenzing's help in handling the Sherpas and porters proved invaluable. The first party entered Nepal on schedule on March 6th, after a heart-warming farewell from the people of Jayanagar and many friends who had come to see us off.

Our two weeks' journey to the acclimatization training camp near Thyangboche Monastery took us through terai jungles, lush padi-fields and over beautiful alpine meadows. Apricot and cherry trees in blossom and blooming rhododendrons and magnolias dotted the landscape along our route. Often local villagers would bring eggs, milk, and fruit, all as a friendly gesture, expecting nothing in return. Our long caravan arrived in Namche Bazar on March 21st. This sleepy-looking village, with about a hundred houses, is in the heart of Sherpa country, not far from Everest, and is an important landmark for all expeditions going to East Nepal. That night a heavy and much needed snowfall blanketed the surrounding country.

Three days later we reached Thyangboche, where we were given an audience by the incarnate Lama in a simple but solemn ceremony. The Lama promised to offer prayers for the safe return of the expedition. That same day we reached our acclimatization training camp at Pangboche at a height of 13,200 feet. Based on this camp, for the next three weeks we carried through a programme which entailed climbing peaks of 16,000 to 19,000 feet. We climbed in different groups and in different areas, carrying varying loads in our rucksacks. We also used this period for familiarizing our-selves with our oxygen and other specialized equipment. Physiologist Das and Doctor Bhagwanani kept a careful watch on our performance and conducted certain physio-logical tests. But so far no one required much medical attention, for we were all in excellent health and enormously enjoyed the good food with which the expedition had been provided. This was also a sure sign of the fact that we were acclimatizing well.

In the second phase of our acclimatization programme, we had divided ourselves into three parties each of four members, and each with a team of ten high-altitude sherpas. Each party was self-sufficient in equipment and stores and had selected its own area for its climbing activity. The plans of all three parties were ready by March 30th.

The first party, consisting of Keki Bunshah, Kohli, Jungalwalla and Ang Temba, moved in the direction of the base of Everest. They did their climbing exercises on the way. This party had been given the task of establishing the base camp and exploring the route through the Khumbu ice-fall.

The second party, consisting of Kumar, Misra, Vohra and Da-Namgyal, went over to the Amadablam area, where they indulged in some interesting rock scrambles. This party climbed the lower slopes of Amadablam and spotted fixed lines and rope-ladders put up by the ill-fated British Expedition to that great mountain in 1959. The party also climbed a relatively difficult rock feature, the Yellow Tower, so-named by the Swiss expedition to Everest in 1956.

The third group, consisting of Sonam, Gyatscho, Chaudhury, Rajendra Vikram and the photographer Gopal, went towards Taweche. They found the mountain very difficult from the southern slopes, but did some useful training climbs on ice and rock faces for three days, after which they moved to the Chukhung glacier.

By the end of the first week of April we had received the welcome news from Grewal that he would join us with oxygen equipment in the following week. Thus, all forces could now rapidly converge on the base camp. Our exciting task was about to begin. We had our equipment, and what is more, we were in good training and excellent health and our morale was high.

Our route towards the summit of Everest lay along the Khumbu glacier, through the Western Cwm, across the Lhotse face to the South Col and finally along the south-west ridge to the top. This was the route followed by the earlier parties because it is the only feasible approach from the Nepalese side of the mountain.

On reaching the base camp we could not see the summit of Everest, but the western shoulders of Everest and Nuptse enclosed the entrance to the Western Cwm above the Khumbu Glacier. Down these faces we could see and hear avalanches thundering intermittently into the valley.

Even without reconnaissance we were aware of the three main hurdles which had to be overcome before reaching the top of Everest. First, the Khumbu ice-fall, an awe-inspiring mass of ice which cascades nearly 2,000 feet down a steep gradient. In its downward plunge, this enormous slab of ice is broken up into gaping crevasses, massive ridges and ice-towers, forming a complicated labyrinth. The ice-fall in some respects is the most difficult obstacle and is constantly changing. Yet throughout our stay on the mountain we had to negotiate it every day. In order to establish higher camps it was also necessary to transport nearly two tons of stores and equipment over this treacherous and dreaded portion of the glacier.

The second hurdle was the Lhotse Face, a very long and steep slope of granite-hard ice and rock rising to 26,000 feet from the Western Cwm at about 22,400 feet. We knew this would tax our energy in cutting steps and fixing rope lines. Here we would also enter the so-called deterioration zone with its extremely rarefied atmosphere. Finally, there was the summit pyramid where, in addition to the technical difficulties, the effects of weather and high altitude were even more pronounced.

By the time all the parties assembled at the base camp on April 13th, the first party, consisting of Ang Temba, Keki, Kohli, Jungalwalla and Bhagwanani, had already established Camp I on April 10th at a height of 19,000 feet. They had also probed forward and made the route a part of the way towards the site of Camp II, but had to return somewhat short of their goal.

In accordance with our pre-arranged plan, the first team had to come off the mountain for a well-earned rest. The second party, composed of Da-Namgyal, Kumar, Vohra and Nisra, took over from the advance party.

I accompanied the second party up the ice-fall and spent the night at Camp I, established in an excellent location by Ang Temba and Kohli. Early next morning we started climbing towards the top of the ice-fall. After nearly three hours we arrived at the point reached by the earlier party. Here the Khumbu Glacier is compressed into a narrow gorge by the massive walls of Everest and Nuptse. Ahead of us, beyond several huge crevasses lay the Western Cwm and Lhotse. At this point we stopped on an ice ridge with Misra and my Sherpa companion, Lakpa. I contemplated the chaotic scene for some time. Looking back down the ice-fall I marvelled at the track-building ability of our climbers. The trail was marked with over 200 multi-coloured silk flags; ropes and ladders were fixed on vertical ice faces and there were many wide crevasses over which bridges had been made with baulks of timber lashed together. Many sections of light aluminium ladders were used for bridging other obstacles. We could see hundreds of feet of rope firmly fixed to the vertical ice ridges to assist the climbers and Sherpas traversing those dangerous sections.

Hours passed. Around three o'clock, Da-Namgyal and the four Sherpas who had gone ahead returned to inform us modestly that Camp II had been established. With a little more work, we could now start ferrying supplies through the ice-fall into the

54

Western Cwm. Thus, with the establishment of Camp II at 20,000 feet, the first obstacle had been overcome; we had found our way through the Khumbu ice-fall.

In spite of a few incidents, we plodded up-hill steadily. For example our liaison officer, Dhanbir Rai, fell ill from acute acclimatization failure. Captain Das, our doctor physiologist, saved Rai's life by prompt administration of oxygen and medicine. Yet we went on. On the ice-fall one of the teams supervised the movement of supplies to Camp II, sometimes using plastic explosives to demolish tottering seracs. Further ahead, in the Western Cwm, Da-Namgyal and Kumar plodded forward, going round crevasses and dodging the artillery of avalanches hurtling down the near-vertical slopes of Everest and Nuptse. They established Camp III on April 17th at a height of 21,200 feet. Although fairly tired, they pressed on towards the Lhotse face and at a height of 22,400 feet marked a site for Camp IV with a flag. Exhausted by their continuous and strenuous march, they handed the task over to the third team. Now Gombu, Sonam and Chaudhury formed the vanguard while the second party went down to Labuje, at 16,000 feet, to recuperate.

We had now reached the high altitude zone where one had not only to guard against the deteriorating effects of reduced oxygen, but to cope with strong prevailing westerly winds beating relentlessly against the Lhotse face. Under such conditions upward progress is agonizingly slow and a man's efficiency and performance drop considerably because his capacity to think and act rationally is reduced to a confused blur. In the face of these heavy odds, after fully establishing Camp IV, Gombu, Sonam and Chaudhury began their work on the formidable Lhotse face on April 20th.

Past expeditions had explored different routes from the Western Cwm to the South Col. The most practical route, however, was up the steep Lhotse Glacier a part of the way, followed by a high traverse towards and over the Geneva Spur to the South Col at nearly 26,000 feet. Sir John Hunt and Albert Eggler's teams were lucky to find fairly long stretches of firm snow in which they were able to kick steps. Unfortunately for us the previous winter had been very mild and there was not much snow on the Lhotse face. Thus we had to hack our way laboriously over the very long ice slope of the Lhotse face.

In addition to these technical difficulties, we now faced very definite logistical problems. Our line of communication was stretched from the base camp at 18,000 feet through the ever-changing Khumbu ice-fall up to Camp IV at 22,400 feet. So far it had not been possible to stock the intermediate camps adequately. Thus, while Gombu, Sonam and Chaudhury were inching their way up the Lhotse face, all remaining available hands were busily engaged in ferrying supplies to Camp III. They succeeded in keeping a small trickle of essential stores and equipment to the forward team. Camp III, which was our advance base camp and the second firm base, was now steadily growing in size.

The Lhotse face was a tough nut to crack. Gombu and Sonam had made good progress on April 20th and nearly reached the site of Camp V, but had expended all their manilla rope and most of their energy. A day or two later Ang Temba and his team took over but, in the face of icy winds, made little headway. One of the Sherpas suffered frost-bite on his fingers. On April 28th, however, the indomitable Da-Namgyal succeeded in pitching a tent at Camp V at an altitude of nearly 24,000 feet. The western disturbances had already set in and the strong winds reduced the temperature to − 22° C. Da-Namgyal and Kumar had worked against heavy odds and this herculean effort took its toll; both the climbers were thoroughly exhausted and had to descend to base and later to the rest camp to recover from their ordeal.

As we could not afford to expend much oxygen at this stage we worked in short shifts and a succession of climbers now took over the lead. Gombu succeeded in passing the Yellow Band and traversed towards the Geneva Spur up to a height of about 25,000 feet before he returned exhausted. Vohra and Chaudhury went next and climbed up to 25,500 feet on May 6th. Finally, on May 9th, without using oxygen, Ang Temba and Jungalwalla, with a party of six Sherpas, reached the inhospitable South Col after crossing the 26,000-feet level. After leaving a tent, a few oxygen cylinders and some stores they climbed down to Camp V and descended to base camp the next day. While exploring the South Col, Ang Temba recovered a diary of Dr Hans Grimm, who was a member of 1956 Swiss Expedition to Lhotse and Everest.

During these hectic days we had our share of casualties. There were a few cases of minor illness and some early stages of frost-bite. All the same we kept up the momentum of our advance for the final bid. While a continuous succession of loads was being transported through the ice-fall and the Cwm to Camps III and IV, Lieutenant Nanda was at work setting up a telephone line from Camp II to the advance base in the Western Cwm, perhaps the highest telephone link ever established.

It would appear logical that, having reached the South Col, we should have maintained the momentum and begun the final and crucial phase of our task at once, but weather conditions frustrated our hopes. Severely cold and strong westerlies permitted no more than two small ferries to be pushed to the South Col. Then, after May 13th, the weather started deteriorating rapidly and snow began to fall intermittently. Faced with these conditions, we had no option but to withdraw to lower camps.

The pre-monsoon lull can generally be expected any time after the middle of May and on average should last for a fortnight. It was, therefore, still not too late, but when the weather showed no signs of clearing up, even after May 16th and 17th, we were a little anxious.

About this time, at the advance base, I was not too well and the doctor, Flight-Lieutenant Bhagwanani, suggested that I should go down. The weather continued bad and I had no option but to descend to the base camp on the 19th. But

20 top: VIEW FROM THE ASCENT to Masherbrum, toward the Gasherbrum Group, Hidden Peak, and Chogolisa. (Photograph from about 24,300 feet by Nick Clinch)

bottom: ON THE WAY TO THE SUMMIT of Masherbrum. Willi Unsoeld at the bergschrund below the couloir to the summit ridge. (Photograph by George Bell)

21 top: VIEW FROM THE SUMMIT of Masherbrum (25,660 ft.) toward Gasherbrum IV, III, II, and Hidden
Peak. (Photographed about 6:15 p.m. by Nick Clinch)
bottom: VIEW FROM THE SUMMIT of Masherbrum (25,660 ft.) toward K2 and Broad Peak. In the depths
is the Baltoro Glacier. (Photograph by Nick Clinch)

22 MASHERBRUM (25,660 ft.) Southeast Flank with West and East Summits, as seen from Camp IV (21,980 ft.) The American climbers, Hornbein and McGowan, are en route to Camp V. (Photograph by Nick Clinch)

23 THE GASHERBRUM GROUP with Hidden Peak as seen from Camp VII (24,900 ft.). Evening. (Photograph by Nick Clinch)

before leaving the advance base I was able to call a conference and announce my summit teams. I had to make a few difficult decisions. First, our most experienced and reliable member, Da-Namgyal, had to be dropped because of illness. Secondly, I had to detail Jungalwalla to the important assignment of supporting the summit teams from the South Col, which I had hoped to do myself. He would otherwise have been considered for one of the summit teams. Finally, I decided on the first summit team: Gombu, Sonam and Kumar. The second party was made up of Ang Temba, Kohli and Vohra. All these climbers possessed the required stamina, determination and experience to tackle the task.

After keeping us in great anxiety for over a week the weather suddenly cleared up on May 20th. We wondered: had the pre-monsoon lull arrived? The met forecast on All-India Radio indicated the monsoon's steady advance up the Bay of Bengal, but there was no mention of the lull.

Although it was clear and bright on May 20th and 21st and there was hardly any wind, we could not send our men up the steep Lhotse face immediately after a heavy snowfall because of the avalanche hazard. After allowing two days for the fresh snow to consolidate and become first on the slope, the first team set out from Camp III on May 22nd. In order to save time they went from Camp III to Camp V, where the three climbers and nine Sherpas spent the night. By the afternoon, accompanied by Jungalwalla and his support party, the team had reached Camp VI on the South Col.

May 24th was a day of good weather and absolute calm. At seven that morning Gombu, Kumar and Sonam, supported by seven of the best high-altitude Sherpas, left the South Col in high spirits and carried with them a tent, butane gas fuel, food, sleeping bags and the indispensable oxygen cylinders. Using oxygen, the party made good progress and set up Camp VII at 27,600 feet. Here the Sherpas wished the climbers God-speed and good luck and trudged slowly back to South Col.

Gombu, Kumar and Sonam settled down for the night. Despite the altitude the three ate well that evening and crawled, fully clothed, into their sleeping bags. In a tent intended for only two, they were somewhat cramped. Excitement and the high altitude prevented sound sleep. They slowly crawled out of their bags at three in the morning and prepared to start.

Till the previous evening everything seemed to be going very smoothly and they were very optimistic about the final outcome. Luck, unfortunately, was no longer with them. The calm atmosphere of the day before had given way to a strong stormy wind which started whipping their tent at ten the night before. The three climbers waited hopefully for wind to abate. At seven there was still no sign of the wind velocity decreasing. There was no time to waste. They decided to take their chance and they set out.

The wind was strong and the going was heavy, but they were fresh and rested and at first made steady progress. The three climbers on one rope moved slowly, haltingly, up the southeast ridge, keeping slightly below the crest. Soon the condensed and frozen moisture from exhaled air blocked the valves of Kumar's oxygen mask. He rapidly changed the mask and bladder, but this incident was an ominous portent of what might happen later when the climbers were obliged to expose themselves on the ridge to the full fury of the gale.

That moment soon arrived, and it became obvious that progress towards their goal was going to be painfully slow. Powder snow, carried by the wind, lashed at the climbers' faces with such force that they had to turn their faces sideways to advance at all. Twice the party halted while Sonam rectified the frozen valves of his mask. The wind was showing no signs of abating. Instead, it increased and particles of drift snow restricted vision. To make matters worse the climbers' goggles were filled with powdered snow, blown in through small ventilation holes. Visibility was practically nil at this stage.

About midday they halted for a little rest. They checked their height and found that they had reached 28,300 feet. They were barely 700 feet from the summit. The temptation to go on was great but the possibility of reaching the summit and returning safely was remote. Fortunately Kumar, Gombu and Sonam were mountaineers of sufficient experience to realize that, unlike a military operation, lives should not be risked unduly on a sporting adventure, no matter how worthy the goal. After a brief consultation they took the wise but difficult decision to retrace their steps.

This was the climax of the expedition. Next day the monsoon reached the Everest region, a week earlier than anticipated. The second team, which had in the meantime moved up to the South Col, waited throughout May 26th for the weather to clear while the weary first summit team descended to the advance base camp. On May 27th the weather was worse and the second summit team was also asked to withdraw from the mountain as fast as it could. Under those conditions further efforts would have been suicidal. Despite dogged determination, the supreme effort had failed. The climbers and Sherpas had done their best; and when you have done your best you can do no better. We were turned back not by the mountain but the "autocratic element", the weather, over which man has no control.

By May 29th, the anniversary of the first ascent of Everest, everyone was back in base camp. It was willed that we should not succeed that year.

If we were disappointed, we also had reasons to be proud. Mountaineering is, for Indians, a relatively new sport. It was heartening to find that our young climbers were fit to challenge the world's loftiest peak. We had organized and conducted a major expedition, solved seemingly impossible logistical problems, and had reached a point higher than any other mountain in the world except Everest itself. What was most important was the fact that every member and Sherpa returned safely. It was also proved that India could make mountaineering equipment which could stand the test of the highest mountain.

Not the least achievement of the expedition was the stimulus to mountain climbing given by our attempt. More and more young Indian men and women are now going out to seek the vigour, health and happiness which only a sojourn in the high mountains can provide. Nearly a dozen Indian expeditions went to Himalayas during 1961, the hard core and leadership for which was provided from amongst the seasoned Everesters of 1960. More than half a dozen peaks have been climbed. Everest is always there, waiting for our successors. These will come and, standing on our shoulders, will one day succeed where we so narrowly failed.

DISTAGHIL SAR

AUSTRIAN KARAKORUM EXPEDITION 1960

By Wolfgang Stefan

"Over there! Nanga Parbat!"—These words struck each of us like lightning. We started from our seats and crowded to the small portholes of the twin-engined Dakota. The steep flanks of the proud mountain soared powerfully into the sky, and a singular feeling of joy and possession gripped us with the view of that rearing Himalayan giant, while the pilot, high above the Indus Valley, steered for the inconspicuous town of Gilgit. Our eyes glanced northwards over the summits of the Malbuting and Haramosh, seeking the Distaghil Sar.

Shortly afterwards the small aircraft settled down on the uneven air-strip at Gilgit. Five men climbed out of the plane with me: Götz Mayr, Herbert Raditschnig, Günther Stärker, Diether Marchant[1] and Captain Mohammed Amanullah Khan, the Pakistani officer who was to accompany us and who had joined us at Rawal-pindi.

We established our quarters in the rest house for the next few days. Gilgit is the centre for the mountain villages of the Pakistani part of Kashmir, and although this town has, because of its tiny airstrip, grown into an important settlement, it has lost hardly any of its original quality. The people still live, as they always have done, in pathetic mud huts, and the bazaars have changed in no essential feature. To get this far earlier expeditions had had to overcome snow-bound passes up to 16,000 feet in an approach march of five weeks, but for us the march to base camp began only at Gilgit. Nevertheless we were still sixty miles from the last village, from which another six marching days would lead us to base camp on the Khiang Glacier. The old caravan route through the Hunza Valley has today expanded into a jeep trail, but it is usually impassable because of erosion, and for only a few days in the year is it possible to drive to its end at Nagar.

Preparational activities kept us in Gilgit for over a week, so we were ready to depart only on May 6th. Six jeeps, piled high with baggage, crossed the hanging bridge over the Gilgit River and began their adventurous journey through the Hunza Valley. The

---

[1] Diether Marchant lost his life on August 27, 1962, in the course of a solo attempt on the North Face of the Eiger. He was one of the best of the younger Austrian climbers. He was 21 years of age. He was a frequent solo climber.—*Editor.*

old vehicles were steered confidently round the dangerous curves; steeply eroded precipices threatened on our right, with an unbroken drop of over a thousand feet into the Hunza River. Unfortunately this adventurous drive was interrupted all too soon: after only twenty miles, at the village of Nomal, we find the road obliterated by a landslide. With heavy hearts we sent the jeeps back and searched for new means of transport. At last sixty donkeys and horses were rounded up and onto them the two tons of expedition baggage and the provisions for the porters were loaded.

With sighs of relief we started moving again. The next village, Chalt, was more than fifteen miles distant. Uphill and downhill, the road leads along the steep bank of the Hunza River. I was often glad not to be sitting in a jeep, but wandering slowly on foot up the valley, which eventually widened until there lay before us the fields and the small mud huts of the village. Only by irrigation is it possible for the people of Nagar to turn the dry earth into fertile ground, a fact which explains why the water laws are among the strictest in the whole country. Each farmer receives his portion of the precious moisture for only a limited time; then he must close the irrigation ditch again so that the water flows on to the neighbouring fields.

Above Minapin, the next and larger village, nature has provided a mighty landmark: Rakaposhi, over 25,000 feet high, the steep slopes of which, at this time of the year, are still covered with snow right down to the valley. There was an old memorial stone at the very roadside, which I would have passed almost without notice had not a native called my attention to it; it commemorated a bloody dispute between the Nagars and the Hunzas. These two neighbouring peoples, divided only by the Hunza River, live in enmity with each other: the Hunzas are Ismaelites and the Nagars Shiites, and their differing creeds lead them into repeated disputes.

In the afternoon of the fifth day after our departure from Gilgit we reached the town of Nagar, and the domain of the Mir of Nagar stood before us. On a big level square he received us in flowing robes, and the white summits in the background provided a fabulous setting. The Mir invited us into his roomy tent, in which he had already lived for a half a year. His old palace has become decrepit, and it will be some time before the new one is built, since every sack of cement has to be brought in on the back of a donkey. A polo game was arranged in our honour: the players, who seemed of one piece with their fiery steeds, showed splendid skill in driving the ball into the enemy field, and minor injuries are no rarity in this game. Bandaging is rudimentary, and the men soon plunge back into the struggle.

On the following day, with 85 valley porters, we left the friendly village of Nagar. A ford brought us to the further bank of the Hispar stream. All day we climbed upwards without a path until we reached a small hanging bridge, leading over the same stream, quiet at this time, to the village of Hispar. The region looked desolate, the squalid habitations built of loose stones, piled on one another, and the fields without the least sign of green. The inhabitants of Hispar were very shy: when we approached, they vanished from sight. Outside the village we settled down on our resting place for the night.

Immediately before us began the vast ice river of the Hispar Glacier, the lower end of which is entirely covered with rubble. Sun glasses were distributed among the valley porters, but it was not long before some of them reported that they had lost them. Most had simply hidden the glasses in order to obtain a second pair, but others, despite the glare, refused to put them on. The further we progressed along the moraine of the Hispar Glacier the steeper became the mountains on both sides of the ice river. At the junction with the Khiang Glacier we set up our next approach camp. Soon the porters had made themselves at home. With water and a coarse meal called *atta* they prepared a dough which they baked on hot stones. These flat cakes they called *chapatis*.

Only two more days of march separated us from the base camp in the innermost cirque of the glacier floor, but on the next day the weather turned bad. A mutiny seemed to be brewing among the porters: some groups showed exemplary skill in building small stone shelters beneath huge boulders, while other groups hardly knew how to help themselves. We gave them bivouac sacks with which they could set up a protective roof.

At last we moved onto the glacier. Uphill and downhill our route proceeded over the coarse stone blocks of the moraine, until at 11 a.m. we reached the old camp site of the British expedition of 1957, where empty tins and scraps of wood were scattered across the wilderness of boulders. It had already begun to snow, and a state of panic broke out among the porters. They dropped their loads, and amid wild shouting we could hear the words "base camp". We tried to persuade them to pick up their loads again, but neither kind words nor the offer of a bonus of a rupee were successful. They would listen to nothing. They were afraid of the new snow, which would obliterate the tracks for their retreat, and of the fog which robbed them of vision. And at last we stood, with our four high-altitude porters, all alone on the Khiang Glacier, still a four hours march from the site of our base camp. Hastily we stacked the loads together, covered them temporarily with a tarpaulin, pitched our tents and crept into them to wait for the snow to cease. Then we and our four porters, heavily laden, climbed every day up to the base camp over the moraines, which in their upper reaches are deeply covered with snow. Above us rose the mighty south flank of the Distaghil, 10,000 feet high.

Two expeditions before us had attempted this proud peak. In 1957 it was the British, led by Alfred Gregory, who attempted to climb directly up the steep south flank. They were forced to turn back, at a height of about 21,000 feet, by bad weather and snowfalls. In 1959 came the Swiss under that well-known Himalayan climber, Raymond Lambert. They chose the southeast ridge, several miles long, as their route of ascent. But this group, too, was not favoured by the weather, and they reached a height of only 23,000 feet. Which route should we choose? The decision was soon made. As a small group, only five men strong, we must attempt the shorter, even though steeper, route through the south flank, for we could set up only a few camps; moreover, in this difficult terrain we could make only limited use of the high-altitude porters.

At first we found the ascent to base camp at 14,000 feet not easy with loads of fifty to sixty pounds, and several days passed before we were accustomed to the altitude. By May 21st sufficient equipment and provisions had accumulated at base for us to move in. But apparently we had arrived too soon, for on the following day winter reigned again about our small town of tents. Again and again we freed our quarters from the new snow, and the snow wall around our camp grew higher.

But this bad weather period, too, passed as quickly as it came, and during the days that followed we were granted splendidly clear weather. Three of us ventured a first reconnoitring trip. We followed the snowy moraine to its end, where we met the mighty floor of the glacier which approaches the steep closed flank over several steps. We pushed our tracks up through endless levels, at first in good hard firn, into which we sank only very slightly. But soon this was supplanted by an ugly crusted surface. Again and again we hoped that the surface would support our weight, but we broke through step after step. Breathing heavily we worked our way upward. A slope threatened by avalanches, which we ought to have climbed as quickly as possible, cost us much time, but when it was passed we let ourselves sink down, relieved, to rest beneath a huge cleft, the upper lip of which offered us a certain measure of protection. Then we broke trail again up another stretch, through the new snow, until we reached a steep gully at about 18,000 feet. The British Camp I already lay beneath us and we hoped to press forward even further, to the second British camp site. This seemed to be much more secure and less exposed to the avalanches. Once again we took a breather. But in the burning sun we became dull and tired. We stowed the loads beneath an overhang and returned to base.

On the following day Götz Mayr and Herbert Raditschnig took their turn. They were already climbing the ice flank when we crept sleepily out of our tents. They ascended the steep gully and reached the indentation of the face which, with the aid of the binoculars, we had singled out for Camp I. In the afternoon our comrades, along with our best high-altitude porter, returned to base. This excellent Hunza porter, whose real name is Hidayat Shah, was given the Bavarian nickname "Sepperl" by Hans Rebitsch during the Batura Expedition on which he served as a high-altitude porter. He made himself quite useful at cooking, too, for he understood how to use the stove. Götz, who served as chief cook, valued him, and with his help produced

63

some delicious meals. Another talent distinguished Sepperl: he understood some fragments of English.

After a brief bad-weather period which kept us at base camp, we all five, together with the porters Sepperl and Shaban, climbed up to Camp I. Since the old tracks had disappeared under the new snow, we had to break a new trail. Towards noon, in great heat, we reached the tiny platform at a height of 18,700 feet. Guarded by a huge ice gendarme, the platform provided a secure camp site. Soon we had set up the tents and the porters departed in the direction of base. It snowed several times during the night and when we opened the tents in the morning a white quilt of glittering new snow lay over them. Anxiously, we peered up at the great ice barrier above our camp. How in the world should we surmount it? While we passed the time in camp with cooking and eating, Herbert and Diether, arming themselves with ice pitons and ropes, decided to come to grips with this obstacle. In a few hours they had fashioned a good ladder of steps, secured by ice pitons and a fixed rope.

In the morning twilight we groped for our boots, parkas and storm trousers. There was hardly room to turn around in the tiny two-man tent in which three of us were making the effort to dress and prepare ourselves. From the other tent Götz passed in a hot drink. Without appetite we crammed down a couple of biscuits with jam, and, one behind the other, we pushed our way out into the open. An icy cold seized our limbs. We roused ourselves to fasten the crampon straps and then, without a sound, the first man climbed up the steep bulge. Our comrades had done good work the day before, which we recognized as we scaled the steep pitch with the aid of the fixed rope. Then we traversed to the right into the steep wall directly beneath the huge trough that cuts through the middle of the face. We were still in the cold shadow; only the peaks far away on the other side of the Hispar Glacier were lit by the morning sun. Breaking trail through the deep snow is fatiguing, and after some hours we let ourselves drop exhausted into the soft snow beneath a big ice tower on the other side of the huge cleft.

A steep slope made it possible for us to gain a few feet of height. Fragments of fog drove down over the face from the summit. Thin veils draped themselves about us and robbed us of vision. At a height of 20,600 feet we suddenly stood before a wide open crevasse, the upper lip of which leant towards us like an overhanging wall of firn. How should we overcome this wall? After some futile attempts to circumvent the crevasse, we were driven back to Camp I by the bad weather.

Two days later Götz, Herbert and Diether set out for a decisive thrust. At the critical point they fixed a rope ladder which they and the porters had brought up from base camp the previous day. Thereafter they pressed on for another 600 feet up the steep slope to a little saddle between the wall and an ice tower which had split away from it. Up there our comrades pitched Camp II and in the evening came back to us.

64

24 EVEREST (29,003 ft.) AND LHOTSE (27,891 ft.) from the west. On the right, in front of Lhotse, is Nuptse (25,850 ft.). In the centre is the Khumbu Glacier with its ice fall, in the left foreground is the ridge of Pumori. (Aerial photograph by the Indian Air Force)

25 EVEREST (29,003 ft.) showing the mighty Southwest Face. On the right, the South Ridge falling away to the South Col. In the foreground, the ridge barrier of Nuptse. (Aerial photograph by the Indian Air Force)

7885 m

7010 m

6500 m

5740 m

4560 m

Distagil Sar (7,885 m). Route and camps of the Austrian Expedition, 1960.

Thus a vital part of the flank had been overcome, so the rest of us left the tents quite early to transport new loads up to Camp II.

The good steps of the previous day were a great help in our ascent through the trough. It was still early in the day when we took a short rest before the steep pitch below the ladder. The first rays of the sun warmed our cold-stiffened limbs. But impatience soon drove us up to the ladder. Apart from the full and rigid rucksacks which we carried, there was still a tent and a gigantic sack of equipment and provisions to be taken up to Camp II. Günther was the first to climb the frail aluminium rungs. Above us a giant white sheet rose to the ridge without a break. From where we were we could get no accurate idea of the monstrous expanse, but we knew from our observations from base camp how far away the ridge still was. Another hour passed before we reached Camp II. It was just before reaching the tiny saddle that we espied the yellow tents that our comrades had erected the previous day. We ought to have brought up the remaining loads from the ladder, but I felt too tired, so we put the job off until the morrow.

We awaited our comrades impatiently; they appeared in the noon heat down by the ladder, and a considerable time passed before they arrived with their high-piled packs. "We're thirsty!" were the first words they forced out of their parched throats. Climbing at high altitude, the body uses up great quantities of moisture; one breathes with an open mouth in order to find enough oxygen, and the dry air dehydrates the throat and body. So our petrol stove worked at full blast and the snow was transformed into a drinkable liquid.

About us lay a grandiose panorama. To our right a sharp snow ridge swung up over steep falls of ice to the summit of a nameless peak of 23,000 feet. Behind it rose Trivor. Immediately before us was the Khinyang Chhish, a Matterhorn of the Himalayas and below was base camp, and in the distance row upon row of mountains to the south.

The shadows crept ever higher up the gigantic flank of the Khinyang Chhish, and the thermometer fell as under the impact of a blow to — 15° C. We fled into our tents. After a day of rest we planned an early departure for a climb up to the ridge.

It was still dark when we fastened our crampons and roped up. Götz and Herbert had started earlier, but they were already back before we left our tents. "I'm cold," Herbert exclaimed without further explanation. They disappeared into their tent. While Günther exerted himself in the deep powder snow above us, our toes gradually stiffened. Diether was the first to retreat, and soon thereafter I noticed how my veins became bloodless.

"We must go back," I said to Günther, who was by no means happy about it. For more than an hour I laboured at massaging my fingers and toes, and only when the sun stood high did we leave our tents. It was a wearisome ascent, yard by yard, over

66

the steep slope above our camp, made the more tedious by our packs, in which we carried the entire Camp III. We gasped for breath, . . . 22,000 feet . . . 22,300 feet . . . Because of our rapid advance we did not allow sufficient time to acclimatize fully, so the thin light air made our labours very heavy. Above the white ridge was the deep blue sky. The minute snow crystals, lifted from the ridge crest by the wind, glittered above us like diamonds.

The altimeter showed 22,500 feet, and a narrow schrund cut across the last slope that separated us from the ridge. Through bottomless powder snow we wallowed up to just beneath the crevasse. Götz, belayed by Herbert, climbed up over a weak snow bridge and toiled step after step up the steep slope. We mustered all our strength, and had nothing left to notice the marvellous panorama or the tremendous view into the depths.

"That's the end of the rope!" Our comrade's words saved us: we sank exhausted. Leaning against the slope we used the break to breathe.

Suddenly the steep flank ended—23,000 feet! To the north the view was open. Before us lay the countless mountain chains of Sinkiang. Silently we stood on the ridge, as though we did not belong to the world at all. It was 6 p.m.! It was getting cold and the tents had to be erected. With our ungainly high-altitude boots we stamped a level place in the snow just below the highest rise in the ridge, and a little later crawled into our sleeping bags.

After a restless night we dozed far into the morning. It was June 9th. Irresolutely we opened the tent flaps. It was no longer as clear as on the previous day and only around 9.30 a.m. did Diether and Günther decide to try a push toward the summit. But it was 11 a.m. before they finished dressing. Mounting along the ridge, which at first had a broad back, they became smaller and smaller. To the south an immense wall of clouds drove slowly nearer. About three in the afternoon Diether and Günther had reached the cliffs that build up to the summit, but fragments of cloud drove down from the peak and enveloped them. Then hours of anxious waiting began. Evening drew on and the darkness grew; yet they had still not returned. Lying in our sleeping bags, we pursued our thoughts. It was impossible to keep awake. I made an effort to prepare a hot drink. Surely they must come soon! It was a whole hour before I was able to get the burner going and melt some snow. I greedily gulped some of the warm liquid and then handed some over to Götz and Herbert. We tried to conceal our anxiety. At 9.30 p.m. we heard voices; we opened the tent flaps and in the uncertain light our two comrades stood unreally before us.

"At six in the evening we were on the summit," was the brief explanation of their late return, and a flash of joy passed over our faces. The summit. With these words the tension subsided.

Even by the weak light of our torches the traces of the extreme cold could be seen on their weather-beaten faces. Soon Diether lay beside me in the tent. The impressions of the day would not let him rest. "There was just no end to the last steep gully on the right of the summit cliffs. We almost climbed too far to the right to a point on the ridge. Only then did we see over there, to the left, a sharp snow crest, the highest point of the Distaghil. A short rest, and it was so late that we had to hurry. Our fingers were stiff, there was no sensation in our toes. I had to fix Günther's crampon straps a couple of times. They were frozen stiff and simply would not hold. A ski pole slipped from his hands and disappeared in the darkness." He paused often as he spoke. Sliding over into the land of dreams, our conversation ended.

Cloud walls advanced towards us and we were caught on the steep flank of the mountains. Even in the forenoon it began to snow. We staggered about in front of the tents with every sign of mild vertigo, for two nights and a day at that altitude had taken too heavy a toll of our strength. Every hour more could become disastrous. The first snow-flakes were only the forerunners of a weather convulsion of great magnitude. Herbert and Götz broke trail down the steep slope, while Günther and Diether, belayed by me, followed. With frozen fingers, they were unable to hold their ice axes; their feet hurt at every step. For hours we fought desperately against the elements, until, exhausted, we reached Camp II in the evening. We ought to have descended even further, but our fatigued limbs refused to obey. The roaring of the storm throughout the night allowed us only little sleep, but next day there was no change in the weather. The masses of new snow rose ever higher around the tents and threatened to press through the thin cloth walls. We spent yet another night at 21,300 feet.

Twilight the following morning broke hopeless and grey; the snow was incessant. The fuel for the stove was used up and we sipped the last of the lukewarm lemonade. We were faced by a difficult decision; whether to climb down the steep avalanchy slopes to Camp I or hold out indefinitely without warm food or drink. We decided to descend, but only after long discussion. We roped up in front of the tents. Herbert and Götz disappeared in the monotonous greyness, leaving a deep furrow in the bottomless powder. The snow clung to our crampons in huge formless clumps, causing our feet to lose their grip in the loose snow. "We are at the ladder!" our friends called joyously upwards, and a weight was lifted from our hearts, for we had had little hope of finding the ladder at the first try in such a fog. The traverse through the great trough was fatiguing; incredible masses of snow had accumulated there. I was seized with admiration for Günther and Diether, who staggered ahead of me on the edge of total exhaustion and collapse, only to rouse again with a tremendous effort.

We could scarcely recognize Camp I, for it was almost buried under the new snow. When the three of us reached the tents, Herbert was already busy, shovelling them free. We were already so used to the storm and driving snow that we did not notice that we were surrounded by an opaque whiteness. The big snowflakes fell incessantly.

We spent only two nights at Camp I, but it was already five days since we had left Camp III. The closer we came to the level glacier, the easier the trail-breaking became, because less snow had fallen. It was so warm that we could take off the down-filled jackets for the first time. Below us appeared the snow-free moraine, and before us spread the wildly torn glacier. The crevasses, which were hardly recognizable during the ascent, now showed their gaping mouths, and soon we were on our way along the moraine toward base camp. Joy reigned among the porters when all five of us suddenly appeared, and they outbid one another in their care and concern for us. And we too were happy to be once more among our fellow human beings.

THE USES OF ADVERSITY

SOME MOUNTAINEERING AND MEDICAL ASPECTS OF THE HIMALAYAN SCIENTIFIC EXPEDITION 1960–61

Michael Ward

SCIENCE IN THE HIMALAYAS

From November 1960 to March 1961 a group of scientists lived and worked in a laboratory situated at 19,000 feet under the east face of Amadablam, about ten miles south of Everest. Under Dr Griffith Pugh of the Medical Research Council of Great Britain, this party carried out research into the long term effects of high altitude on man. This research programme was the pivot of the Himalayan Scientific and Mountaineering Expedition led by Sir Edmund Hillary and very generously sponsored by the World Book Encyclopedia Inc, an American educational organization.

The expedition was divided into three phases. During the first phase, from August to November 1960, Sir Edmund Hillary led a party investigating the legend of the yeti and at the same time found a suitable site for the Silver Hut and other camps used by the wintering party. During the second phase Dr Pugh directed the research programme at the Silver Hut, and four members of the wintering party made the first ascent of Amadablam. Finally, in March 1961, Hillary returned with a fresh climbing party to join the scientific party and attempted to climb Makalu without the aid of oxygen. During this assault, physiological work was carried on up to a height of 26,000 feet.

In this account I will make no attempt to discuss the findings of the first part of the expedition. Briefly, the quest for the yeti was carried out in and around the Rolwaling Valley, which lies to the west of Everest and just south of Gaurisankar and Menlungtse. It was in this region that Eric Shipton and I in 1951 saw some footprints which could be attributed to the yeti. No direct evidence for the existence of the yeti was found by our expedition. At the end of October the party traversed the Tesi Lapcha into Sola Khumbu and there examined the yeti scalps kept at Dingboche Monastery and also at Khumjung. The elders of Khumjung were persuaded to part with their scalp, which was taken by Hillary, Desmond Doig and Kumbo Chumbi on a world trip. The scalp was examined by experts in America, France and Britain, and was considered to have been manufactured from the skin of a goat.

Himalayan Winter

In order to carry out our physiological programme it was necessary to find a site that was safe from the dangers of avalanche and rock fall, and also relatively easy of access and sufficiently high to serve our purpose. The upper part of the Mingbo Valley had been entered by a col (19,500 feet) from the Hongu Glacier by Eric Shipton and Hillary during the 1951 Everest reconnaissance. They called this the Amadablam Col and it was our first choice as a site for the Silver Hut. But it was found that the col was extremely cold and windy and also very difficult of access, so the hut was placed below the col on the Rakpa Glacier, at the head of the Mingbo Valley. This hut was designed by Ezra Levin of the Timber Research Association with the help of Dr Pugh, and a great deal of work was involved in its development. It looked like a section of a London tube train and measured 22 feet by 12 feet. It was carried in in pre-fabricated sections, each weighing about forty-five pounds. The whole hut weighed just over a ton and took little more than a day to assemble. Inside there were eight bunks, a stove specially adapted for use at high altitudes, and a table. We had electric light powered by a wind generator and also a two-stroke engine for the same purpose. There was a porch at one end with double doors, and at the other a work-bench extending for about thirty feet around the walls of the hut. The M.R.C. provided laboratory equipment comparable to any available for similar work at sea level. This included electronic apparatus for measuring minute accounts of carbon monoxide, a stationary bicycle for measuring work rates, a Haldane gas analysis apparatus, a portable electrocardiogram, and apparatus for measuring the amounts of carbon dioxide and oxygen in the blood.

Over the hut wire guys were stretched and attached to ice-filled sacks countersunk six feet into the ground; these made the hut very stable even in the winds of up to eighty miles an hour that were measured during the winter. Our main problem throughout the winter was not the low temperatures that we had expected but the difficulty we found in keeping the hut from getting too hot. If the temperature inside fell below freezing point much of our apparatus, which contained water, would have cracked, so the stove had to be kept alight. As a result the temperature was often tropical. Several members of the party slept in tents, finding this less enervating.

Next to the hut was a twelve-man domed tent which was used as a store, in which the Sherpas, who cooked for us in rotation, lived. Several smaller tents were used as stores and for laboratory work when the weather became warmer in the spring. We had two ice-caves, one of which was used as a lavatory and the other as a food store.

This little colony was set on the edge of a small glacier in the midst of a formidable cirque of vertical faces and fluted ice peaks dominated by the east face of Amadablam, 3,500 feet above us. A few feet from the end of the hut the steep side of the glacier dropped into the lower part of the Mingbo Glacier. To the south the great peaks surrounding Namche squandered their beauty on the indifferent sky.

Some 1,300 feet below us the Green Hut, constructed by Wally Romanes out of

71

canvas and wood, served as a staging point between the base camp at Mingbo and the Silver Hut. At Mingbo, 15,500 feet, a high yak grazing pasture under the southwest face of Amadablam, we built an airstrip which was used from February 1961 onwards by planes and helicoptors.

Our day began at seven with meteorological readings, followed by breakfast. We worked throughout the morning, often having only a light lunch, and continued in the afternoon until about four o'clock. By this time we were ready for a change and skied down the glacier and in amongst the crevasses until dark. Apart from Pugh, who had skied in the 1936 Winter Olympics, we were all relative novices. However, this daily interlude kept us reasonably fit and I think contributed greatly to the easy-going atmosphere enjoyed by this party throughout the winter months.

Each member of the party had his own programme to complete and this could only be done with the full co-operation of other members acting as "guinea pigs". Dr Pugh investigated the effects of altitude on blood volume and cardiac output; Dr John West, a respiratory physiologist from the Postgraduate Medical School, London, was mainly concerned with lung diffusion studies; Dr J. Milledge, a physician working with the M.R.C., investigated the sensitivity of the respiratory centre to oxygen and carbon dioxide; Professor S. Lahiri, of the Presidency College, Calcutta, worked on blood gas analysis; Michael Gill, a medical student from Dunedin, New Zealand, assisted other members of the party and was responsible for the psychometric investigations—he also supervised the daily menus; Dr Tom Nevison, of the U.S.A.F., was present for part of the winter and during this time he measured water turnover with deuterium oxide. Wally Romanes, a builder and electrician from New Zealand, stayed with us throughout the winter and was responsible for the general maintenance of the hut and electrical equipment. Barry Bishop, a member of the staff of the National Geographic Society and a glaciologist, made a survey of the Mingbo Valley, carried out temperature studies of the Rakpa Glacier and solar radiation studies. Captain Motwani, of the Indian Army Medical Corps, stayed for most of the winter at Mingbo, acting as a liaison officer. Finally, myself, a surgeon at the London Hospital, carried out haematological and urine studies.

Before leaving home similar observations and experiments had been done on members of the wintering party at sea level. Thus it was possible by the end of the expedition to have more or less complete records of the results of experiments done at sea level, 15,000 feet (Mingbo), 19,000 feet, and 24,500 feet (Makalu Col). In this way a composite picture of man's adaption to long residence at high altitudes (especially at 19,000 feet and above) was available. However, the individual observations were in many instances complete in themselves as well as contributing to the overall assessment. In addition, the medical observations that I made on climbers using oxygen on Everest in 1953, taken in conjunction with the observations at the Silver Hut and during the attempt without oxygen on Makalu, have provided me with detailed data of the diseases likely to occur over 17,500 feet.

We had radio contact with Katmandu. Dr Pugh considered this was essential and we were in fact able to order replacements of apparatus from England by this means. When Peter Mulgrew came in with the spring party he established contact with radio hams in all parts of the world and in this way Nevison heard of the birth of his son via a radio contact in Florida. Our call sign, 9N3pm, was the rarest on record and many enthusiasts attempted to work us.

In order to complete our scientific programme we were forced to work for much longer hours over a four-week period in the spring—often until midnight and later. This is of interest when comparing the performance of members of the wintering party on Makalu with that of the spring party, as I think this extra pressure of work took a lot out of us. The scientific work continued on Makalu. The stationary bicycle was taken to 24,500 feet and used by West and myself to carry out a simple programme at this height. Gill was able to obtain alveolar air samples at 26,000 feet.

Surprisingly, the temperatures never fell as low as we had expected and we had many hours of sunshine and very little snow until a few weeks prior to the onset of the monsoon in May. The lowest temperature recorded was −30° C. We had few storms and were sheltered from the prevailing wind.

In addition to our daily ski-ing we made one ski-mountaineering expedition, climbing up to the Amadablam Col and ski-ing down the Hongu Glacier beyond. We then put on skins and ascended to what we knew as the South Col. From there we had to make a very steep descent towards the Green Hut. For part of this descent steps had to be cut across a bergschrund before we could reach the lower part of the glacier leading to the Green Hut. We found this a most exhausting outing, partly because we were unused to ski-touring.

As the winter passed we studied the south ridge of Amadablam and wondered whether it would be possible to climb this beautiful and challenging peak by this route. The upper slopes of Amadablam appeared to average about 45°, and in order to get some idea of what conditions might be like on these upper slopes Gill and I decided to climb a fluted peak behind the Silver Hut, which we called Rakpa Peak, after our small Tibetan terrier. The upper slopes of Rakpa were about 60°. In addition to being a good climbing expedition this enabled me to carry out a simple experiment on the effects of stress on the human body.

Milledge, Gill and I set out with skis one Sunday morning. We descended 500 feet to the glacier which led to the foot of our peak. We skied up, using skins, and about noon reached the foot of Rakpa. Here we left Milledge, who descended on skis. Gill and I started cutting steps up a steep snow slope until we reached the ridge. Up this we climbed, negotiating on the way some extraordinary grotesque ice towers balanced, in many cases precariously, on a knife edge. The last two to three hundred feet were very steep and provided ice climbing of a high standard. Gill climbed magnificently and did most of the step cutting on the upper portion. We descended quickly at dusk, reaching our skis again after dark. We were too tired to ski properly and had to carry them. At the foot of the 500 feet climb to the Silver Hut we were met by Milledge and some Sherpas and we thankfully gave them our loads. It took us a long time to reach the hut and twenty-four to forty-eight hours to recover fully. However, this climb left us convinced that the upper slopes of Amadablam were possible.

The completion of the scientific programme shows that field work of a high degree of accuracy can be carried out provided that adequate preparation for prevailing conditions is made. The main scientific investigations were originated and organized by Dr Pugh, who must take a great deal of credit for the successful outcome of the primary objective of this expedition.

MAKALU

Prelude

Hillary returned to the field in the middle of March and arrived at Mingbo to find that the Nepalese government had decided to take a serious view of what they considered to be the "unauthorized ascent of Amadablam". As they were threatening to expel the expedition, Hillary returned by plane to Katmandu and spent over a week waiting for them to reverse this decision. In the meantime, John Harrison, who had come in from New Zealand, and who had brought up the rear, was arrested by the Nepalese at their checkpost at Namche Bazaar. However, we carried on with our preparations for crossing to Makalu and were finally rejoined by both Hillary and Harrison. The route to Makalu involved the crossing of three 19,000 feet passes and this took about a month to accomplish. Whilst the members of the spring party under Hillary's direction carried out this complicated move, the members of the wintering party worked on at the Silver Hut.

The traverse to Makalu took either two or three days, depending on whether the climber was energetic or not. There was one camp in the upper reaches of the Hongu Valley and a further camp at about 20,000 feet on the Barun plateau. The country that we crossed was not too exacting from the mountaineering angle and it was possible to use skis for large sections. Camp I, at the foot of Makalu, was placed on the southern bank of the Barun Glacier and this formed the base camp for our attempt on the mountain.

Makalu was first climbed in 1955 by a French expedition led by Jean Franco. Oxygen was used on this ascent and every European member of the expedition gained the summit during three successive days. This was a triumph of organization and leadership. Previous to this successful ascent, a New Zealand party led by Hillary in

74

1954 had reconnoitred the route used by the French to the Makalu Col. Incidentally, the successful route on Makalu was first noted from the upper reaches of Everest in 1953. In 1954, also, an American expedition had attempted to climb the southeast ridge of Makalu but had had to turn back at a height of about 22,000 feet due to considerable rock-climbing difficulties.

We chose Makalu because it combined height with moderate technical difficulty. We hoped that the members of the wintering party would be so well acclimatized that they would find an ascent to nearly 28,000 feet not too difficult. Thus, in addition to the normal challenge of climbing a high Himalayan peak, we hoped to extend our knowledge of the effects of altitude on man. (It should be noted that eight people have already ascended to 28,000 feet on Everest without oxygen and we knew therefore that this was feasible.)

The first four camps on Makalu were established by the spring party—Leigh Ortenburger and Dr Tom Nevison, American; John Harrison and Peter Mulgrew, New Zealanders. Gill, Milledge, West and I went down to a yak grazing pasture at Shershon, 15,000 feet, for five days' rest. Romanes decided to stay up at Camp I. Bishop, Lahiri, Motwani and Pugh remained at the Silver Hut to work. Desmond Doig joined them and provided radio contact between Makalu and Katmandu.

The lower camps on Makalu were on the same sites as those used by the French; however, there were to be two camps between the Makalu Col and the summit. Camp III, at about 21,000 feet, served as our advance base camp. As Gill and I arrived at Camp II we saw Camp IV being established on the far side of a snow gully connecting two shelves which ran across this part Makalu. The small dots of the climbers making their way across the face seemed to move very slowly, such was the immensity of the slopes. Ropes were fixed in the gully and, in fact, from Camp IV to the Makalu Col they were continuous and proved life-saving.

The plan was for Gill and myself to establish a route through to the Makalu Col. This would be followed next day by a supply lift. We moved up to Camp IV on May 3rd; Hillary was at Camp III, organizing this lift.

Camp IV was in an exposed position with magnificent views over into Tibet and across to Everest and Chamlang. On our first attempt to get through to the col we were deceived by a fixed rope left by the French. By the time we had climbed to the top of it and found that it led nowhere it was too late to do anything except return to camp.

Next day we found the correct route. Gill led most of the upper part of this, as I was not going well. The Makalu Col was very cold, with a biting but gentle wind. We could not see the upper slopes of Makalu, as they were covered by drifting cloud, but Chomolonzo, climbed by the French in the autumn of 1955, looked magnificent. We did not stay long, but came back slowly to Camp IV. Earlier that day we had put in fixed ropes and were very glad of them. (During the next three days all the equipment and stores needed for the assault parties, including the bicycle ergometer, were brought up to the south col and dumped there). On the 6th we returned to Camp III, feeling very tired but not completely exhausted.

Next day Hillary, who had not been well for the past two days, decided that he should descend to Camp II. I knew that he had had a headache but was surprised that it had not passed off. We descended to Camp II in the afternoon and settled in for a restful evening. The next day, just after supper, as the sun was fading from the mountains, I heard a weak shout from Hillary's tent. I called to him, but there was no reply. I hurriedly pulled on my boots and went to his tent. I found that he could not speak properly and had an obvious paralysis of the right side of his face. I immediately called Dr Milledge, who was in a tent close by, and we rigged up an oxygen set within minutes. We gave Hillary oxygen throughout the rest of the night. I also gave him a pain-killing drug, as it was obvious that his headache was extremely bad. Milledge and I took turns to sit up for the remainder of the night to make sure that the oxygen tubes did not kink and that the cylinder did not run out. Within an hour or so the facial palsy had recovered, although Hillary still complained of severe headache between bouts of sleeping. After an uncomfortable night Milledge and I decided that the best plan would be for Hillary to go down to Shershon and return to lower levels, if possible to Katmandu. We considered that he had had a transient stroke and that it would be dangerous for him to remain above 15,000 feet. I thought he should be accompanied by a doctor, and as I was in any case the *chef d'attaque* of the expedition, Milledge had this unenviable task. Hillary was still aphasic, but could walk slowly. They took a radio with them, but communication was bad and from then on, apart from one letter which Hillary wrote to me from Camp I, we had little contact with this small party.

I gave the news of Hillary's illness to Desmond Doig, who was stationed at the Silver Hut, and with whom we had radio contact.

The Assault

One great difficulty was that only Hillary and Mulgrew knew the exact details of the stores and equipment that were on the Col. Mulgrew had gone down to Hillary at Camp I, but he returned later and solved this problem.

Despite the reduction in the number of climbers, I thought that if I took Milledge's place on the Makalu Col, doing physiological work with West, we should still be able to complete our scientific programme as well as climb Makalu. Camp V on the Makalu Col was therefore established, and West and I started work, using the stationary bicycle.

The first assault party, consisting of Romanes, Gill and Ortenburger, established

76

Camp VI at about 25,800 feet on the near side of the glacier coming down from the summit of Makalu. The following day Gill, Romanes and Ortenburger started to cut steps across the glacier. This cost them an incredible effort in poor weather and, although they managed to get across the glacier and dump some material for the last camp, Camp VII, they could not establish it. On their return to Camp VI they had what might have been a nasty fall. The weather throughout these two days was cold, with a severe and bitter wind. Gill's nose was very badly frostbitten. Romanes, too, was in a very exhausted state when they returned to the Makalu Col and he had to have oxygen (which was available for medical purposes). They all three descended next day.

It was obvious that our plan would have to be changed; accordingly, I decided that Mulgrew and Nevison should establish Camp VII with Annalu and if possible push on next day to the summit, whilst Harrison, Urkien and myself would follow. On May 16th Nevison, Mulgrew, Annalu and seven Sherpas set off from Camp V and spent that night at Camp VI. The next day they crossed the glacier.

The trail-breaking was left by and large to the Sherpas, in order to save Mulgrew and Nevison. On the way up the Sherpas had a fall and Ang Temba hurt his ankle. Both he and another Sherpa returned to Camp VI. Mulgrew took this extra load, and Nevison then led the whole way to Camp VII. There is no doubt that this unfortunate incident imposed a considerable strain on the assault trio. After slow but steady progress a camp site at the bottom of a rock was reached. The height was about 27,000 feet. The Sherpas descended, leaving Mulgrew, Nevison and Annalu to make the site for Camp VII.

The next day, May 18th, they set off for the summit. At first the wind was not bad, but higher up snow clouds were being driven from the summit ridge. They ascended steadily; Annalu complained of a pain in his ribs but kept going. They thought they would reach the summit and return by dark. Suddenly Mulgrew developed a terrible pain in his chest and collapsed. For some time he could not move; he begged the other two to continue to the summit. Annalu, however, complained of the cold and said the pain in his chest was worse (he had probably cracked a rib in the accident the day before). There was only one possible decision; they started down. Mulgrew, helped by Nevison, crawled and slipped back to Camp. Every now and again he had to stop to cough up dark red blood.

The Descent

In the late afternoon they regained Camp VII. After a poor night they set off again. It soon became obvious that Mulgrew could not reach Camp VI that night. Annalu descended to get help, and in the afternoon two Sherpas arrived from Camp VI with a tent. In this Mulgrew and Nevison spent a very bad night.

In the meantime things had been going far from well lower down the mountain. Romanes and Gill had descended to Camp III whilst West and I remained at the Col. It soon became obvious that I was not fit enough to take part in an assault, so when I heard that Ang Temba had injured his ankle I went up to Camp VI to spare Harrison and Ortenburger, the third assault party (West had descended by this time). I climbed up to Camp VI using oxygen and took Pemba Tensing with me. We arrived in fair condition (May 18th) and I looked at Ang Temba's ankle. He could not walk and would have to be carried down. I radioed to Harrison and Ortenburger, and next day they came up again to Camp VI with Sherpas to carry Ang Temba off the mountain. I remember that when they arrived I thought for some reason that the assault party had succeeded. I told them this, much to their astonishment; this was in fact the first indication that I was becoming ill.

The Sherpas descended, carrying Ang Temba, whilst I followed by myself, leaving Harrison and Ortenburger at Camp VI. As I descended the Sherpas gradually began to disappear into the mist and, although carrying Ang Temba, they were going faster than I was. At one point I felt most apprehensive, for they disappeared from view into the clouds. I realized I was going too slowly and was in fact in a bad way, but by a great effort I managed to catch them up. About quarter of a mile short of Camp V I fell off a small boss of ice and was almost unable to get up. I managed to shout to Urkien, who came back with another Sherpa to help me. By hanging on to both of these Sherpas I got into camp. There I had a tremendous fit of shivering and remembered nothing more for nearly forty-eight hours. My next recollection is of West's face on May 22nd, as he came into the tent. He had in fact been down to Camp III and had come up again in charge of rescue operations. West and Nevison helped me out of my sleeping bag and told me what had happened; I did not understand them.

West, Nevison, some Sherpas and myself went down slowly—for me this was an effort of great concentration. At the start of the long traverse to Camp IV West left and went up again to the Col alone. Incidentally this was the first big mountain he had climbed, yet far from being overwhelmed by the disasters, and despite the fact that he was not a climber, he played a prominent part in the rescue operations. The descent took many hours and the fixed ropes were life-saving. Although fully clothed, I felt a terrible inner coldness; all my fingers and toes were frostbitten and my pace became slower and slower. As darkness fell I was still about a hundred feet above Camp IV, to which Nevison had descended to prepare a meal and to warm sleeping bags. Two Sherpas supported me throughout this time and I began to get hallucinations just before I reached Camp. Nevison forced some fluid, terramycin tablets and stew down my throat. Evidently I was then talking nonsense in between using the oxygen. I have a vivid memory of a dream concerning an underground house in

Switzerland. Next day Gill arrived and we set off, myself little better than before. By evening I had not reached Camp III, but eventually made it some time after dark.

The full enormity of the disaster that had overtaken us was now apparent to me. I talked to Doig at the Silver Hut on the radio—a disjointed and breathless conversation. Up on the Makalu Col the struggle to rescue Mulgrew continued.

On May 20th, after I had left Harrison and Ortenburger at Camp VI, Annalu staggered into Camp bringing news of Mulgrew's illness. Fortunately, I had left a half-empty bottle of oxygen at Camp VI. Two Sherpas were sent up to Mulgrew and Nevison with this oxygen and a tent. Annalu continued down to Camp V with a note for me to send up more oxygen. Then, since no contact could be made with me by radio, and as assistance from below was essential, Harrison and Ortenburger tossed up for who should descend. Harrison lost and came down. At Camp V he found me cyanosed and very breathless and I did not recognize him. The situation was now desperate, with two sick men, one at 26,500 and the other at 24,500 feet.

In the meantime Ortenburger had climbed up to Mulgrew and Nevison. Nevison and two Sherpas descended whilst Ortenburger and Mulgrew, who was using oxygen brought up by a 'low-altitude Sherpa', managed to start down. Harrison at the Makalu Col radioed down to Camp III, where Romanes and Gill were, to send oxygen up to the Col, which by then was almost denuded of personnel except for myself and one or two Sherpas. On the 21st Mulgrew was brought down to Camp VI by some Sherpas who spent the night there without sleeping bags. On the 22nd Urkien and some Sherpas appeared at Camp V on the Makalu Col without either Mulgrew or Ortenburger.

Mulgrew was now helpless, they told Harrison, but they were too heavily laden to bring him down. After a quick meal they set off again, and later in the evening brought in Mulgrew, who appeared almost lifeless. His hands were very badly frost-bitten. However, after some warm food and drink both Ortenburger and Mulgrew improved. On the 23rd Ortenburger descended and arrangements were made for Romanes and some Sherpas to come up to the col the next day, bringing further supplies of oxygen. On the 24th, West, Harrison and the Sherpas set off from the Makalu Col with Mulgrew. It soon became apparent that he could not be carried and he soon became unconscious. The situation had once again become desperate. However, Harrison made a makeshift sledge out of rucksack frames, which worked extremely well. Mulgrew, in a sleeping bag, was strapped onto this vehicle and the whole journey to Camp III was achieved that day. I saw Mulgrew for the first time at Camp III and it was obvious that he had to be evacuated as soon as possible. Arrangements had already been made to fly us out by helicopter from Shershon.

Mulgrew was carried on the backs of relays of Sherpas. I managed to walk down, as did Ang Temba. We arrived at Shershon in the evening and next day the helicopter collected us, taking Mulgrew, West (who had come to look after us), Ang Temba and myself in relays to the United Mission Hospital at Katmandu.

Mulgrew's life had been saved by quick thinking, devotion and extraordinary endurance on the part of all members of the expedition, while the Sherpas, almost without exception, were magnificent. Most of the Sherpas who helped to bring Mulgrew down were so-called 'low-altitude' Sherpas. Some of them had spent nights at Camp V and VI without sleeping bags or lilos. That Mulgrew had managed to live through the nightmare days of his descent was unbelievable. His will to live had triumphed where that of a lesser man would have failed.

For the interest and information of those who climb high mountains, I think it is worthwhile to discuss the adaptions of the human body to high altitude and comment on the complications that can occur with special reference to this expedition.

Medical Aspects of High Altitude Climbing

At sea level the normal barometric pressure is equivalent to the weight of 760 mm of mercury. As the climber ascends the weight of air decreases, so that at 19,000 feet it is equivalent to only 380 mm of mercury. The percentage of oxygen in the air, however, remains the same whatever the height, i.e. 21 per cent.

Thus the amount of pressure driving oxygen from the lungs into the blood becomes less the higher the climber ascends. It is this drop in oxygen pressure that is the major factor in high altitude climbing. To combat it the body attempts to compensate with two major adaptive mechanisms. In the first place more air and therefore more oxygen is passed through the lungs; in the second place there is an increase in the number of red cells, and therefore of oxygen-carrying capacity, in the blood. This enables the same amount of oxygen to be carried in the blood at 19,000 feet as at sea-level. However, it must be remembered that the pressure of oxygen in the blood is very much less than it is at sea-level, therefore the maximum amount of oxygen that can be delivered to the tissues is very much less than at sea-level and the capacity for physical exercise is reduced.

The cells that are most sensitive to lack of oxygen are those of the brain and this explains why accounts of climbing at high altitude are sometimes incomplete and bizarre. It explains, too, the hallucinations, forgetfulness and callousness that climbers often show when high on a mountain, quite unlike their sea-level behaviour.

The two main adaptive processes—an increase in breathing rate and an increase in the number of red cells—may themselves cause medical complications and illness.

Increased breathing and the dry atmosphere at extreme altitudes increase the rate of water loss from the lungs by as much as three-fold. This is one reason why climbers tend to become dehydrated; other reasons are the difficulty of obtaining enough fluid from the snow because of limited fuel supplies and inefficient stoves, and the blunting

27 AMA DABLAM (22,495 ft.) in the Everest massif (Nepal Himalaya). The East Flank. (Photograph by M. Ward)

of the sensation of thirst. Drying of the respiratory tract, coupled with lack of oxygen, seems to predispose to respiratory infections, the most serious of which is pneumonia.

The increase in the number of red cells in the blood probably causes an increased liability to thrombosis. The normal ratio of red cells to plasma is 45 per cent red cells to 55 per cent plasma. At high altitude this ratio can change to 65 per cent red cells to 35 per cent plasma. The blood becomes very sticky and more difficult for the heart to circulate.

Frostbite is an almost inevitable sequel to sickness or accident. Warmth depends on the flow of blood around the body. In any condition where there is "shock", the peripheral blood vessels contract and the supply of heat to the limbs is greatly reduced or cut off. The extremities, therefore, cool down to the same temperature as the surrounding air, which at extreme altitudes is below freezing, and no matter how much clothing is worn, frostbite is inevitable.

Lack of oxygen constricts the blood vessels of the lungs and causes a rise in pulmonary blood pressure. This increases the work on the right side of the heart and the heart enlarges. At high altitude, where the climber is continuously exposed to lack of oxygen, any lung condition which further impedes the absorption of oxygen is extremely dangerous. He may lose consciousness as an early symptom and signs of heart failure with pulmonary œdema may occur.

To examine the major illnesses that occurred on Makalu in the light of this knowledge is interesting and informative. To take my own case first: I developed a chest infection, probably at Camp VI (26,000 feet), after a period of eight days on the Makalu Col, doing work connected with our physiology programme and involving a maximum of effort. This illness first manifested itself by the hallucinations I had at Camp VI, followed by an inability to *descend* at a reasonable rate. I became progressively weaker and had to be dragged into a tent on the col. Here, after rigor, I became delirious—another manifestation of anoxia, as the brain cells are most sensitive to lack of oxygen. I was treated with antibiotics and oxygen and descended forty-eight hours later with Nevison. On this descent I was occasionally delirious and felt a most extraordinary central coldness, despite being fully clothed. I suffered frostbite of all my fingers, toes and of my nose. The explanation is that the lung infection, diagnosed by Nevison as pneumonia, strained an already strained heart, resulting in a shutdown of the circulation. Blood, and therefore heat and oxygen, were not available to my peripheral vessels during the descent. My cardiac output was sufficient for lying in a sleeping bag but not sufficient for any form of exercise. An X-ray of my chest at Katmandu, taken within twenty-four hours of returning by helicopter, showed an enlarged heart. Later X-rays at the London Hospital showed a gradual diminution in the size of my heart until it became normal after three months.

In the case of Mulgrew the sequence of events was probably as follows: a clot of blood formed in his lungs at 27,000 feet and this led to "shock", constriction of the peripheral vessels and diminution in cardiac output. This explains the coughing up of blood, his complete collapse and his very severe frostbite. After his evacuation to Katmandu, and to Australia and New Zealand, he developed an infection of the legs, both of which had to be amputated below the knee; some fingers were also amputated. The clot of blood in his lungs became infected and pus formed, which had to be drained off in New Zealand.

Sir Edmund Hillary suffered what appeared to be a transient stroke. This may have been due to a spasm of the cerebral blood vessels secondary to a transient thrombosis. Three other cases, in respect of young and fit personnel, with similar clinical features, have occurred on expeditions to the Himalayas. Two of these patients subsequently died and one recovered.

Nevison considered that he had an attack of pulmonary œdema at Camp VI, for his sputum was frothy and tinged with blood; he was also very breathless at rest. An X-ray, taken in America some time later, showed no cardiac enlargement.

If medical oxygen had not been available on Makalu in all probability there would have been three deaths.

The precipitating factor in these three serious illnesses is not known, but I had just spent the winter at 19,000 feet. This had obviously taken more out of me than was thought at the time. In fact, as a result of the winter, although the full programme of work was carried out satisfactorily, the general condition of the whole wintering party was less good than that of the party coming in during the spring. The ascent of Amadablam, with the subsequent carrying off of a Sherpa, was a great strain, but I believe we recovered from this. The subsequent month, spent working often till after midnight at the Silver Hut, tired us more than we realized. In fact, 19,000 feet is too high for plainsmen for long periods, and 17,000 feet, or even 15,000 feet is probably the best height to get maximum acclimatization.

Hillary had spent a month on a world trip with the yeti scalp after being with the expedition in the field from August to the end of November. The scalp was flown by him to Kumjung on January 5th. He returned the same day and went back to New Zealand for a holiday and to organize the spring party. After his return to the Silver Hut in March he had to fly back to Katmandu, where he spent some ten days clearing up the difficulties arising from the ascent of Amadablam. As well as being eight years older, his physical condition in 1961 did not compare in any way with his superb fitness in 1953.

Mulgrew had spent the autumn on the yeti hunt and had returned with the spring party. His general health appeared as good as any other member of the expedition.

The contrast between the physical condition of the climbers of this expedition and that of the French expedition to Makalu is quite remarkable. The same contrast was made between members of the successful Everest expedition in 1953 (using oxygen) and the pre-war Everest expeditions which did not use oxygen.

The main effect of oxygen appears to be to combat deterioration, and by doing this and by increasing the speed of movement on the mountains the climber can ascend more quickly, more efficiently and more safely. *Oxygen should always be taken on expeditions to Himalayan peaks, and should always be available in the high camps,* as it is of life-saving value in cases of acute pulmonary œdema and pneumonia. Both of these conditions can occur below 19,000 feet. Climbing oxygen, too, should be taken by climbers who are trying to ascend peaks of over 24,000 feet, as it combats deterioration, which accelerates at these heights, and therefore increases the margin of safety.

THE ASCENT OF AMADABLAM

Reconnaissance

The Silver Hut was not only the highest laboratory in the world but it also had the most spectacular backyard. After three months we had grown accustomed to the impossible looking mountains around us, dominated by Amadablam, remote, beautiful and increasingly tempting. Encouraged by the ascent of Rakpa Peak, we decided to have a closer look and at the end of February Romanes and Gumen Dorje set off to reconnoitre the south ridge. Three days later they returned with the verdict that it would be a good climb in the New Zealand Alps. Romanes had reached the Yellow Tower that had turned back Cunningham. However, a few days later the hut became overcrowded due to a series of space-consuming experiments, and Pugh agreed that Bishop and I could be spared to have another look at the Yellow Tower. I also confirmed with Pugh that we had permission to climb mountains in the Mingbo Valley.

We took two Sherpas and, after a night spent at a camp below the crest of the ridge, we climbed along to the Yellow Tower. The first surprise was the character of the ridge, casually described by Romanes as being "fairly difficult". The route included a tower on which a nylon rope placed by Cunningham flapped listlessly, a gully with an overhang, and beyond this the ridge became a series of ragged and jagged turrets. The route wandered in and out of these, first on one side and then on the other; cold, sunless and windy on the west, while on the east, where luckily all the more difficult pitches were, the sun warmed the rocks. A small hanging glacier, twenty yards square, nuzzled at the foot of the Yellow Tower. Just before we reached this we negotiated a narrow piece of ridge, along which we progressed *à cheval*, followed by a proper finger and toe traverse.

By then Barry and I were most impressed; the mountain was showing its calibre and we wondered what would happen if we had a snowfall of even two inches. On the small glacier, a natural camp site, we had our lunch. We then climbed fairly

83

easily up to the ledge on the Yellow Tower from which the difficult climbing began. We now understood what Romanes meant by "a good route". Beyond the right-hand edge of the ledge on which we stood we could climb straight up over an overhang on to the ridge again. Once on the ridge there were thirty feet of difficult rock before easier ground was reached. Alternatively we could traverse upwards and to the right across the face of the tower, which was steep and rather exposed.

We decided on balance to try the traverse first and I started off. After a very awkward ten feet and three pitons I landed on the top of a diamond-shaped rock. From there I could either go straight up over the overhang or continue right, where a smooth ten feet barred the way from what appeared to be easier though exposed rock. I could not find a good crack for a piton and so continued upwards to the overhang. I could not get over this and returned to Bishop on the ledge. We were finding that climbing of some difficulty could be done provided one got one's breathing right. Holding one's breath at 20,000 feet cannot be prolonged.

Bishop continued up to the overhang and managed to climb it, using some etriers. He put in a piton above and, after having a good look, came down; he said he thought we could get to the crest of the ridge. We had spent a considerable time on our attempt and decided that it would be best to pitch a camp on the glacier next day, so that we could tackle the tower when fresh. This we did on February 25th.

We returned to the attack on the 26th, and to start with I went up to and over the overhang, using etriers. Above, the rock was very loose, and even if we reached the crest of the ridge there were still considerable difficulties. I returned to the ledge on the diamond-shaped rock, and after a search found a fairly good crack for a piton. By using an attenuated foothold I put in a further piton, on which I hung an etrier. I stood up in this, moved up a rung, made a further long stride and was across the difficulty. Somewhat selfishly I then belayed onto a really firm piton and invited Barry to continue across the face up to the tower some fifty feet away. The first thirty feet proved relatively easy, then the rock began to overhang again. Barry retreated, banged in another piton and then went up. He put in another piton, clipped in a karabiner, and then rested on the tight rope; a few further contortions and he was up. I followed; the last ten feet or so before the ridge were most awkward and exposed.

From the top of the Yellow Tower we made our way easily over another tower of reddish rock (the Red Tower) and were soon in the Notch. From the Notch a vertical step, seamed by a crack, led to what appeared to be an easier ridge. This led to a further tower and beyond this we could see the upper slopes of the mountain. This vertical step, which we called the First Step, was obviously going to be troublesome. We returned to the top of the Yellow Tower and traversed down its crest until we found a convenient spot to put a wire ladder. This just reached to the ledge. From then on we used the ladder for our ascent and descent of the Tower.

84

That afternoon Romanes, Pemba Tensing and Gumen Dorje arrived at Camp II at the foot of the Yellow Tower.

Next day Romanes, Bishop and I climbed the wire ladder and continued into the Notch. There an ice-slope led to the foot of the First Step. We cut steps up this slope, unfortunately now on the west side of the ridge. The vertical crack for which we then aimed was just sheltered from the fierce wind. The fact that all the hardest climbing was done out of the wind in the sun was of the greatest help.

The first portion of the crack overhung and could be classed as "severe". Further up it became much more difficult. Romanes started on this whilst Bishop and I sheltered behind the crest of the ice-slope and enjoyed the tremendous view downwards. The wind boomed and shrieked and every now and then blew the rope horizontal. Romanes continued up for about thirty feet and then started traversing right out of the crack. He put in a few rather insecure pitons and came down. Bishop then went up and spent a long time trying to put in some reasonable ones. Evidently the crack would go but pitons and crack size did not coincide; some *coins de bois* would have helped. We descended and next day Bishop climbed up, put in a few rather shaky pitons, hung some etriers, and climbed the crack. I then took over the lead and went up the ridge above. The climbing was a good deal easier but most exposed; again the thought of a few inches of snow was unnerving. We got to the foot of an ice ridge leading to the Second Step. There we left some rope and ironmongery. On the way down we put in pitons at convenient belay points.

At Camp II that night we found Gill; he had come up from the Silver Hut after being the last subject for a series of experiments on cardiac output by Dr Pugh. On March 1st Romanes and Gill continued up the ridge and got to the top of the Second Step; this they managed by traversing left across the foot of the Second Step and climbing a very rotten snow gully. Higher up the snow improved, but this section of the route was always the most dangerous. At the top of the Second Step a mixed snow and rock ridge led to the proposed site of our last camp, a hanging glacier at the foot of the upper ice flutings.

Bishop and I spent the day taking up reserve supplies to the ledge below the ice ridge leading to the Second Step, and putting a wire ladder down the First Step. Next day Bishop, Romanes and I descended to the Green Hut while Gill remained to consolidate the route. This sudden interruption may appear unusual, but our climbing on Amadablam was still a reconnaissance. A plane had managed to land on the airfield at Mingbo, but in doing so the tail had been badly damaged. By radio Pugh had asked me to go down and see what I could do to help.

After this break we were ready to continue the attempt on Amadablam, and I had to decide whether we could really spare the time and whether it was safe. A further talk with Pugh settled the first point—they were still busy at the Silver Hut. The question remained whether it was safe enough. We had four climbers: the two New Zealanders, Romanes and Gill; one American, Bishop; and an Englishman, myself. There were only two Sherpas who were really good and who could be spared. What would happen if we had an accident? The remainder of the party would not be able to mount a strong rescue operation; we would therefore have to be entirely self-supporting. Amadablam was technically difficult so far and on the whole route there was nowhere we could relax. All of the climbing was by pitches and the Sherpas, never very keen on belaying, had to be thoroughly drilled. In fact both Sherpas were very apprehensive of the mountain; its reputation after 1959, its difficulty and in-accessability, made them say it was a "Sahib's path" and not a "Sherpa path". Sherpas are not strong in the arm and most of them do not excel in rock-climbing. So far Amadablam had been a continuous rock climb and they did not like it much. It was also the wrong time of year and many prophecies of snow were made.

I decided, therefore, that any final attempt should be made by the four of us together. In this way we would be self-supporting. Another safety factor was our easy and direct communication with the Silver Hut through our portable radio. The fact remained, however, that we four were the only mountaineers in the wintering party and we should have to fend for ourselves. On March 6th we rejoined Gill at Camp II.

Gill and the two Sherpas had improved the route between I and II and also taken 100 pounds of food and equipment to the Notch. We then followed Gill's suggestion that we should move our camp from below the Yellow Tower to beyond the Red Tower. This was a good plan, because the ascent of the two wire ladders slowed our initial impetus to get through to the ice shelf.

Next day we woke to see three to four inches of snow on the rocks. This cleared towards midday and the six of us spent the whole day moving our camp up 200 feet along a quarter of a mile of the ridge. The new site was not so comfortable, but after the Sherpas had spent a day or two improving it (they did not climb above this camp) it became quite habitable.

The "Illicit" Summit

On the 8th Gill and Romanes set off to get through to the ice-shelf, whilst Bishop and I took up more loads to the ledge below the Second Step. We also put more ropes and pitons in to safeguard the route. In the evening they returned, looking very depressed. They had gone to within 100 yards of the ice-shelf, but there they had found an ice ridge on which tottering mushroom-like towers balanced precariously. They reckoned it would go, but thought it would take longer than we had time, or food or equipment for. Next day, I decided that Bishop and I should have a look at it before retreating.

We set off early and climbed quickly. The gully by which we traversed the Second

86

Step was unpleasant and loose. The initial part of the ridge above the Second Step was not too difficult. We got to the mushroom area at about midday. It looked un-inviting and beyond it the edge of the ice-shelf was vertical for about twenty feet and would, we thought, have to be climbed by artificial means.

We started off at once to maintain our morale. The ice towers were of fantastic shape, often overhanging on both sides; they were balanced on a steep-sided ridge along which it would take too long to cut, so we had to go over the towers directly. We found that we could usually belay safely in a crevasse at the end of each pitch. Some of the towers were very rickety, and we climbed them as nearly in the line of the crest of the ridge as possible. After some time we reached the foot of the ice-shelf, which luckily did not look too formidable. We climbed it using some ice pitons, ice-screws and an etrier. Next day Romanes, choosing a different route, managed to get up without resort to artificial aids.

The ice-shelf was a sloping snow-field about an acre in extent. The consistency of the snow was ideal for an ice-cave. The views were impressive, looking down the south face and into the Dudh Kosi. Thyangboche and Namche Bazaar we could just see, and beyond them the range of mountains south of Namche. The immediate problem above us was an immense ice-cliff stretching completely across the south face. About 150 feet high, this threatened our camp site; it would be impossible to climb it or to traverse beneath it. A broad highly polished ice-swept runnel ran down from this cliff and bounded the ice-shelf on the West. Obviously some ice, too, got swept down a narrow runnel on our right. The apex of the shelf divided the two runnels. We would have to cross the right-hand runnel, but as it was only thirty to forty feet wide the danger would not be great; the ice-field showed no evidence of avalanche debris and was, therefore, we considered, quite safe.

The upper slopes did not look at all steep; this, however, may have been pure relief. We were still 1,500 feet from the summit, and the only breach in the ice-cliff above was between its right end and the edge of the east face, where there was a horizontal snow ridge. Up to this ridge a snow slope led and this was plainly our first objective; it looked like the key to the upper slopes.

As we descended the weather looked threatening; black clouds began to loom up beyond the Dudh Kosi and light snow fell. As we reached the ledge Romanes and Gill climbed up to us; we told them our news and swiftly descended to our camp on top of the Red Tower.

Later that evening the weather cleared and the stars came out. Throughout these last few days the weather had not been very settled and we would watch with anxiety the mountains to the southwest. It seemed that, contrary to experience in the European Alps, the appearance of high cirrus did not necessarily presage a front, whereas towering cumuli often meant a snow-storm.

We decided not to take tents for our last camp but to rely on a snow cave. This would lighten our loads. We would have to get to the shelf early to build an ice-cave, which would be tiring after a full day's climbing at 21,000 feet. I also felt that we should rope the gully by which we avoided the Second Step, in addition to a few more difficult pieces on the ridge beyond; this would facilitate our retreat in the event of a bad snow-storm. Next day Romanes and Gill took some loads up the ice-shelf and also fixed ropes on the portions above the Second Tower, whilst Bishop and I roped the loose gully.

On the 11th we all arrived on the ice-shelf at 4.0 p.m., and under the direction of Romanes, an expert, started to make an ice-cave. To begin with only one person at a time could work, which we each did at full throttle for ten minutes. When the entrance widened out we could work two at a time, while the other two recovered debris. We used a light aluminium snow-shovel and a special ice block cutter (actually a sort of saw with two cutting surfaces, one being jagged and the other sharp). There was a beautiful sunset—I remember especially how Menlungtse stood out—but we were far from finished. In fact, after five or six hours hard work we had just managed to make a sleeping-shelf wide enough. We cooked a sparse meal and, being squashed together, spent a warm if relatively uncomfortable night.

Next day Romanes and I reconnoitred the first half of the route to the summit. We cramponed up the first 200 feet of the ice runnel to a natural ice-cave. To cross the runnel we cut steps and emerged quickly on the far side. We climbed a small rock buttress which gave onto the snow slope leading to the right edge of the ice-cliff. The top of the snow slope was a narrow ridge; its far side fell steeply into the monstrous precipice of the east face. To our left the ice-cliff was broken, and we could sidle round it, cross a narrow gully and get on to some rocks. This short section was menaced by the ice-cliff, and as quickly as possible we cut steps across and got to the safety of the rocks on the far side. We climbed this for three rope-lengths and then traversed onto the snow above the hanging glacier. By now we were both tired. As far as we could see the main difficulties between us and the top were a series of snow and ice flutings; if these were in good condition we should get to the top. On our descent we fixed more ropes and got back to the ice cave. Here Gill and Bishop had spent the day enlarging the cave and making it more comfortable. We got everything organized for the next morning and went to bed after a good meal.

At 8.30 a.m. we set out. We quickly gained height and were soon at the flutings. These were very impressive as they swept in parallel lines towards the blue sky and summit ridge. The weather was more settled and, although there was the usual cold wind, we were sheltered most of the day. At the foot of the final slope we found a convenient fluting which appeared to run diagonally across the others; this started at the bottom right-hand corner and ran up to the centre of the summit ridge. We

88

followed this the whole way. The consistency of the snow varied considerably, sometimes becoming very icy and steep, so that handholds had to be cut. In general the angle was between forty and fifty degrees and on the whole less steep than the upper part of Rakpa Peak. Romanes and I had been leading from the start and after a few rope lengths handed over to Bishop and Gill. We gained height steadily and at about 2.30 p.m. we saw the front pair disappear from view and heard a short yell. In a few minutes we were gathered on the top. Instead of the narrow ridge we had expected, the summit turned out to be a snow-cap, seamed by a crevasse, about 100 yards by thirty.

The upper part of the north ridge looked very difficult and the final hundred or more feet of the ice cap appeared extremely steep. To the east we could just make out the Silver Hut. The Everest group dominated all the other mountains and we could see a formidable array of the world's highest peaks. As we took photographs I realized we were the same height as the foot of the Lhotse face. We did not stay long at the top and reached the ice-cave at sunset.

Early next morning we descended to Camp II, clearing the rocks of the pitons and other impedimenta as we went. The Sherpas were genuinely pleased to see us, for they had been very apprehensive. That night we talked to the Silver Hut; they had seen us on the top for a fleeting moment. We arranged for Sherpas to come up next day to carry off our gear, and planned to meet them at the foot of the Yellow Tower. Romanes and Gill rigged up an aerial ropeway to send down loads. Bishop and I, Gumen and Pemba ferried loads to the ropeway. All went well and soon the loads were hurtling down with gay abandon—a suggestion that we should follow was not taken up. By midday the last loads were down; the Sherpas followed and Romanes dismantled his fine ropeway and we abseiled off knocking out as many pitons as we could.

The Ides of March

We had seen our Sherpas set off with immense loads; I must admit with some misgivings. We all took quite heavy rucksacks and started down. About a quarter of an hour down the ridge, just before the toe traverse and the *à cheval* ridge, I came across a frightened group of Sherpas. In their midst was Gumen; he said he had broken his leg. He was right, the foot was at a right angle to the knee and there was a thin trickle of blood from the fracture site. The Sherpas were stunned; their morale vanished. I quickly twisted Gumen's leg straight. The Sherpas had been carrying some high altitude rations in cardboard boxes; I tore the cardboard up and with puttees made a serviceable splint to above the knee. I gave Gumen morphia and some sulphonamide. I injected the morphia into his abdominal muscles, as the skin there is often warm when the limbs are cold; the morphia therefore acts more quickly.

The tension that always eases after climbing a difficult mountain now returned with relentless pressure.

Gumen told us that a rock had broken under him; he had no chance with his heavy load and his leg had snapped like a twig. The main problem was how to get him off, as he was heavier than the other Sherpas and they would not, and indeed could not, carry him. Normally, climbing involves as much balance and co-ordination as pure strength. But to take Gumen, who weighed about 120 lbs, along the ridge required as much brute strength as anything else. Gill and I were the strongest in our party and we fashioned a sling out of the climbing rope and started to carry him on our backs. Any other method when climbing a horizontal ridge is out of the question. Romanes went off with Penuri and a note for Pugh, telling him about the accident and asking for food, morphia and a wire splint. We, of course, were out of food and fuel, as we had expected to get off the mountain to the Green Hut that evening. Once Penuri had reached Camp I Romanes returned to help. Bishop was to get the loads off the mountain with the other Sherpas who were still in a trance.

Gill started by carrying Gumen whilst I belayed him. Our progress was extremely slow and after five or ten minutes he was exhausted. For about an hour we alternated our carries. It was too dangerous and we were getting progressively more tired. Romanes then appeared, having made very rapid time. We evolved a system that either Gill or I would carry Gumen while Romanes did all the ropework and reconnoitred the next few feet. We worked out each step and hold, found the best belay— the best rest spot. Our limit was ten minutes. The carrier was helped by the other Sahib and Ang Pemba; they steadied him, made footholds, protected Gumen's legs and generally made life as easy as possible. Only Romanes and the carrying Sahib were roped.

Behind us Bishop was exhorting the Sherpas to get our loads off the mountain and carrying immense ones himself. It soon became obvious that we would not get off the mountain that day, and as the afternoon passed we looked for a camp site. There was only one which would serve, just before the Tower roped by Cunningham's party. About one hour before sunset we reached this site and snow began to fall.

We just managed to scrape two rudimentary platforms and put up two tents. Wally pressed on to Camp I to extract a reluctant Sherpa sent up by Pugh (contacted that afternoon by radio) with kerosene and food. He returned, a yeti-like figure, and disappeared again in the swirling snow. We settled in for the night. Gumen's general state was very good; he had never become shocked and the morphia kept him relatively happy.

We woke next morning to a grisly outlook. There were about six inches of snow on the rocks and it looked as if more was on the way. It would have been dangerous to move in such conditions and we waited. The sun came out later and began stripping

90

the rocks. The problem of the tower was overcome by penduluming across its face. This was Gill's idea; the route over the top was still snow-clad and too risky.

We fixed the rope at the top of the tower, where Romanes manipulated it. Leaning well against the rope Gill carried Gumen across in an arc. I held his feet in doubtful places. This was most spectacular, but we had no alternative. After a few more hours of alternate carrying we reached easier ground about 100 yards short of Camp I. Here one of the Sherpas took over.

The weather then broke again and at 3.0 p.m. it began to snow. There were still a lot of large boulders to get through and I asked Da Tensing II, who was carrying Gumen, what he thought. He was all for going on, saying that it would get worse. He then did a very fine carry over the most fiendishly slippery snow-covered boulders; another Sherpa and I steadied him. In the meantime the others, plus some more Sherpas, had managed to get all the loads off the mountain. We finally made our camp in a dismal waste of boulders with over four inches of snow on the ground.

In the morning we attempted to get Gumen carried on a stretcher. Both he and the Sherpas refused, so a very dirty and tough customer called Tenzing from Dingboche chose to carry him almost unaided to Mingbo. Tenzing was immediately booked for Makalu and was in fact one of the so-called low-altitude Sherpas who cheerfully went to 26,000 feet to get Pete Mulgrew off.

That afternoon we arrived at Mingbo. Two days later Gumen was in the United Mission Hospital at Shantah Bhawan in Katmandu, having been flown out by plane. His X-ray showed no displacement of the fracture, this being a tribute to the efficiency of cardboard and the Kramer wire splint. His general condition remained very good throughout, due to adequate morphia, adequate warmth (we kept him in a big down jacket all the time) and his own constitution.

After these strenuous few days we returned to Changmatang, where by solid eating and sleeping we put on weight at the rate of a pound a day.

Amadablam seemed to be a mountain of Alpine calibre; the route by which we climbed it was a very good one, providing climbing of every variety. By and large the difficulties had to be overcome rather than avoided and there were sections of artificial rock and artificial ice climbing. The solitary situation of Amadablam, the great beauty and character of the mountain, made this a memorable climb.

> "Sweet are the uses of adversity,
> Which like the toad, ugly and venomous,
> Wears yet a precious jewel in his head;
> And this our life exempt from public haunt,
> Finds tongues in trees, books in running brooks,
> Sermons in stones, and good in everything."
>
> *As You Like It*

UNEXPLORED WEST NEPAL

By John Tyson

One cannot wander far from the main trade routes without discovering what a large part of the earth's surface still remains unexplored. This is a very pleasant discovery to make. Explorers and mountaineers, turning their attention to Greenland, to the Antarctic or to the great fjords and ice-fields of Patagonia, are finding even today an almost untouched field for discovery. Certainly in the Himalayas, despite a century of climbing and charting, there are still to be found entire ranges about which no accurate information exists, and where no peaks have been mapped, climbed or even visited.

Much of Nepal is still in this happy state. The chance to visit this country first came my way in 1953 when I travelled with W. H. Murray up the Nepalese bank of the Kaliganga in the extreme west of Nepal to explore the western approaches of Mount Api. Later we climbed in the splendid but savage Yokapahar Himal, which stretches between the main Himalayan range and Tibet, and circling the Api and Nampa massif descended the valley of the Setiganga, at that time still unvisited by any European. The countryside was one of great poverty, and this ten-week journey seemed to show that in the little-known interior of Nepal the small lightly-equipped party would operate most easily and would cause least hardship to the villagers in regions where food is often scarce. Indeed it seemed that the majority of the west of the country was still in the phase of reconnaissance mountaineering, where the small expedition, often with scientific aims, comes most fully into its own. Marcel Kurz supported this view, encouraging us and suggesting a particularly remote section of the Great Himalayas where the maps in his recent *Chronique Himalayenne* were plentifully scattered with question marks. It was in fact at his châlet at Saleinaz that the plans of the 1961 expedition were laid, and we shall always be grateful for the kindly advice he gave us.

Our 1961 journey had similar aims of exploratory mountaineering and mapping to those of 1953, this time a little further to the east in the mountain chains of the Jagdula Lekh and of the Sisne, Patrasi and Kanjiroba Himal—probably the least-known ranges of the entire Himalayas. Though several European explorers had skirted the fringes of the region—notably the botanist Oleg Polunin, and the famous Italian Orientalist Giuseppe Tucci—from a purely mountaineering standpoint the only

92

successful ascents in this entire area had been carried out by Dr Herbert Tichy of Vienna, with his Sherpas, in the course of his pioneering trip through western Nepal from the capital, Katmandu, to Pithoragarh in 1953. Even the fabulous Toni Hagen, who has been almost everywhere in Nepal, had missed this group in his wanderings. The long approach march is the main reason for the neglect of this part by explorers, for here Nepal is at its widest—150 miles from the jungly terai in the south to the Tibetan Plateau. This approach journey of almost a month on foot persuaded us once again to keep our numbers down to only three, besides Sherpas, and to travel light.

Our party assembled on the Nepalese frontier at the end of March. John Earle, the expedition quartermaster, had travelled ahead of us with the equipment. James Burnet and I found him, tired and perspiring, in the Indian customs shed, battling to clear our equipment out of India. The frontier post was Nepalganj, an oppressive, sinister shanty-town, and one which has witnessed the downfall of many a Gurkha soldier returning to his home in the hills. Here we drew enough money in Nepalese and Indian coin and notes to last us the next three months. Significantly, no-one could tell us what currencies would be acceptable in the regions we proposed to visit, for even in Nepal itself almost nothing is known about these outlying parts.

At Nepalganj we were joined by a youth from Katmandu, Manik Tuladhar, who announced himself as our liaison officer, and by the three Sherpas we had engaged through the Himalayan Society in Katmandu. It would be hard to find better men for the job than the hardworking Angtemba III and the jovial and very experienced Mingma Tsering. As sirdar we had engaged Ang Dawa, a most impressive and imposing figure. He had been with Max Eiselin the previous year on Dhaulagiri. Our only regret is that he brought along an unexpected fourth Sherpa as cook, something of a trouble-maker, who later turned out to be the sirdar's younger brother!

Although Nepalganj is one of the five permitted points of entry into Nepal, ours appeared to be the first 'expedition' to have gone in by this route. This had some drawbacks, for the officials were unfamiliar with the regulations and viewed our pile of crates despondently while the matter was referred to 'higher authority'. Yet there were also many advantages: all our shopping for supplies was done in the presence of such a large crowd of interested and curious well-wishers that none of the shop-keepers dared swindle us, and soon we had hired ponies for the first stage of the journey and bought mountains of local food at very low prices. Those who come after us may not be so fortunate.

The ponies were laden not only with the usual mountaineering gear but also with several heavy crates containing the delicate survey instruments, when on April 5th we set off eastwards across the monotonous and densely wooded plains of the terai towards Sallyana, the first town on our route. The Tharu cultivators and stock-raisers who inhabit these tracts live precariously in jungle villages stockaded against wild animals. Transport between the villages, on tracks passable only in the dry season, is by carts pulled by water-buffaloes. The wagons of these timid, primitive Tharus were in fact the only wheeled vehicles we saw in west Nepal—indeed the only wheels of any sort.

Throughout the terai the malignant *awal* fever is rife, and it is said that these Tharus survive through having built up a resistance to it. No hill-dweller, however, will venture into this jungle during the rainy season for fear of the *awal*, as we discovered when we descended from the hills and recrossed the terai three months later during the monsoon.

But now it was the hot season and on the main jungle tracks we passed many buffalo carts and pony trains carrying the trade between the Nepalese interior and the great marts of the Indian border. Our own pony-men insisted that we travel with a rifle at the head of our column, as a precaution against the armed dacoits who prey on these baggage trains.

Our route crossed the main ridge of the low Siwalik hills, youngest and outermost wrinkle of the Himalayas. To the north, clearly visible, stretched the higher, darkly forested Mahabharat Lekh, with the Babai River winding across a wide *dun*-valley between the ranges. This broad plain of Dang was the last flat country we were to see for three months. With our ponies grunting under their heavy loads we climbed by torchlight the steep Mahabharat Lekh to emerge on the crest in sunshine amid forests of rhododendron, oak and magnolia.

A week's journey through a varied landscape of terraced hills brought us to the attractive fortress town of Sallyana. Here we were given a most friendly reception from the Bada Hakim. He had great plans for the development of his district: a school had already been opened (as schoolmasters we inspected it with great interest) and a hospital was being built in a belated but worthy attempt to modernize this backward region. To emphasize the point, a helicopter with a load of building materials suddenly appeared overhead. There are no roads in the province.

From Sallyana four days' march through the fertile and agriculturally varied Midlands took us to Jajarkot, finely situated on a high bluff above the Bheri River. Especially memorable on this stage was a high-level trek through thickets of flowering rhododendron with glimpses of the whole range of the Dhaulagiri Himal floating above the afternoon heat-haze. Later the track dropped to the sultry Bheri River valley carved from beds of conglomerate hundreds of feet thick. Near Jajarkot we were astonished to cross this river on a fine steel wire suspension bridge bearing the name 'Henderson, Aberdeen'. It had been ordered during the last years of the rule of Maharajah Chandra Shamsher, the Rana Prime Minister, who had been anxious to improve the internal, though not the external, communications of Nepal. The sections

94

of the bridge had been carried across the hills by porters and assembled here in 1927 by Indian engineers.

North of Jajarkot the track is no longer suitable for ponies. Man is the beast of burden along the whole length of the Bheri Gorge where the river pierces the southern branch of the Himalayan range itself.

With our loads on the backs of thirty coolies we followed the right bank of the Bheri northwards to Dali. From now on the villages became smaller, the country poorer and our progress slower. Generally messages had to be sent to several villages before porters could be found for the next stage. There was sometimes confusion as to how far each stage should be. We would have preferred to make a *bandobast* right to Kaigaon, but it soon became clear that none of the men had heard of Kaigaon and that few had travelled more than a day's journey above their village. Despite these problems the coolies were friendly and willing, and carried heavy loads, often through the heat of the day, for very low wages. At Tallon an agreement was made for the rest of the journey to Kaigaon, reputed to be still six days distant. The track climbed and descended for thousands of feet over successions of rocky spurs, passing alternately through the dense bamboo thickets of the river-bed, and the temperate forests of the high ridges with their conifers and rhododendrons. From the high crests we obtained further tantalizing views of snowy ranges to the north. Eastwards, beyond the Bheri, rose the delicate fluted spires of Hiunchuli Patan.

Not a single doctor visits this huge area of country, and each night many pathetic cases were brought to us for treatment, often from distant valleys. Most were beyond cure—goitre, cataracts or tuberculosis of many years' standing, but we did our best and from time to time were rewarded with decisive cures—a small boy with pneumonia, for example. Not all our visitors came for treatment. The majority came to stare, for no white man had ever been seen in this part of the Upper Bheri. Each evening the semi-circle of squatting figures remained around our tent door until long after dark, and began to form again in the morning before we were awake. Binoculars, watches and cameras were all examined minutely; but the greatest miracle was the wireless set which could speak to them from Katmandu in their own language.

In 1924 Maharajah Chandra Shamsher had asked for the help of Indian officers of the Survey of India in mapping the whole of Nepal, and the result was the ¼-inch Reconnaissance Survey Map of 1925-7. This was an astonishing achievement considering the short time available. However, the triangulation covered only a part of the country and in the areas beyond its reach the topographical work deteriorated. The mountain chains of the Himalayas north and east of the Bheri Gorge were never triangulated or surveyed. They were in fact the least-known mountain ranges of Nepal, and the main purpose of our journey was to complete the map of this region.

95

So when, two weeks after leaving Sallyana, we crossed the main river at Ila and climbed up out of the sunless gorge to a pass from which we could have our first sight of those peaks, it was an exciting moment.

As we stood on the pass the icy crests of the Jagdula Lekh dominated the view. Beyond lay a maze of 20,000 feet summits of the Sisne Himal and Kanjiroba Himal. Our track then dropped through birch-forest and across alpine meadows, where yaks grazed, to the little village of Kaigaon, fifteen flat-roofed houses of Tibetan style standing in ploughed fields beside the rushing Ilagarh River.

Near Kaigaon we began our mapping. Our survey method was to compute an astronomical base-line between two peaks some seven miles apart, and to fix their altitudes by elevation from the Chaukri snow peak and Hiunchuli Patan, the most northerly known positions of the Survey of India triangulation in this region. This 'astro-fix' method involved measuring by theodolite the altitudes of four stars in the four quadrants of the sky at precisely known times—hence the radio. From this base-line we would later carry a photo-theodolite triangulation northwards into the heart of the mountain group.

It was while we were camped on a rocky summit near Kaigaon, preparing for a star-fix, that we had a most unpleasant and frightening experience. During the night a severe thunderstorm developed and lightning struck a few feet from our tents. We struggled out into the blizzard and, grabbing the Sherpas, stumbled down the steep snow to a safer spot. While we were cowering here, lightning once more struck the ridge just above our heads, the air was filled with an acrid cordite smell and the zips of our down jackets glowed with an eerie light. An hour later we heard the storm boom and echo away to the south-east and we crawled back to our tents feeling very shaken. The survey cairn had been shattered, and the precious wireless set, left inside the tent, had been knocked out of action.

On May 4th Earle set up base camp on an alpine meadow two days' journey up the Jagdula Khola. Here Burnet and I later joined him after computing our base-line and finishing some survey stations below. During the weeks that followed the map progressed steadily. Our survey stations were mostly at heights of between 13,000 feet and 17,000 feet. The climbs up to these stations, often through snow-covered forests of great beauty, were among the most enjoyable days of the expedition. The forests abounded in game—bear, bharal, wild goat and ram chukor. Rhododendrons and azaleas flowered side by side, and primulas, anemones and potentillas covered the open slopes. Some of our survey stations could be completed in a day; others took several days and involved high camps, splendidly situated with views extending over nearly half the length of Nepal. As an additional check on position, resections were taken from Dhaulagiri and, far to the north-west, the peaks of Saipal. On clear days the white dome of Api, 110 miles distant, was also visible and towards Tibet the

28 AMA DABLAM (22,495 ft.) as seen from the west. Photographed from a nameless summit to the south of Everest.
29 ON THE ASCENT TO AMA DABLAM (Everest massif). (Photograph by M. Ward)

30 VIEW FROM THE WEST BANK OF THE KHOLA toward the snowcapped peaks between the two main sources of the Jagdula Khola. (Photograph by John Tyson)

31 SATAL PRASAD, the best Shikari (hunter) and guide of the forests and gorges around Kaigaon, was of great assistance to the mapping programme. (Photograph by John Earle)

range of the Yokapahar Himal which Da Norbu and I had attempted to cross during the monsoon eight years before.

During the six weeks which we spent in the area we came to know well many of the people both of Kaigaon and at the nearby town of Jumla. One of our luckiest meetings was with Satal Prasad, the finest *shikari* in the region, whose detailed knowledge of the gorges north of Kaigaon was of the greatest value to our survey work.

Satal Prasad's father had migrated to Kaigaon from Tukuche, an important trading centre in the Kali Gandaki valley, between Dhaulagiri and Annapurna Himal. He was a Thakali, member of a racial group of Tibetan origin closely related to the Sherpas of east Nepal with whom they formed a single tribe until the Middle Ages. His younger brother, Krishnaram, also accompanied us frequently, and was one of our most reliable porters—fully the equal of the Sherpas who gladly accepted him as such.

While Earle and Burnet mapped the valley to the west of base camp, I set out with Ang Dawa and the shikari on a three-day reconnaissance up the Jagdula Khola. The valley divided into two branches, one draining the glaciers of the Sisne Himal, and the other eastern one flowing down from the north of the Kanjiroba Himal. Between was the group of high snow peaks shown in the photograph of the Jagdula Khola and conspicuous also in Tichy's pictures.[1] On the second day Ang Dawa and I crossed to the east bank and climbed for 3,000 feet for a view up the line of the valley towards the Sisne Himal. Progress along the steep, trackless and heavily eroded valley sides was desperately slow. Only on the decaying avalanche debris of the river bed, or in the river itself, could reasonable speed be kept up. I felt that if only time could be spared, this was indeed a possible route towards the great circle of unknown peaks to the north.

One of the finest viewpoints was Earle's and Burnet's camp on an easterly spur of the Patrasi Himal. To the north they could see and map parts of the complex glacier systems of the Sisne Himal, whilst southwards their uninterrupted view over the whole range of the Jagdula Lekh enabled them to examine and plan an interesting route there. Tichy and his Sherpas had climbed two summits of this range in 1953, naming them Dui Tal Chuli and Pasang Peak. The village of Kaigaon lies at the foot of this ridge; the local Kaigaon names for these two are Dudh Kundali (Pond of Milk) and Ghyuthumba (Butter Mountain). To the north of Dudh Kundali is a high mountain dominating the side-valley above our base camp and called by the natives 'Kansirolba', allegedly after a local god. Probably this peak gave its name to the so-called 'Kanjiroba Himal' of the Survey of India, but none of the natives on this side

[1] *Chronique Himalayenne*, by Marcel Kurz, Fondation Suisse pour Explorations Alpines, Zurich 1959. (Planche 54).

H

of the group apply the name to the range so marked on the existing sheet; instead they call the whole group 'Sisne Himal'.

East of Ghyuthumba is Matathumba (Mother Mountain), the fine end-peak of the Jagdula Lekh, an ascent of which would be both valuable to the survey and technically interesting. And so on May 14th the three of us, with Mingma Tsering and Angtemba, placed our Camp I on a northerly moraine of the Matathumba Glacier. Next day we carried Camp II up onto the glacier, and as we arrived before mid-day we were able to prospect the first part of the route which we had planned up steep snow to the col between Ghythumba and Matathumba. Here we found to our dismay a desperately narrow ridge with a sheer drop on the far side, and where we had hoped to climb eastwards along the main arête to Matathumba it was impossibly steep and thin. Disappointed, we returned to camp. From here we again studied the north face of the mountain, at length picking out a new route which we felt might go.

At 7.30 next morning, in the crisp cold air, we set off, Earle and Burnet in the lead, myself following with Angtemba III and Mingma Tsering. We climbed steadily up steep snow slopes with icy patches, passing as quickly as possible beneath the line of séracs. A high wind was blowing and powdered snow hissed and poured down on us from the ice-cliffs. Above these cliffs a dangerous windslab forced us to the left up steep ice-slopes to the corniced north-east arête, which to our surprise and relief gave easy access to the summit. This was a perfect snow dome, and we asked Mingma Tsering to go first to the top, carrying the Nepalese flag.

Below our base camp were the ruins of a Buddhist monastery. According to Satal Prasad it had been destroyed long ago, perhaps in the Nepal-Tibet war of 1792-3, but stories were still told of a route northwards across the snows to Dolpo which the Lamas had followed. Such legends of lost passes are widespread in the Himalayas, as they are in the Alps: none of the present inhabitants could point out the line of the supposed route.

We had had tantalizing glimpses of great snow peaks to the north, drained by the Jagdula Khola, and we now hoped to force a way up the river into the heart of this unexplored region. Earle and Burnet were keen to examine the Jagdula gorge for themselves, and while I completed some survey stations they set out with a week's supplies to find the Lamas' route. In John Earle's own words: "Little did James Burnet and I realize, as we set out with four coolies and three Sherpas, what a frustrating and utterly exhausting week we were to have. The first day we made three or four miles, climbing along the side of the steep valley, 1,000 ft. or so above the river. The going was easy but awkward. Loose shale, tough stunted juniper and thorn bushes and interminable little side gorges made progress slow. Soon the angle of the gorge steepened, and it was rock climbing for most of the way. For a while we descended to the river bed and went onto the snow beneath which we heard the roaring

98

of the water. It did not look or feel too safe and we hastily climbed back again on to the rotten rock. Late in the evening we came to the snow-filled gorge of a side valley and camped in a forest of silver birches near an overhanging cliff.

"Dismayed by what we had seen in the gorge itself, we decided next day to follow a side valley which would lead to a col at about 16,500 feet which we had noted earlier from a survey peak. In this way we would by-pass the gorge and reach the main massif from the side. But at once we were up against difficulties that were to dog us throughout the week: loose shale and stunted bushes made the climbing in and out of the side gullies dangerous and slow. After traversing a rotten cliff face we reached the snows—soft and wet. At every step we plunged in up to the knees, sometimes even to the waist, and progress was painfully slow and breathless. The col appeared to get no nearer. I had given up looking at it, and was delighted at length to glance up and see we were almost there. With high hopes we kicked up the final snow slope and looked over: three thousand feet of sheer, loose rock, covered with snow and ice, plunged down to another gorge even more unpromising than the one we had left; and still on the other side rose the great line of magnificent peaks.

"For five days we tried everything in our power to get through to the mountains beyond. We waded in the icy waters of the river; we tried to climb along the water-smoothed rocks just above it; we clambered over the melting snow bridges beneath which the brown waters frothed and raged. Trying to by-pass the valley bottom yet another way, we were caught in a blizzard on the ridge and spent an unpleasant time climbing down a shattered cliff face which was rapidly becoming covered in wet snow. It soon became obvious that even if we found a way through there would be little hope of getting laden coolies along the route. In the end we had to admit defeat. Although we were at it throughout the hours of daylight we never made more than a mile and each night returned exhausted to our camp."

Having now completed our triangulation[1] of the area we had to decide whether to spend further time battling with the gorge or whether to move rapidly round to the other side of the group for further exploration before the monsoon broke. We chose the latter course and within ten days had reached Maharigaon on the western side of the massif.

From Maharigaon a track runs north across the mountains to the village of Dalphu on the Langu River, and for two more days we followed this route through beautiful valleys reminiscent of North Wales in contour and colouring. The air was damp and the peaks around us were wreathed in cloud as we carried our tents through the snow to a high corrie on the east of the Dalphu track; luckily a brief clearance

[1] The map extends from latitude 29° 05′ N. to 29° 25′ N. and from longitude 82° 30′ E. to 82° 50′ E.

99

enabled us to choose one high central peak from amongst the confusion of unexplored ranges.

Our alarm clock was set for 4 a.m. but when the three of us, with Mingma Tsering, left our top camp after the usual hasty meal the weather seemed unpromising and heavy stormclouds still filled the valley. Our climb started up a fine granite arête, alpine in character, later deteriorating into shale and slate, then soft snow and finally a long ice ridge which we climbed in crampons. As we reached the summit, a delicate snow cornice, the mist closed in, depriving us of the extensive view north to the Langu

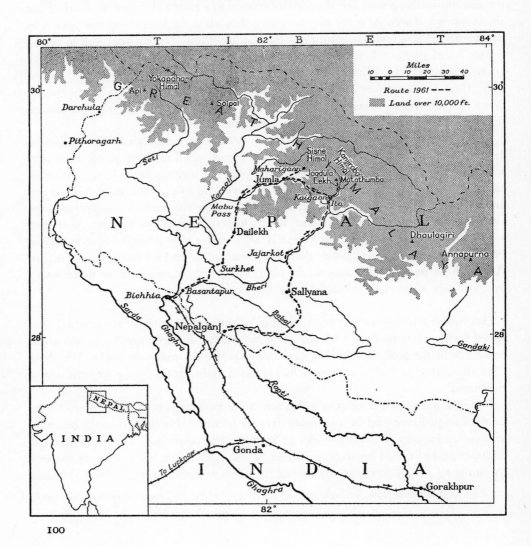

valley and Tibet for which we had hoped. Our altimeters read 21,000 feet though we think this an overestimate. We turned at once, as the weather was worsening rapidly, and snow fell steadily as we descended the icy ridge to our top camp.

On the way back to Maharigaon, James Burnet stopped at the snowline to include in his collection of plants for the British Museum some fine clusters of a rare and undescribed species of yellow primula. In torrential rain we crossed back to Maharigaon.

By now it was the middle of June and we realized sadly that the time had come to leave this corner of Nepal. Satal Prasad and Krishnaram came with us as far as Jumla to see us on our way. Already the monsoon was breaking and soon all movement on the hill tracks would cease. Rivers would wash away paths and bridges, and down in the terai the dreaded *awal* fever would again hold sway. We waved farewell and quickened our pace towards India, three weeks' journey away.

12/27

NANGA PARBAT BY THE DIAMIR FLANK

By Karl M. Herrligkoffer

The name Nanga Parbat, which is what the natives of Kashmir call the mountain, has its origin in the Sanskrit words *nanga parvata*, which mean "naked mountain". The mountain also has another name: *Diamir* or *Diamar*. It means "king of the mountains". But this more beautiful name has only maintained itself on the mountain's western flanks; on all the maps the massif bears the name Nanga Parbat, a name which has acquired an aura of tragedy. Richard Finsterwalder, who participated as cartographer in the Willy Merkl Expedition of 1934, worked together with Walter Raechl and by photogrammetric methods firmly established the height of the peak as 26,658 feet.

Nanga Parbat towers 23,000 feet above the valley of the Indus as a mighty western bastion of the Himalayas. Fifteen hundred miles separate it from Everest. Regarded with awe, and avoided by the natives as one of the "thrones of the gods", Nanga Parbat remained unknown to Europeans until quite late. In 1856, scarcely a hundred years before the conquest of its summit, an Asian explorer from Munich, Adolf Schlagintweit, became the first traveller to advance to the foot of the mountain; from there he journeyed northwards to Kashgar. There, in August 1857, the warlike Wali Khan had him beheaded on the suspicion that he was a spy.

MUMMERY'S BOLD ATTACK

It was not until 1895 that a mountaineering assault was made on Nanga Parbat, by a small group of proved British climbers, A. F. Mummery, G. Hastings, J. Norman Collie, and Major C. G. Bruce. Their plan to attack the giant from the Rupal Valley, to the southeast, foundered in the face of the monstrously steep cliff which plunges 14,800 feet from the main summit—the highest precipice in the world. The Englishmen then moved over the Mazeno Pass (17,590 feet) onto the western flank of the massif so as to reconnoitre a route over the Diamir Glacier. Having been temporarily left alone on the mountain, Mummery attempted with only two Gurkhas to reach the main summit over the western flank. Misled by his experience of Alpine proportions, he thought that he could apply the same scale to these Himalayan giants which are nearly twice as high. He hoped with a single porter (the second had dropped out) to reach the summit within one or two days. But at a height of 20,000 feet he was compelled to retreat. Back on the Diamir Glacier he met his friends and it was decided to try to climb the mountain from the north. While Collie and Hastings and the porters circled the mountain over several passes on the Chilas side to the Rakiot Valley, Mummery decided to climb with his two Gurkhas over the Diama Glacier to the northwest ridge and cross one of the two Diama notches (20,340 feet) to the Rakiot Glacier. He did not know that on the far side these notches break off in unpassable precipices. On August 24, 1895, he and his two companions parted from their friends and since then no trace of them has been found. One suspects that Mummery and the two Gurkhas never reached the ridge, and that they were killed by one of the frequent avalanches during their ascent over the glacier.

For many years thereafter things were quiet around Nanga Parbat. In 1931 the extraordinary ice-climber Welzenbach planned a Nanga Parbat expedition, but this ran aground very early. Then in 1932 Welzenbach's climbing companion, Willy Merkl, succeeded in pushing through the first German Himalayan Expedition to the mountain.

Instead of following Mummery's route, Merkl chose the Rakiot side for his attempt, and all later expeditions, including those of 1934, 1937 and 1938, chose the same route from the Rakiot Valley over Rakiot Peak and the east ridge to the Silver Saddle. But all the exertions of these German expeditions failed to achieve victory over the summit. Although the route over the northeast side of the mountain had no unsurmountable difficulties, it was exceedingly long. The route between the base camp and the main summit comprised no less than eight and a half miles and necessitated at least five high camps with their complicated supply system. Long before the actual summit assault, a huge expenditure of energy and time had occurred. It was therefore not surprising that the possibilities of a shorter and quicker route were considered. Such a route could only be found on the Diamir flank on which Mummery had already made an attempt. Whether the summit could be reached this way could not be unequivocally ascertained from the material at hand. Neither the exceptionally sharp and clear aerial photos which were taken from the Ju 52, nor the photographs and observations which Luft and Zuck brought with them from the Diamir Valley, gave a reliable lead. One could be certain only that on this flank the avalanche danger would be markedly greater than on the Rakiot side.

The decision as to which route should be chosen by the next big expedition could only be made after a reconnaissance of the Diamir flank. It was therefore decided to send a small but strong and able team into the flank with that object in the spring of 1939. Peter Aufschnaiter, a Tirolean, was chosen to lead it.

THE RECONNAISSANCE OF 1939

Camp II was set up at about 15,500 feet, below the cliff gateway to the Diama Glacier, and on June 13th four sahibs, with their three Bothia porters, climbed over the glacier to the foot of the rock rib which Mummery had climbed in 1895 and which he had called the "second rib". On this rock spur Chicken and Lobenhoffer found a foot-long piece of firewood at a height of about 16,500 feet. It appeared to be a relic of Mummery's camp-site, a last mysterious memento of the man who disappeared forty-four years earlier. They held it meditatively in their hands. Then they climbed on, but the terrain became so difficult—in fact impassable—that on the same day they were back at Camp II. On the following day an enormous ice-avalanche plunged from the upper Bazhin Glacier into the valley, flooding the entire "Mummery Rib" like a sea-swell breaking over a reef. Though this "direttissima" to the summit of Nanga Parbat had tempted the four explorers strongly, it now revealed itself as exceptionally deadly, and all thought of climbing it had to be abandoned. Since there was now no possibility of approach by the Diamir Glacier, they tried their luck on the neighbouring Diama Glacier which descended from the northeast, over which they hoped to attain the North Summit I. But here, too, observations from the lower part of the glacier showed that regular avalanches would make impossible any attempt to get through.

Consequently the attack was shifted to the rock ribs parallel and to the northeast of the "Mummery Rib", rising in the fall-line of the North Summit. On June 15th, Aufschnaiter and Harrer were able to set up Camp III on the right edge of the lower Diama Glacier at about 17,230 feet. This camp was situated above the ice-fall, at the foot of the so-called Middle Rib on which, in the days that followed, the two men strenuously worked their way upwards. The higher the sun rose, the thicker became the barrage of falling rock, and by noon all hell broke loose on the wall. Nevertheless they eventually reached a height of 19,350 feet. Aufschnaiter and Harrer now believed that the route they had chosen offered the only possibility of climbing the Diamir flank, but would call for the greatest measure of skill and effort from both sahibs and porters. The successful Diamir expeditions of 1961 and 1962 completely contradicted this premature conclusion.

Between July 16th and 18th the German reconnaissance of 1939, after a brief interval on Diamirai Peak, succeeded in building up new Camps I to III. But this time the Bothia porters could not be persuaded to advance any further under the continual threat of rock-falls and avalanches, so that the sahibs were thrown back on their own greatly reduced resources. But they were still of no mind to give up. In the wall itself the rock-falls were now so dangerous that Aufschnaiter and Chicken found it necessary to turn back. Harrer and Lobenhoffer, however, climbed on. They climbed for more than ten hours up the murderous wall until they were able to set up Camp IV at about 19,690 feet. The next morning saw them descending. They had to hurry to get out of the dangerous wall before the avalanches of ice and powder snow began their deadly barrage.

THE GERMAN DIAMIR EXPEDITION OF 1961

On April 29, 1961, the German Institute for Foreign Research, of Munich, began its fourth Himalayan expedition. The participants were: Dr Karl Herrligkoffer of Munich, expedition leader, doctor and cameraman; Rudl Marek of Munich, deputy expedition leader; Michl Anderl of Bad Tölz; Dr Ludwig Delp of Munich, in charge of the camps; Toni Kinshofer of Bad Weissee; Jörg Lehne of Rosenheim-Pfraundorf; Siegfried Löw of Rosenheim-Salzburg; Toni Messner of Munich-Lenggries; Harry Rost of Gendorf-Burghausen; and Gerhard Wagner of Munich, the expedition's geographer.

The aims of the expedition were: 1, to reconnoitre a route of ascent on the Diamir flank of Nanga Parbat; 2, once the route had been found, to climb it to where it joined the Bazhin trough; 3, an assault over the Diamir flank to the summit; 4, to survey cartographically the area of the Diamir Glacier not yet covered; 5, to organize medical-scientific observations; 6, to shoot a 16 mm colour film of the expedition and of the inhabitants of the Diamir Valley.

The main group, travelling by ship from Genoa, arrived in Karachi on May 12th. Anderl, Delp and Herrligkoffer followed by air. After quickly solving the usual customs difficulties with the baggage, it was possible to reach Rawalpindi by as early as May 14th, and on the 17th the entire expedition arrived in the little Himalayan town of Gilgit. On May 19th eleven highly laden jeeps started off with four tons of baggage (160 crates and sacks), the members of the expedition, and the accompanying Pakistani officer, Captain Malik, as well as eight high-altitude porters from the Hunza Valley.

After some hot days at the Bunar Bridge, and after porter difficulties (too few coolies had been ordered), an advance party under Toni Messner could begin their march to the Diamir Valley. During the next two days Rudl Marek left for Bunar with eighty porters; and finally, a rear-party under Ludwig Delp, left with the rest of the baggage. Contrary to our intentions, the porters refused to ascend through the narrow Diamir Valley, ostensibly because of the two dangerous ascents directly above the river, though their real reason was probably to lengthen the approach march from three to six days. The route through the Diamir Valley was chosen on the return, and it went quite according to plan. The story of the approach march from the Bunar Bridge in the Indus Valley to the base camp at 13,450 feet, is told by Ludwig Delp:

At the Bunar Bridge

May 21st was a very long day! Captain Malik and I had just left our places beneath the Bunar Bridge, until then the only shaded place in this sandy basin. Clouds had arisen and had alleviated the heat a little. A wind arose that was full of fine sand. Soon thick squalls blew the sand into all the crannies of our remaining baggage. It was hard to know which was the better, the windless heat or a somewhat cooling sand-storm, but all I wanted to do was to get out of that inhospitable basin. We were expecting the missing porters to show up soon, to take on the last of the baggage and free us from the interminable waiting.

Evening was already approaching when the Lambadar from Bunar appeared. Captain Malik, interpreting, told us that the porters who had started early in the morning, were sitting tight at a steep place and could get no further, so our baggage could not be picked up that day. But tomorrow, certainly, they would arrive ... It was only too clear that the men were simply prolonging the march in order to increase their wages. What could we do but have patience?

On the northern side of the Indus the cloud veils hung low upon the mountains, and it seemed to be raining. Sand squalls swept over us repeatedly. I was slightly anxious about the porters' provisions, which were packed in porous sacks: a down-pour of rain would ruin them. A few hundred yards upstream I discovered a small stone hut, but very dirty. Isa Khan quickly cleaned it. Everyone lent a hand, and soon all the baggage was under cover. But light rain did not fall until the next morning, and by then the porters had returned, and we were able to leave that uncomfortable valley floor.

Beyond the Bunar Bridge the path climbed along the left bank of the Bunar. First it crossed a small terrace of rubble until, high above the river, it led into the western precipice. Constantly ascending and descending, we had to cross innumerable gullies torn deep into the slope, while further up there was a gorge where, from between the steep walls, the water poured in fury. To get around those cliff walls a side valley had to be followed, where the going was quite pleasant in the light and silent rain. After several rests, we reached a gigantic and ancient juniper with mighty roots that ran widely in all directions; and in a few more yards we came to the upper edge of the precipice and before us there spread a gently rising, sandy basin, with clumps of coarse grass and, higher up, of conifers. We were surprised to find there a view of the middle section of the Bunar Valley: to the east lay the deep depression of the lower Diamir Valley, and where it joined the Bunar Valley, we could see, on a high terrace that broke off vertically to the valley floor, a small area of green. There, below mighty trees, we saw the inconspicuous huts of Diamirai. Above them towered Airl, nearly 16,400 feet high. High above the steep slopes of rubble the timber line was clearly visible, with mighty evergreens and small meadows reminding us of our own high alpine meadows. The Bunar Valley ran directly southwards from where we stood: in the distance it was blocked by gigantic snow-covered peaks. Somewhere to the west, in a broad side-valley of the Bunar, we felt we should see villages, and where another green region showed, in front of the western precipice in the yellow-grey stone desert, was the village of Halala. The path led down to it over boulder slopes. My assumption that we should take the path which, branching off at the height of Diamirai, led down to the valley floor, and that we should then pass up the Diamir Valley, proved to be mistaken. The porters explained that our column had not climbed into the Diamir Valley, but had entered the next eastern side-valley further up the Bunar, and they assured us that the Diamir Valley was impassable at several points. This was an unpleasant surprise, for detours cost time and money.

The Rest in Halala

The path now followed the high western bank. We climbed in order to circumvent a gorge that fell steeply into the Bunar Valley, and after a turn in the path we saw the village of Halala ahead. The deep gash of one more gorge separated us from the groups of trees. We descended to the bed of the stream, past a deep sandy area which is the village graveyard. Then we quickly scrambled up the steep bank beyond, with wooden pipes carrying water which the villagers have diverted high above the gorge. In a mighty jet, this water poured into a roofed stone tub. The branches of nut trees and apricot trees arched above us.

In the village there were few inhabitants, but this was not surprising, as most of the men were employed as porters on our expedition, while the women had to remain invisible. Furthermore, some of the population were already away with the beasts on a high pasture in the mountains. Sometimes, on rounding a corner, one caught sight of a figure fleeing into a doorway: a woman who had been lying in wait to catch a glimpse of the strangers. We learned that our main group had arrived on the previous evening and had spent the night there. On the day before, our advance group had passed through. We were shown the camp-site used by our comrades below the village, in the corner between the northern and eastern precipices above the Bunar Valley, and we learned that they had actually passed up the Bunar stream to Gashut so as to cross from there the 13,100-foot Airl Pass into the Loiba and Diamir Valley. The porters had obstinately refused to climb straight over Diamirai into the Diamir Valley, and as our rear party was obliged to follow the main group, we had no choice but to march the next day in the direction of Bunar and then choose the southern side-valley to the Airl Pass.

Towards the Bunar Villages

On May 23rd we went on up the Bunar Valley. Below the small oasis, Halala, we crossed the river, balancing on two beams. During the morning we passed three more villages like the one we had left: Thamrus, Gatudas and Gashut, all situated on the right bank of the Bunar. During a rest at Thamrus an old man approached me, and with a friendly air indicated by sign language that he would like to massage my feet. I did not protest, for the porters seated nearby nodded encouragingly. The old man

107

crouched before me and systematically worked over my legs and feet. From my thighs to my toes, he massaged and relaxed each separate joint and muscle. The pain at the beginning soon gave way to a feeling of ease which lasted for quite a while during the ensuing march. I later learned that such treatment was regarded as a gesture of respect for a guest.

The valley forked at the level of Gatudas, and at this point there were several small settlements, relatively close together. The huts of Manrun Gush and Karo stood on a rubble point where the Bunar, flowing from the southeast, was joined by another stream from the southwest. Beyond the side-stream we saw the settlements of Kalubai and Nishkin and, a little deeper in the side-valley, Charodaat. Compared with the dry wastes in the Indus and Bunar Valleys, these small villages, lying on the brink of turbulent brooks between scanty vegetation areas, shaded by nut and mulberry trees and dominated by steep mountain walls, can be regarded as idyllic. In spite of the gradually increasing heat of noon, there was a light, refreshing breeze.

A Night Raid

We had left the Bunar Valley at the village of Gashut and had passed up the side-valley that descended from the east. The endless chalky slopes lay behind us, and we climbed into an entirely new landscape. A brook had cut deeply into the valley and built up a yard-high wall of boulders. It had washed the soil from beneath a gigantic fir tree which practically barred the valley. Men were busy on the slopes cutting wood. There was a smell of resin. In the afternoon we arrived at an enormous boulder which leaned against the northern slope. At its base it overhung several yards, thus forming a roof over an area of several square yards, surrounded by stone walls.

Siegi Löw awaited us here, to tell us that these were to be our quarters for the night. The place was called Dekowa. He reported that our main party had the same day crossed the pass in the east and was now descending into the Diamir Valley. A few pieces of baggage had been left behind and were to be carried by us and the returning porters. Siegi then left in order to catch up with the main group by evening. I looked somewhat doubtfully at the end of the valley where, high above the cliffs, and the stunted pines and birches of the timber line, lay the 13,100-foot pass which the porter-lambadars had talked us into. But Siegi did catch up with the main party on the far side of the pass by nightfall, thus covering a distance which would take us and our porters the whole of the next day.

We made ourselves at home under the boulder, the sahibs in front, the porters behind, and a fine fire was soon burning. As the sun sank, one of the porters lifted his voice in prayer. The others mumbled their way through the prayer routine, the firelight flickering over their pensive faces.

108

A cool wind had risen. Soon we were soundly asleep. On the following morning two of the crates between which we had been sleeping were missing, and Captain Malik was beside himself with anger. He sent a porter at once over the pass to find the police inspector from Chilas, the Raja Sahib, who was with the main group. Our porters were called together and interrogated. Finally we offered a Judas-fee of twenty rupees to the one who would identify the thieves or bring back the cases. Naturally, our first suspicion fell upon the porters who had spent the night with us, and a search was made in the vicinity because the heavy cases could not be far away. Nothing could be found, however, and so, empty-handed, we broke camp for the Airl Pass. Shortly before the path left the timberline the Raja Sahib came down to meet us, accompanied by two musket-carrying policemen. He took the porters aside and carried out a time-consuming cross-examination.

In the afternoon, while the Raja descended to the valley with his attendants, we crossed the pass, which was marked by a stone cairn. Meanwhile, snow had begun to fall, and the wind drove the wet flakes into our faces. The hoped-for view of the Ganalo ridge and the summit of Nanga Parbat was veiled by fog. With big strides we hastened down the slope. Stunted pines and junipers appeared out of the mist, and then mighty pines, at first singly and then in thicker and thicker groups. The snow had changed to rain; the slopes became slippery, and occasionally a porter lost his footing with his heavy load. At the edge of a thick fir wood the porters sat down together with their lambadars and declared that they would wait for the rain to stop. but we got the column back on its feet, not without some strong Bavarian language, and climbed down through the dripping forest. Great clumps of mud stuck to the soles of our boots, while from the tops of the giant firs the rain dripped upon us and ran down us.

Airl Gali, the fairy-tale Meadow

At last the forest thinned out, and we found ourselves on the edge of a slanting mountain meadow, where small huts stood beneath the last trees. We had arrived at Airl, high above the Loiba Valley. We quickly lit a fire and cooked our supper, and while the rain poured down outside in the growing darkness, we sat comfortably on crates and sacks and enjoyed our food in the smoke of our fire.

The morning brought splendid sunshine; the air was sweet and fresh. At breakfast in front of the hut we judged that we could easily reach the village of Diamir during the day and move a good way beyond it towards Nakatun. Then came a messenger from the Raja Sahib, ordering all the porters to return to Gashut, where the Raja would investigate the theft of our crates. We cursed not a little over this new inter-ruption, nor were the porters happy about having to recross the pass and make a third journey to rejoin us. Captain Malik thought that we should acquiesce in the Raja

Sahib's order and soon the porters had disappeared in the mountain forest. The all-powerful Raja Sahib was successful, for on the following day the stolen crates were back. He had discovered that men from the Bunar Valley had secretly crept into our boulder camp and carried the crates by night to Gashut. It was well that we all slept, for they had been armed with muskets, ready to fire. Now they were under arrest in Gashut and would probably spend several years in prison. The poor fellows had been very unfortunate, for they would anyway not have known what to do with the radio transistor which the cases contained.

From Nakatun to the Glacier

Diamir and the pastures of Nakatun are the end of human habitation. The sky was overcast, and Nanga Parbat was not to be seen. Behind Diamir we climbed into the gorge of the Diamir brook; it was overgrown with brush, but the path that led to the last and highest pastures was well worn. A soft rain fell as we arrived at a mighty boulder in the middle of a green meadow, and in its shelter were tiny stone huts, room for sheep and goats and their herdsmen when the bad weather came. Here the path branched off to the huts of Nakatun, where Gerhard Wagner rejoined us after his scouting trip through the middle Diamir Valley. After spending a rainy night there, we left the next morning; high above us in the east, set off against the steel-blue sky by the first rays of the sun, our mountain towered above the terminal moraine of the Diamir Glacier. The furrowed gullies and mounds of the moraine were green with birches, pines and firs.

There was no further reason for delay: a wash in the ice-cold brook, a quick breakfast, and we were soon climbing towards our goal. The landscape increasingly reminded us of our high alpine valleys, as we ascended a dark green meadow slope, passed around the rocks of an old landslide, through a low shrubbery and then a thin deciduous wood, and finally over a mountain brook. The high basin of the glacier, surrounded by snow-covered slopes, drew nearer and nearer. To the north of the path an extended moraine slope became ever more conspicuous. It was twice the height of a railway embankment and seemed to stretch endlessly into the valley. To the south we could see the saddle in the Mazeno ridge, through which Mummery, in 1895, and his companions entered the inner sanctuary of Nanga Parbat. The way taken by our porters passed between the southern marginal moraine and the slope that leads to the Mazeno ridge. We climbed the moraine and then followed its crest. After a few miles we suddenly met Jörg Lehne and Toni Kinshofer, who were to pilot us across the dangerous glacier. It was a joyous meeting, for we had not met for a week, so far had the column been extended.

In the meantime our troop of porters had arrived at our own level, and by shouts and gestures we directed them to join us; then we descended to the glacier. Soon we were looking at one another between mounds as high as church steeples; we stumbled over rotten snowfields and past glacier lakes. After an hour we reached the edge of the northern moraine, which led us due east to the Diamir flank. We spent another half hour advancing over stunted vegetation, when suddenly we saw the tents of our base camp beneath a towering rock wall. In a few strides we had joined our comrades, and our expedition was fully assembled at the right place. We were just in time, for we had scarcely arrived when rain began to drum on the roofs of the tents. Only when we had erected the big supply tent and stowed the loads could we call it a day.

(Here Ludwig Delp's story ends).

Camp I is set up

Base camp was set up on May 24, 1961, two days ahead of our planned arrival, and our first concern was to find a suitable and secure place for Camp I. We also wanted to reconnoitre a route of ascent through the Diamir flank. We had planned to choose the mighty buttress to the north of the Mummery Rib for our ascent, so that is where we began our reconnoitring. At the foot of this rock rib, directly under a cliff, there was a narrow but safe camp-site for Camp I. From now on forty-four-pound loads were carried from base camp to Camp I, which lay at about 16,400 feet. Kinshofer, Lehne, Löw and Rost moved up to Camp I so as to scout out the route above. The climb up the cliff was very difficult and not suitable for the porters. To set up safety ropes would be a long and difficult task, so we decided to force a route up the ice couloir which ascends on the northern side of the rib. In its lower part this couloir has an inclination of about 40°, and after climbing for two or three hours one arrives at the depot camp, which is at the lower end of a rock rib. Here the couloir steepened to 50°, and the last part led over iced cliffs to a rock pulpit which afforded just enough room for a single tent. We named this bivouac place the Eagle's Eyrie. It stands at 19,360 feet.

For the climb from Camp I to the Eagle's Eyrie the porters, carrying loads of twenty-six pounds, required eight hours, and only at the so-called depot had they an opportunity for a sitting rest. As an additional safety precaution for the high-level porters, and to make the ice couloir passable even under bad conditions or during a difficult descent, we decided to fix steel cables along the route. Altogether we anchored 2,300 feet of steel cable and an equal length of rope. Fastening the storm tent to the rock pulpit of the Eagle's Eyrie was especially difficult. There was enough room for the tent, but there was no possibility of anchoring the tent pegs. Dangling stones had to serve instead. Immediately in front of the tent the icy wall dropped 3,000 feet. It was an airy camp-site, but secure against objective dangers and valuable for the carrying of loads to Camp II. The way from the Eagle's Eyrie to Camp II at 19,690 feet was very difficult (fifth degree) in parts, and the loads had to be pulled up these pitches with doubled ropes. It was tedious and time-consuming work, requiring a whole day for a couple of loads.

Camp II, above the Ice Couloir

The intention was to develop Camp II into a base for the attempt on the summit. It was set up in bad weather on June 12th by Kinshofer, Lehne and Löw. At first it consisted only of a waterproof tent with some rucksacks full of provisions. Meanwhile Harry Rost and Hidayat Shah had settled down for the night in the Eagle's Eyrie. On the next day the advance party would haul up their loads to Camp II. On June 14th three twenty-six-pound loads were hauled up with considerable difficulty. A snowstorm continued relentlessly, so that late in the evening Kinshofer and Löw came back to Camp II looking like ice-men. Meanwhile Löw had explored part of the way to Camp III, so far as this was possible through the masses of new snow. June 15th was again a day of bad weather, and all three stayed in their tent at Camp II, preparing for the next day and waiting for sunshine.

On June 16th the weather was intermittently cloudy and the men in all the camps were up early. Four porters climbed up from Camp I. One of them turned back half-way; he could not make it up the couloir. Towards noon two porters climbed up from base camp with their loads, and in the distance red and yellow stains suddenly appeared on the glacier, where Gerhard Wagner, our scientist was at work. On the same day the advance party pushed up towards the planned site of Camp III at 21,650 feet. They made good progress in spite of the trail-breaking and many time-consuming safety precautions. The difficulties continued. After a steep gendarme followed a short and level ridge, which then sloped increasingly until it ran into an ice slope covered with powder snow and situated beneath a cornice. This was the Kinshofer icefield. Roped up and carrying heavy loads, the three climbed simultaneously, using only the front prongs of their crampons. In the middle of the slope Siegi Löw began to consider whether climbing so steep an ice slope without pitons was not a bit too risky; then the three men suddenly became conscious of the danger of their position. If one should slip, all three would sail down 3,000 feet, past Camp II to the Mummery Spur. With special caution they proceeded a little further to a rock outcrop. There they laid down their rucksacks and belayed as well as they could. Then they climbed carefully back down to Camp II, knowing that this stretch too must be secured with fixed ropes. At three in the afternoon the trio were back in their tent.

An hour later Isa Khan, Amino and Ali Johar, the porters who had climbed up to the Eagle's Eyrie during the morning, arrived back at Camp I in a state of utter exhaustion. For eight hours they had climbed up the 3,000-foot ice-wall, carrying loads of from twenty-six to thirty pounds, and relying only on their crampons and the fixed ropes. Hour after hour the forward prongs of their crampons clawed into the smooth

32 IN THE PRIMARY SCHOOL of Sallyana (West-Nepal) the children learn to read and write. (Photograph by John Earle)

33 THE ICY SUMMITS of the Kanjiroba Himalaya seen from Jagdula Lekh. (Photograph by John Earle)

34 THE DIAMIR FLANK of Nanga Parbat (26,658 ft.) seen from below base camp. (Photograph courtesy of the Deutsches Institut für Auslandforschung, Munich)

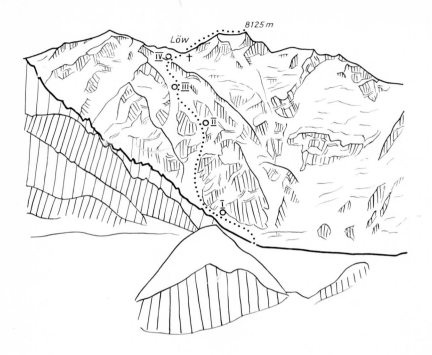

THE DIAMIR FLANK OF NANGA PARBAT (26,658 ft.). The route of the German Diamir Expedition of 1962, showing the high camps. (Sketch by Herrligkoffer)

ice, and throughout the climb there was no opportunity to rest. They could regain their breath only while standing, and even the least unpremeditated effort would spoil their rhythm, for the scarcity of oxygen had already made itself felt. In addition to this, the sun at noon was merciless: its rays were reflected a thousand-fold by the glacier and reduced their already diminished strength still further.

The next two days were spent in hauling up loads. Meanwhile Michl Anderl climbed up to the Eagle's Eyrie to relieve Harry Rost. Altogether thirteen half-loads reached Camp II, and on the evening of June 18th this high camp, with its three tents at 19,690 feet, was occupied by Anderl, Kinshofer, Lehne, Löw, Rost and two Hunza porters.

Camp III, above the Cornice

At six o'clock on June 19th Kinshofer, Löw and Lehne started from Camp II. The two porters, Hidayat Shah and Hidayat Khan, followed, and Rost and Anderl brought up the rear of this ascending party. At first they climbed at a good pace. But the last pitches to the ridge were extremely steep and covered with snow and ice. The 1,300-foot ice slope had to be secured with fixed ropes and much time was lost on this job. At noon it began to snow, and only towards three in the afternoon did the party reach the intended site of Camp III, above the cornice, at 21,650 feet. They pitched the perlon tent in driving snow, and Rost and Anderl then returned to Camp II, leaving the advance party (Kinshofer, Lehne, Löw) in their new camp.

The advance party wanted to make a start for the summit early on the morning of June 20th, but it snowed and a vehement wind blew over the steep flank. During the morning the weather conditions improved, and at noon I advised Lehne in Camp III by radio telephone that the monsoon had already reached the Garhwal Himalaya, that it was raining in Delhi, and that we must reckon that the monsoon would reach us in a few days. I therefore advised them to start for the summit this same day. The weather seemed to co-operate, and the advance group declared themselves ready. Shortly after three in the afternoon the summit trio—Kinshofer, Lehne and Löw— well-equipped, started climbing in the direction of the north summit. Lehne gives us the following details of the climb:

A Start for the Summit

We started from Camp III at 3.15 p.m. It was sultry, and far to the west hung a wall of clouds. The first steep slope necessitated strenuous trail-breaking: twenty steps, then a pause—later only five steps, then a pause. An intermittent zone of glare ice provided some relief. We now climbed relatively quickly, for the ice was good. We took a rest by a rock outcrop, but not for long, for the weather grew ever more threatening. We now kept to the left, on the rocks, because we hoped to find more

I

opportunities there for belays. The terrain inclined at about 50° and was more covered with ice than anything we had known on this mountain. We all climbed together, and we were at about 23,000 feet when darkness began to fall. Toni headed for a big rock; he gabbled something about a cave, but it was only a downward-sloping ledge on which we could, however, sit close together. We had forgotten the thermos-flasks, and the petrol stove at first would not function. We had to change the fuel cartridges and fiddle about with the jet needle before eventually we had two pots of Ovomaltine heated. Then we pulled our sacks over our feet. We wore our down jackets, but the zipper of mine would not close. The wall of clouds in the west had meanwhile drawn closer, but we were still above it. I could not sleep and every five minutes I looked at the weather. At midnight I thought: "Tomorrow at three o'clock we will be on the summit!" But it was not long before the wall of cloud towered above us; the storm and the snow began. In the dawn we emerged from our bivouac like snow men. It was still snowing. We had to go back.

The Retreat

June 21, 1961. The trio had scarcely descended several rope-lengths when it was bathed in sunshine. But they continued their descent, although with heavy hearts, for under such conditions there was no sense in considering a push to the summit. The route which they had covered the day before had worsened considerably. Six inches of fresh snow lay on the glare ice, and they took the precaution of belaying each other. Toni Kinshofer went last and he was the first to slip. Siegi Löw, who was attached to the rope only by a carabiner, was able to arrest the fall. Further down Siegi Löw fell three times, and Toni Kinshofer a second time. Then Lehne lost a crampon and had to hobble on without. Down the last slope to Camp III the trio broke trail through deep powder snow. A strong wind was blowing, and the tent was snowed up. At ten o'clock they renewed contact through the radio with headquarters, whence their every movement on the Kinshofer icefield had been watched. A storm raged outside the tents and by three in the afternoon it began to snow once more.

June 22nd: Avalanches thundered down the walls of the Mazeno Ridge. Six inches of snow lay at Camp I and the porters were unable to climb to the Eagle's Eyrie. The renewed snowfall meant that we could not count on any improvement in the weather that day. Michl Anderl thought that a retreat to base camp was called for. By radio at six o'clock, Harry Rost expressed the feeling that he should descend, for he felt the situation was precarious. I advised him to wait until noon. Perhaps by then the sky would have cleared and the early avalanches would already have passed down the couloir. At first the situation seemed rather hopeless. If only the sun would shine again, we might regain our nerves. But the snow fell wildly, and the sky was grey. A radio conversation with the trio in Camp III at eight o'clock led to the decision that they should descend to join Michl Anderl and the two porters at Camp II. There they would wait and then, if the weather on the day after next should permit a renewed assault, two ropes would advance to Camp III, Anderl and Kinshofer forming one, and Lehne and Löw the other.

I also wished to make a change among the porters, for these too had been over-worked. The weather was really abominable, and the snow fell unceasingly. Only the lowest 2,000 feet of the mountain were visible beneath the clouds. Snow or hail fell for hours, and the wind was too weak to tear a hole in the clouds. So we waited for the morrow and the final throw of the dice. At noon I suggested that one of the trio should break trail down to Camp II; Lehne decided to do it and at 2 p.m. arrived at Camp II, which was occupied by two sahibs and two porters. The weather report forecast snow-fall and strong winds; the report was accurate and in the night the predictions were fulfilled.

June 23rd. From Camp I Isa Khan and Amino climbed up to the Eagle's Eyrie. Camp II (Anderl and Lehne) reported snowfall and strong winds. There was no question of climbing up to Camp III. This same report was repeated hour after hour, until at eight o'clock I decided that they should go up alone without porters. But Anderl said it was impossible. The porters, whose provisions were growing short, wanted to descend. Agonizing conversations ensued at every hour. Marek declared repeatedly that he could no longer take responsibility for the porters who had to climb the couloir, because the new snow and the repeated avalanches had made it too dangerous. At ten o'clock we heard from Camp III (Kinshofer-Löw) that it was storm-ing up there and that the two men would retreat to Camp II during the afternoon. At Camp II it was snowing so hard that an ascent to Camp III was out of the question. During the morning the two porters were sent down to the Eagle's Eyrie to await the porters bringing provisions up from Camp I. Hidayat Khan wanted to descend and had now to be relieved by Amino. Kinshofer and Löw must return to Camp II, but because of the storm they waited until the afternoon to come down. The weather worsened, with furious wind and snow. I gave the order that everyone was to retreat to Camp I the next day, for the radio had reported that the monsoon had begun. The masses of snow which the monsoon would bring could turn the couloir between Camps I and II into a nightmare of avalanches and Camp II would be cut off.

The Descent to Base Camp

Of June 24th Lehne reported: "There were four of us in Michl Anderl's tent. Two of us were holding the poles to keep the tent from flying away. When it blew especially strongly, we played at airships: Anderl was in the bows and was pilot. We were in the stern, and at his command we pulled the release cord. We then imagined how we would circle around Camp I as a gesture of respect and sail down to base camp. On the radio we were told to bring all the tents with us, which was then impossible. We had to wait. At noon we broke camp and took down the tents, for the storm had quietened a bit. Hidayat Shah and I went down to the Eagle's Eyrie, while the others lowered the loads, which repeatedly got stuck. It took many hours to get them down to the Eagle's Eyrie and at four in the afternoon we went down."

After a coffee break at Camp I we all returned to base camp. Siegi Löw was last, wet through and hungry.

The march back was not as smooth as those of earlier expeditions. Our liaison officer had agreed with the lambadars of the neighbouring villages on a lump sum of thirty rupees for the transport of each porter's load. But because of the deliberate delays during the approach march, the coolies were still thinking of sixty-five rupees, and for such a wage they would take only a fifty-five pound load. As they crossed the Diamir Glacier, the coolies who were willing to work, about twenty in number, suddenly found themselves confronted by an ascending troop of their countrymen who tried to force them with sticks and stones to drop their loads. The police were called upon to mediate, but they were unsuccessful. After such a "parley" between the police and the local peasants, I was obliged to treat several policemen for injuries, and some of them were invalided for several days. In the end we had to call the militia, who climbed up into the Diamir Valley, arrested the trouble-makers and took them away to Chilas. The upshot of the coolie battle on the glacier was that we had to call upon people from neighbouring valleys, which involved waiting for several days for them to arrive. We sat on our loads at the already broken base camp and were wholly dependent on the services of mountain peasants. As we descended to Diamir on June 28th, there were barely enough porters to carry our remaining loads. Ahead of us was a wild descent of the Bunar Gorge with several dangerous climbing pitches. After three days we reached the hottest camp-site of the expedition, the Bunar Bridge.

The actual goal of the expedition was achieved: the Diamir flank was reconnoitred and climbed in its entire height. Only the summit assault was prevented by the monsoon.

THE GERMAN DIAMIR EXPEDITION OF 1962

The task that had been begun the previous year was to be completed in 1962. All the difficulties of the Diamir Flank were now known to us, and we could plan accordingly. Firstly, I wished to make use of our experience on the return march through the Diamir Gorge, and I insisted that our approach should lead through that gorge with its shepherd paths and climbing pitches. To offer real security to the coolies with their sixty-two-pound loads, the Hunza high-altitude porters were to secure the dangerous pitches with fixed ropes and give direct aid to the coolies on the exposed places. The second problem, which had not been solved the previous year, was how to master the 3,000-foot couloir between Camp I (16,000 feet) and Camp II (19,700 feet). The loads must be transported as quickly as possible from Camp I to the depot (18,000 feet) and on over the upper part of the couloir, where we had fixed steel cables. So in Gilgit we enlisted ten qualified high-altitude porters under their experienced Sirdar Isa Khan. Among the men from Hunza there were four from the previous year, who were already acquainted with their task. I also took along some husky fellows who proved quite competent, and one of the three best high porters of 1953, Hadji Beg.

Our Camp II, at an altitude of 19,700 feet, which could be reached only after surmounting a 600-foot cliff, was this time to be an enlarged and to become an acclimatization station. This meant that tents and provisions had to be brought up to enable a team of several men and some porters to hold out through a bad weather period of up to eight days. To develop Camp II in this way it would be essential to replace the previous year's primitive rope-lift with a real transport cable. In the end we used a winch from mountain rescue equipment with a wire, one thousand feet in length, of five millimeter gauge. Eventually it had a length of 820 feet, was set up in a few days, and with it in a single hour a 100-pound load could be lifted over the cliff to a point seventy-five feet below Camp II. From there two or three men had to pull the heavy sacks up the steep slope to the tents.

The Herrligkoffer route, which crossed the Kinshofer icefield almost immediately above Camp II, was this time changed by Toni Kinshofer so as to reach the firn ridge, ascending to Camp III by a big traverse which one began immediately after leaving the cliff ridge, about an hour's climb above Camp II. This variation in the route between Camp II and Camp III proved to be considerably less dangerous: there was no glare ice, only deep snow in which one had to force one's way up to the knees.

There were some changes in the personnel of the previous year. Lehne and Messner were indispensable, but I wanted to strengthen the party for the summit assault, and so the participants of the previous year, Toni Kinshofer and Siegi Löw, were given the support of the Himalayan novices, Anderl, Mannhardt (Kinshofer's companion in the first winter ascent of the north face of the Eiger), Manfred Sturm and Hubert Schmidbauer. Michl Anderl was intended as cable transport specialist and contact-man between Camp I and the advance group. Rudolf Marek this time dealt exclusively with supply problems. The leadership and medical care of the expedition were again my own main duties. In the fulfilling of twenty-four medical-scientific assignments I could rely on the aid of my medical-technical assistant Sieglinde Ulbrich, who also assumed responbility for the medical care for the porters.

On April 29th the group left Munich and on the following day boarded the m.s. *Asia* in Genoa. With the mountaineers went four and a half tons of baggage.

Marek, Ulbrich and I flew ahead of the expedition to settle formalities. Thus it was possible for the baggage to be put on the train the day after its arrival in Karachi (May 12th, 1962) and sent on its way to Rawalpindi. The team flew the next day to Rawalpindi, and received the baggage there on Monday, May 14th. The next two days, May 14th and 15th, were the main holidays of the moslems, and there was nothing we could do. Even our written entry permits had still not arrived from Karachi. Thus eight valuable and expensive days were wasted in Rawalpindi. But on May 24th we were able to depart from the friendly town of Gilgit in eleven jeeps, piled high with luggage, in the direction of the Indus Valley.

At 4 p.m. on the same day we reached the Bunar Bridge and had covered eighty miles from Gilgit. Awaiting us were the lambadars of the previous year. At first the porters, some of whom had come with donkeys, wanted again to carry the loads over the remote Bunar Valley and the 13,000-foot pass to the Diamiri Valley and base camp, but I declined this proposal. After much negotiation we finally reached agreement.

We climbed up the sheep trails toward Diamirai, and on the following day into the gorge as far as Jail and Diamir. The third stage ended at Nakatun, the uppermost pasture huts of the Diamir Valley, and in the morning hours of the fourth day we crossed the glacier and, still before noon, arrived at the site of our base camp.

Of course, the site of Camp I was already determined. To provision it with essentials as quickly as possible, ten Hunzas and five Diamir men were sent up the next day. Ahead of them went Kinshofer, Schmidbauer, Sturm and Mannhardt, to break the first trail upwards. All returned to base in the evening. On the following day fifteen forty-four-pound loads were transported to Camp I. The weather was not very good, for repeated snow flurries ran through the valley. Snow was still lying at base camp.

On June 1st Kinshofer and Löw climbed in the direction of the depot above Camp I. Schmidbauer and Anderl were at base, working on rope ladders to surmount the cliff wall below Camp II. At the same time Sturm and Marek were at work enlarging Camp I, while Mannhardt was getting the steel cables carried up from the moraine depot.

Siegi Löw was no man of letters. His diary is brief and covers only the first two weeks on the mountain. Nevertheless I would like, in memory of this outstanding comrade and mountaineer, to include in this account the little which his diary has retained about Nanga Parbat.

From Siegi Löw's Diary

June 4th. The alarm sounded at a quarter past four. Kinshofer and I climbed from Camp I towards the couloir. Mannhardt followed some distance behind with six porters. On the previous day a tent had been set up at the depot, and we were to move into it in the evening. At the middle stretch of the couloir Kinshofer and I carried a steel cable on our backs so as to push ahead with the work of safety precautions. It was tedious work, for much snow still lay in the couloir. Behind us three Hunzas were laboriously trying to drag the heavy thousand-foot cable which would be used to pull up the loads. The rest of us were occupied with securing the fixed ropes. About 2 p.m., after the Hunzas had gone down, we too descended, for in the heat there was considerable danger of avalanches. The snow was very soft, and while we descended big balls of snow formed under our crampons. Toward 3 p.m. we are all back in our tents at Camp I, and we were just in time, for half an hour later two sizeable avalanches swept down the couloir.

June 5th. First thing in the morning, Toni Kinshofer and I entered the couloir again to make more progress with fixing the ropes. By early afternoon, after hard work, we had fixed a total of 750 feet of steel cable. We descended to the depot for a well-earned rest.

June 6th. At 4.30 a.m. we are awakened by a gigantic wave of air pressure. The tent structure collapsed and a big avalanche roared down towards Camp I. Each of us grabbed a tent pole to save the tent from caving in, but the poles had snapped. Helplessly, we stared at each other. But then we fell asleep again under the collapsed tent. We awakened again to the sound of porters ascending, and then realized with astonishment that a gigantic avalanche has actually grazed us. Because of the great danger we decided to descend to Camp I with the porters.

June 7th. Toni and I climbed into the couloir again with 600 feet of steel cable, so as to secure the last part of the way to the Eagle's Eyrie. But we could not quite complete the work. We hung part of the rope ladders to the cliff and then descended to the Eagle's Eyrie and bivouaced there.

June 8th. During the morning we secured the cliff wall and reached Camp II at 19,700 feet. In the meantime, Anderl and Mannhardt had come up. Anderl selected the points of attachment for the cable hoist. Together we descended to the Eagle's Eyrie, picked up loads, and dragged them up the wall to Camp II. While Toni Kinshofer and Mannhardt set up a tent which was left there the previous year, I scratched in the snow for provisions that had also been left behind. It was quite a while before some canned goods showed up to our general pleasure.

June 9th. Early in the morning Toni began to prepare the points which Anderl had selected. He cleared away the ice and snow and applied a drill. Anderl and I descended to the Eagle's Eyrie. While my comrade took the winch on his back, I carried the line, and after several strenuous hours on the cliff face, we arrived back at Camp II. After setting up the winch, Kinshofer and Anderl pulled up the cable and fastened it into position. In the meantime I continued my digging for preserves, for we were still short of provisions. But by evening the hoist had been set up, except for the support which we intended to haul up the next day.

June 10th. After the cables had been anchored, we hauled up the needed support. The fastening and arranging of this support caused some headaches. At last, towards noon, the highest hoist in the world was completed. In the afternoon we hauled up the first load, and to begin with it worked without a hitch; but with the next load the winch jammed. We had forgotten the oil. So we fried some bacon and poured the liquid fat over the winch, and it began to turn once more.

June 11th. Two of us went down to the cable hoist station, while the other three remained to haul up the loads. A break in a cable held us up for several hours, but after the damage had been repaired hauling was resumed and we now had the feeling that things were functioning properly. In the days to come we would know whether or not the hoist would prove its worth. At any rate we could now hoist up to 100 pounds at a time, whereas previously a porter could only take twenty-six to thirty pounds up to the Eagle's Eyrie.

June 12th. The weather noticeably worsened. Kinshofer and Sturm climbed down to the hoist station. It began to snow. We hauled up loads until 1 p.m., but then we had to stop, for the driving snow grew too wild, and the two men at the bottom of the hoist had still to climb up through the couloir, in danger of avalanche. After four loads had been hauled up, the work had to be broken off. Then Kinshofer, Sturm and Schmidbauer, who had climbed up to join those two, in two hours fought their way up the 600 feet to the shelter of our tents at Camp II. On the following day Schmidbauer suffered an attack of altitude sickness and his companion, Toni Kinshofer, tried to revive him with hot drinks. Persistent bad weather forced us to take a rest day.

A Battle against the Snow

Snow fell at base camp too, and the porters, who had to carry loads of twenty-five pounds to Camp I, needed several hours longer than usual. On June 14th snow was falling high up and everyone in the high camps remained in the tents, sleeping and eating, and recuperating. Nevertheless, during the morning I tried to get the high-altitude porters moving up towards the depot, and after much discussion they decided to go. Their column crept slowly upwards through the waist-deep snow, but only three were able to reach the depot and leave their small loads. But the great gain was that a trail had been broken for the next day. On June 15th the weather cleared; the wind was still blowing strongly across the flank, but everyone was active again and anxious to make up for the lost days. The two high-porters, Hadji Beg and Goriat, decided to move their quarters to Camp II, and at about 8.30 a.m. they climbed up the couloir with their personal loads. To be able to hoist the loads which had meanwhile been brought to the bottom station of the hoist, Mannhardt and Löw descended from

Camp II, bringing Schmidbauer down at the same time. They handed him over to the two porters who had come up from Camp I, and these accompanied him down. Others were busy pulling three loads up on the winch.

The weather remained uncertain and stormy, so that the six men at Camp II had a very restless night. Nevertheless, in the morning of the following day, Kinshofer and Löw climbed up from Camp II towards the site of Camp III in order to secure part of the route with a perlon rope. They completed 1,000 feet that day and then returned to Camp II. As I have already noted, Kinshofer made a variation in the route, according to which an immediate traverse was made to the ridge that led up to Camp III. The traverse was not easy, for it passed through waist-deep powder snow, yet the ascent was considerably safer than that of the previous year over the Kinshofer ice-field.

The next day, June 17th, Kinshofer and Löw moved into Camp III; Mannhardt and their two porters, Goriat and Hadji Beg, accompanied them on the ascent, which was not easy, because at times they sank into the boundless powder snow up to their bellies. Eventually they reached the ridge, and on the same day were able to secure the whole stretch except for a small section below Camp III. While Kinshofer and Löw moved into Camp III, Anderl, Sturm and Mannhardt returned with the porters to Camp II. At the site of Camp III, above the big cornice, the tent of the previous year was found; it was all squashed down, but the air mattress inside still contained some air and could be used at once. While Kinshofer was busy erecting the tent, Siegi Löw, the eternally hungry one, dug for old canned food and after much searching was rewarded. The meagre menu at Camp III was thus pleasantly augmented.

On June 18th the two men in Camp III would have preferred to sleep really late, but by ten o'clock the two Hunzas arrived from Camp II with the rope for securing the last 600 feet below Camp III. On June 19th cloudy and stormy weather reigned over Nanga Parbat, and in Camp III especially the mountain wind blew sharply across the tents. Nevertheless, Kinshofer and Löw got out of their sleeping bags early and at 8.30 a.m. they were climbing, breaking through the snow-crust, towards the southern rock ridge which leads to the northern summit. After about 1,000 feet they had climbed around the ice-fall and were turning to the right in the direction of the Bazhin trough. During their traverse they fastened about 600 feet of their 7 mm rope and towards noon returned to Camp III. On the same day Anderl, Mannhardt and Sturm, together with their heavily laden porters, reached the same camp, and one more tent had to be erected. While the porters prepared to descend, the newcomers were still busy levelling a site.

June 20th. On the same day of the month, but exactly a year later, there was a great departure from Camp III at 21,650 feet on the Diamir Flank. In 1961 the rope made up of Kinshofer, Lehne and Löw, had kept to the northern rock rim of the ice-field, but this time the ascent was directed toward the southern rock rim so as to make as directly as possible for the Bazhin trough. They left at six in the morning; Kinshofer broke trail, followed by Mannhardt, Sturm and Anderl, all carrying fourteen- to twenty-pound rucksacks. Mannhardt carried the perlon tent, and the others carried the petrol burner and provisions. During the ascent Löw began to complain about his toes, which had been frost-bitten while fixing the ropes above Camp II on the 16th. One toe had already split, but he wanted to endure it and to be on the summit assault at any cost. Towards noon the ridge had been reached. The wind blew icily over the Bazhin trough and swept long plumes of snow into the azure sky. The sun was still shining, but out over the Diamir Valley a thick cloud bank already lay waiting. Slowly but surely it thrust closer and closer to the mountain. The big perlon tent was set up in the shelter of an ice fall immediately behind the ridge which leads up to the northern summit, and it gave all five men just enough room to sit. It was without the comfort of an air mattress or a sleeping bag. There were many crevasses around the tent, and a safe way had to be found for an early departure, which would be before daylight. A view across the Bazhin trough, two-and-a-half miles wide, reached to the summit structure. To the left and eastward of it stood the storm-stricken outlier summit of 25,952 feet, connected with the main summit by the Bazhin Notch (25,630 feet). The party was still separated from the summit by over 3,000 feet of elevation.

No Summit Weather

It was their hope that this night they would start the final climb. They crouched on their rucksacks, penned inside the tent while the condensation ran coldly down the perlon walls. But the next day (June 21st) brought anything but summit weather. A thick haze lay over the Diamir Valley. Clouds gathered and towards 2 p.m. a high thunderstorm lashed at the tent. Thunder and the roar of avalanches competed with one another. There was no choice: the party could only hold out in the protection of the tent until the storm had blown itself out. But squatting in such narrow space gradually became a torture, and provisions were growing short. A decision would soon have to be taken. If the weather should clear, they could start for the summit; but if it remained stormy there could only be a retreat to Camp III, or even Camp II.

But in the early hours of June 22nd, the storm cleared, though an icy wind continued to rage over the ridges. It was very cold. Nevertheless they decided to start. Anderl realized that his limit had been reached and he remained at the camp, and so it was four young men who started out in darkness on their way to the summit of Nanga Parbat. Siegi Löw was in good form and broke trail; then came Kinshofer and Mannhardt.

Sturm soon began to feel unwell. He had a pain in his side and after two hours found himself unable to keep up with the others; he decided to turn back. The moon was practically full and its cold light aided the three lonely men. Towards four in the morning the eastern sky grew light above the Bazhin Notch; the so-called death-zone (24,500 feet) had been passed, above which the human organism is no longer able to regenerate its strength, even in rest. The three had already been under way for hours. Toni Kinshofer's idea that they might reach the summit cliffs below the shoulder in four hours proved false. At home and on paper we had reckoned that six to seven hours must be reckoned for this stretch, but the clear air at high altitude often misleads climbers into underestimating distances. Only at nine o'clock did they reach the Bazhin Notch after having searched in vain for a suitable route onto the face of the shoulder. Here, at 25,750 feet, the party of three joined the route of Hermann Buhl's ascent of 1953. They had taken eight hours for 2,000 feet, and there was now no question of reaching the summit and returning to Camp III the same day. A bivouac in the open had to be faced. Just as Hermann Buhl in his time, they too had grossly miscalculated the distances, and in their confidence of being back at Camp III or IV by evening had brought neither bivouac sack nor provisions. The little food they had was in their pockets.

After a half-hour's rest the three tied into a hundred-foot rope. Kinshofer led. Löw and Mannhardt followed. The rocks were iced and therefore quite dangerous. The technical difficulties were between second and third degree, but half-way up they had to overcome a tower on which two rope-lengths of fifth degree had to be mastered. The summit trio chose the ascent to the shoulder over the ridge. To their left the mighty southeast face of Nanga Parbat fell away 14,500 feet into the Rupi Valley. The view into the depths was of grandiose proportions.

Suddenly the rope jerked taut: Siegi Löw had broken through a snow-bridge, but Mannhardt had caught him. After quite a while Siegi Löw was brought back to the surface, coughing and utterly out of breath. This time things had turned out well: only his ice axe had been lost. The conditions on the ridge were bad, and a party of three naturally climbs more slowly than a man alone. This can be the only explanation why, in contrast to Hermann Buhl, who climbed the shoulder ridge in four hours, these three were on the go for seven hours. When, towards 4 p.m., they reached the 26,480-foot shoulder, the summit had long since been enveloped in cloud. Only occasionally were they granted a glimpse into the Diamir or Rupi Valley or backwards to the Silver Plateau.

The approach to the 150-foot summit rise ran along the long summit ridge of the trapezoid-shaped cliff. They stumbled up the ridge on its Diamir side, and at 5 p.m., thoroughly exhausted, they were on the top (26,657 feet) of Nanga Parbat. A little below the ice calotte of the summit, they found the small cairn which Hermann Buhl built at seven in the evening of July 3rd, 1953.

Sixteen hours earlier they had started from Camp IV. A long tedious way lay behind them, but they were in a good mood, except that Siegi Löw had lost all feeling in his feet. The other two felt the cold in their toes. They shot a few summit photos of each other and then prepared to descend. There was not enough time to return over the shoulder, so they decided to bivouac in a cleft at about 26,510 feet. For protection they had only the clothes they wore. They pressed against the rock and crowded together so as to shield at least their backs and sides against the storm which swept unremittently over this high open bivouac. During the night Kinshofer and Mannhardt lost all sensation in their feet. They tried to stay awake. Occasionally they were able to doze briefly, only to be wakened by the shudders that shook their bodies. Little was spoken. Drowsily they looked into the night and yearningly awaited the sun. During the night Siegi Löw was overcome by weakness; he was suffering severely from frost bite. He may have taken too much katovit during the ascent, a stimulant that mobilizes the reserves of strength for some hours, but increasingly drains the body. Circulation disturbances, enfeeblement, hallucinations and anxiety are the results.

As the morning turned grey the climbers left their ice-cold bivouac and climbed a few yards to the ridge to warm themselves in the first rays of the sun. At about six they began the descent. Over the horizontal ridge they reached the shoulder at about seven and climbed down to the tower. They tried to circumvent the difficulties they had met on the ascent, and on the Diamir side eventually found a relatively easy gully which emptied into the upper part of the Bazhin Trough. Technically the terrain was not difficult, and in the upper part of the ice gully they could descend standing up. So as to move more quickly, and since no dangers seemed to threaten, the three men untied.

The high wind drove the snow constantly into the faces of the exhausted men. Their beards and eyebrows were iced up. The openings of their parkas and sweaters were frozen stiff. With half-closed eyes they tried from time to time to see where they were. Then they lost sight of Löw. Kinshofer shouted back, and from 600 feet above them they heard his voice shouting: "Come up here!" Toni thought that Siegi had had another of his spells of dizziness and climbed upwards in the direction of the voice. He had not covered 150 feet when a shadow flashed past him; it was Siegi Löw falling! His arms stretched wide, he hurtled on his back into the depths without uttering a sound and without making a move to save himself. At the bottom of the gully he was thrown from a bulge in the ground as from a ski jump. He was flung head first upon one of the last rock outcrops and received fatal injuries. Mannhardt, who was far in the lead, at first saw nothing of all this. He was alerted by a shout from Toni, and both men hurried down to their comrade. Löw had a gaping wound above his brow. He was unconscious; his head and arms and legs hung as if lifeless.

After the two men had overcome their first shock, they decided to take the badly wounded man down to Camp IV. But after only a few yards they were forced to

124

realize that they were incapable of such superhuman exertions at that altitude, and that they themselves were practically at the end of their strength. Toni Kinshofer wanted to remain with the dying man, while Mannhardt went as quickly as possible to Camp III for help. Camp IV was empty and the way there was most dangerous for a man alone, because of the many crevasses around it. Mannhardt, therefore, kept a bit higher, and after three hours reached the upper edge of the slope which drops from the summit ridge to the Kinshofer ice-field. Putting all mountaineering caution aside, he climbed down the last slope to Camp III in the direct fall-line. Even before his arrival in Camp III, we could see by his pace that something exceptional must have happened. Then, towards six o'clock in the evening, the staggering news reached us: Siegi Löw lay unconscious with his comrade Toni Kinshofer at 24,600 feet, and Toni was waiting for our help.

The hour at which Siegi Löw ended his rich mountaineering career in the arms of his friend in the Bazhin Trough, without regaining consciousness, will remain indelibly in Kinshofer's mind. Alone with the dying man, in the mistaken expectation that in a few hours help would arrive, he kept his vigil. In this heroic solitude he was hardly aware of his own condition, for he was already suffering from hallucinations, seeing phantom figures, hearing his name called, until the icy wind recalled him to actuality.

After 7 p.m. the ever-cheerful Siegi passed away in the arms of his friend. It was then time for Kinshofer to think of himself. At about 8.30 p.m. he started on his way. He followed Mannhardt's tracks so long as these were recognizable. He had lost his ice axe. He had long since forgotten that the two cameras with the summit photos were in the rucksack into which he had thrust Siegi's feet. As he crossed the wide snowfield of the trough in a northerly direction, one of his crampons came loose, but he stumbled on in the illusion that he was wandering through a tobacco plantation. The heights had completely confused his senses. All night long he climbed towards the ridge near Camp IV. Now and again he rested in a snow hollow which he dug with his elbows, in order to gather the remains of his strength. The great danger of falling asleep was prevented by the high wind, which repeatedly shook the solitary wanderer awake. Slowly the moonlit night passed, and in the morning, at eight o'clock, Toni, whom we had thought to be in Camp IV, appeared at the top of the slope that led down to Camp III and safety. He had made his way round the crevassed area. At 8.55 the rescue party met Toni an hour above the camp. The long suspicion that Siegi Löw was dead became a certainty. Our sorrow was great, but great too was our joy at Toni's return. In that frightful night he found his way back to life. Without food or drink or rest, he had faced those deathly conditions for fifty-six hours.

In the circumstances we could not think of bringing down the body of the dead climber. Rescue operations were indeed still in preparation in the various camps during the night of June 24th, but now we had to bring the survivors, with their badly frozen feet, down to base camp and hospital as quickly as possible.

At base camp we erected a cairn on the site of Siegi Löw's tent and held a service in his memory. On the following day, amid driving rain and snow, we moved off towards the lower levels of the Indus Valley. In carrying away the incapacitated climbers, the mountain peasants behaved with extraordinary skill. They carried them down the precipitous climbing pitches of the Diamir Gorge in hammocks and on their backs in slings. Early in the morning of the third day we reached the Bunar Bridge. Jeeps were waiting and on the following day we were already flying home.

To please us, the pilot flew once more around the mountainside on which we had struggled for weeks and where we had now left our comrade. The mountain had covered its summit with clouds and only permitted us a scant glimpse of its ice-armoured precipices. Thus we bade farewell to the "German Mountain of Destiny", but we promised to come again.

POSTSCRIPT

A year later, on June 10, 1963, we actually returned to Nanga Parbat. This time there were only four of us: Toni Kinshofer (29), who had reached the summit in the previous year and since then had had all his toes amputated; Gerhard Haller (31), a climber to whom botanical work had been entrusted as an extra duty; Klaus Scheck (23) and the author as director, doctor and photographer.

This time no ascent was to be attempted. We only wanted to reconnoitre the Rupal side of the mountain, the world's greatest precipice, with a sheer drop of almost 16,000 feet from summit to foot, in case a possibility of ascending it should reveal itself. In a few days we found a line of ascent secure against avalanches, which in a year or two will give a strong team of young Himalaya climbers a chance of showing its metal.

K. M. Herligkoffer, 15.7.63

PUMORI—THE DAUGHTER MOUNTAIN

GERMAN-SWISS HIMALAYAN EXPEDITION, 1962

By Gerhard Lenser

First encounters with Pumori have probably followed much the same course with all contenders, and I will admit that we were no exception. This mountain, the Virgin Jewel of the Khumbu, as Marcel Kurz has called it, is seen for the first time when Everest with its eternal toga of clouds, wild Lhotse and the Nuptse wall have long been part of the daily landscape. One is out of breath from coming up over the old green tongue of the Khumbu Glacier, that heap of rubble which is as ugly as it is famous. We were dumbfounded, and our Sherpas too. Pumori had played no part in the plans of the expeditions with which they had previously been in this region. "You will never get up there!" they said.

When you see the mountain for the first time, you can stare your eyes out searching for a route of ascent, even if at home you have already puzzled out the best possibilities with the help of the splendid photographs that are available.

We set up our base camp at approximately 18,000 feet, in a small hollow between the uppermost yak pasture of the Pangboche people, which is called Gorak Shep, and the Pumori Glacier. I had chosen this site because I had thought we would be protected there from the unremitting winds from the Dudh Kosi Valley and the Khumbu Glacier. That was a mistake. The hollow proved to be a sort of wind channel. However, this did have one advantage. The cold Dudh Kosi wind prevented us from prolonging our comfortable breakfast until lunchtime. In the late mornings it regularly drove us back to our air mattresses for a brief nap.

After a week had passed I became uneasy and reckoned that our somnolent group was the most unsuitable expeditionary team that ever sojourned in the Himalayas. I was indignant, but unjustly so, as it later turned out. We were indebted for this long period of rest to the wise advice of Ernst Forrer, who was experienced in the Himalayas. It gave us an ideal time for adjustment to the rarefied atmospheric conditions of this altitude, a good preparation for our coming trials in the difficult cliffs of the south face and on the incredible northeast ridge of Pumori.

The first aspect of Pumori, however grandiose an impression it may produce, discourages the sahib as well as the Sherpa. However, the closer one approaches the mountain, the more simple everything appears. Undoubtedly, our unsuccessful predecessors were taken in by this, and so, to begin with, were we.

127

On April 4, 1862, we had established our base camp on Gorak Shep, and on the 12th we took an exploratory stroll. We climbed over slag slopes to the foot of the red cliffs of Pumori's south spur and returned rather sobered.

I incline more to rock routes; Ernst Forrer, by contrast, is an ice-man. Sometimes we had wild disputes; but as a result of this first advance all our hopes for a short steep ascent, that would be different from the attempts of our predecessors, sank to zero. I still consider the south spur of Pumori to be possible. We wanted, however, to climb the mountain and not merely solve a minor problem.

The Nepal side of Pumori presents the southeast face and the west flank. The entire southeast face is two-and-a-half miles broad. Everything that, until our visit, had been attempted on Pumori, including the catastrophe of December 1961, had taken place there. Far in advance, I had furnished this southeast face with a series of theoretical intermediary camps, depots and routes of ascent, but such theories are a normal part of an adventure.

On our exploratory climb under the "shoulder spur", the ice ridge which runs down the icewall below the shoulder, the end point of the northeast ridge below the summit pyramid, we found numerous traces of predecessors, but no route of ascent that could be taken seriously. Here one can get up to well above 20,000 feet, and one can take magnificent photographs of Everest opposite; then one suddenly finds one-self beneath monstrous ice bulges and towers and cracks ripe and ready to break off, so that in all modesty one climbs down again. This was one more futile venture. We still searched with the big field glasses for a weak point, but in vain. Only far towards the east there still remained a spur, almost below the wild Lingtren-Pumori ravine. We climbed down in order to have a go at our "secret tip".

In general I put little trust in "secret tips", which someone gives you casually. Here the tip was: West Col.

We climbed about on the Changri Shar Glacier so as to scan the West Col and the secretive west flank, which on the map inspires ideas of an ascent. But we soon climbed down again, though we had obtained a good view of the south spur from the west, of which we now had an exact idea. However, the west flank is murderous. There you will find no nicely graded west glacier: only a vile icefall and fearful avalanche walls. Therefore I decided to establish our Camp I in the closest proximity to the eastern cliff spur, and from there to make a new attempt to find a way to the mountain itself.

With the attempt to pitch a usable camp at the right point beneath the southeast face there seemed to appear the first symptoms of moral dissolution among both sahibs and Sherpas. There was a Camp Ia, another which might be called Ib, and a third, Ic.

At base camp, disregarding the cold valley wind which arose about 10 a.m., we

128

35 ON THE NORTHEAST RIDGE OF PUMORI. Camp III (20,400 ft.) of the Lenser Expedition. The view toward the West Shoulder of Everest and, in the background to the right, Lhotse. (Photograph by the German and Swiss Nepal-Himalaya Expedition of 1962)

36 PUMORI (23,442 ft.), one of the most beautiful mountains in the world. (Photograph courtesy of the Swiss Foundation for Alpine Research)

had our first days of fair weather. There was an atmosphere of spring, when one might expect to find larks and other tiny songsters that might help one to forget the harshness of the scene. But there were only the impertinent jackdaws and fussy ptarmigans.

On the day when I despatched the first loads to a hypothetical Camp I came the first really bad weather. It hailed, stormed and snowed wildly, and with minor pauses continued thus into the middle of May. The famous fair weather period before the summer monsoon failed us completely. Though this did not lead us into a retreat or a catastrophe, it nevertheless brought us into a hopeless organizational mess. The base camp of the Indian Everest Expedition, not far away, was also dominated by an atmosphere of nervousness, although softened by Asian resignation.

The Sherpas, Nima Tensing and Nima Dorje (the Nima Dorje who had been on Dhaulagiri), and I, were the first to resume our ascent. In our first serious attempt, carrying rucksacks heavy with ropes and pitons, we climbed a goodly portion of the face of the cliff spur. I had spied out a snowfield which looked from below like a broad ledge, and wanted to bring up the smallest tent as the first stage in the face. The climbing on the spur varied between the third and fourth degree of difficulty, and the snow-ledge proved illusory. But we had covered 600 feet of the Pumori face, and a good start had been made. We fixed ropes all the way down to the bottom of the face and we now had a really good beginning of a route, which encouraged us to proceed.

Unfortunately, the weather continued bad. On the following days we climbed up twice more, each time a little higher, until we reached a chimney which we examined closely. Ueli Hürlemann, the youngest member of our party, but physically the strongest, until now had had difficulty in acclimatizing to the oxygen-poor altitude, so he remained at the base camp to start with and organized the transportation of supplies to Camp I, which stood at 18,000 feet at the foot of the southeast face. Hans Rützel and Ernst Forrer, together with the two Nimas, took part in attempts to climb higher.

The chimney was a real trap. I climbed a rope-length up it, here and there hammering a piton into the ice with which it was plastered, until I could go no further. It took me hours to get down again and I still marvel that I made it; in any case, I have become much more critical of climbing on rotten vertically-stratified rocks. Snowfall and storm followed, and we went down.

Two days later Forrer made a new attempt from the point whence we had retreated below the chimney, and on a protruding pulpit-like site he succeeded in hacking out a level place from the ice, where our small tent could be pitched. This was Camp II. It was at least a shelter for the nights, and in the later stages of the ascent it played a decisive role. Ernst Forrer and I were now no longer obliged to climb down the entire wall; instead we could make use of every slight improvement in the weather to press forward. The Nimas and the two others, as well as Ueli Hürlemann, who could not be kept idle below, climbed up daily, even in the worst weather—in fog, storm and snow showers—along the fixed ropes, and brought us new supplies. In the end there were probably a hundred ice and rock pitons in the wall, with more than 2,000 feet of rope attached. There were all kinds of pitches: walls, chimneys and corners, everything to delight the heart of a climber. We climbed everything at first without direct aid, except for one holdless wall where the cracks were buried under deep new snow; there we fastened a sling. While we did this the weather raged down at us from the northeast ridge, and when we again reached a good ledge, we wound the rappel ropes about us and swooped down again to the camp on the face. It was quite comfortable in this tent, although Forrer lay on the piled up snow wall, beyond which the mountain fell away for nearly 1,200 feet. But inside the tent we saw nothing of this.

On April 23rd I had started the first part of the face. On the evening of May 3rd, around five o'clock, we deposited our heavy packs on the soft slopes of the col between Pumori and Lingtren. We had already reached this point the previous day, but had had to return to the camp on the cliff.

I have named this pass the "Pass of the Disappointed". Later we crossed it part of the way down to the Rongphu Glacier in Tibet. Mallory had been there in 1921, and Shipton in 1938, when searching around Mount Everest for better possibilities of ascent. And indeed, to the north, lovely ski slopes fall away in soft waves. The east-west shadow, which here must be called an icy one, also does not make the climber's life easier.

At 20,180 feet (according to Erwin Schneider's map of 1957) the Pass of the Disappointed might count as the highest and most difficult pass that has been crossed so far, but I would advise against the trip.

The southeast face, on the same scale as the north face of the Eiger, lay below us, and our disappointment at the appearance of the northeast ridge was indescribable. Judging from the photographs, we had reckoned on a friendly firm crest, and the map suggested the same. But before our eyes began the wildest and steepest corniced ridge that we had ever seen.

A little above the col we pitched a double nylon tent for Camp II. The altimeter indicated 20,400 feet. Forrer, the ice climber, announced that he would avoid the ridge and use the north face instead, and at that very moment there thundered, as if in greeting, down from the ridge and over the icy north face, hardly fifty yards away from our tent, a huge and glassy chunk of cornice.

At night the temperature fell to an unusual degree. Neither of us could find any sleep, although we had become well accustomed to the cold since our nights in the wall began.

130

The good route we had prepared up the southeast face now brought its rewards. The Sherpas, with Rützel and Hürlemann, constantly brought up supplies, even in bad weather. Because of the danger of falling cornices, Forrer and I made our first attempt on the northeast ridge. It failed. Then we climbed down to the Rongphu Glacier, reconnoitred the north face, and started up it in good weather. Eventually we had to retreat to safety out of a practically vertical, furrowed, firn wall in driving snow and in constant danger of avalanches.

By this time we had had enough, so we went all the way down for a rest. We had been eleven days on the mountain without interruption, and we gave way to our two comrades. On May 9th I climbed down to base camp with Forrer. On May 13th we returned to Camp III on the pass. During this time Hürlemann and Rützel had made two more attempts along the northeast ridge and had then given up. Both had come back over the wall to Camp I.

When one has sat for a day at base camp, read the mail from home with encouraging words from friends, the world looks quite different. We decided to remain in Camp III until either the weather improved or our provisions ran out. If the good weather arrived we wanted to push forward with our "Pumori-method", that is, without any further build-up of camps, carrying all necessary equipment with us—a small tent and five days' provisions—and wearing as many clothes as possible. In this manner we wanted to push on over the ridge and over the summit wall. It would entail a greater risk, but we had considered it long and carefully. In the event of a severe turn in the weather we should be able to pitch the tent wherever we were and wait from eight to ten days for an improvement. The question remained as to whether, on that exceptionally steep ridge, a camp site could be found.

The hoped-for weather came with a fresh cold wind out of the brown infinity of Tibet. On May 15th, after 6 a.m., the three of us (Rützel had not yet come up again) left Camp III. By noon the two wildest pitches on the ridge, on which all attempts had failed until then, had been overcome. The second decisive point on this important day was a level cornice in the middle of the northeast ridge. There we set up the small light tent. This was our Camp IV. Beside it stood an ice-tower, which was not to be climbed and which involved a vital decision. We had to climb around it to the right in the icy north face. About noon on the 16th we climbed, one after the other, hand over hand, back onto the ridge above the tower. Towards evening, in a light fog, we arrived, fairly exhausted, at the "shoulder", where we pitched our small narrow tent on the level spot we had been yearning for. At 21,820 feet, it was our last and most important camp. Ueli Hürlemann named it the "Pumori Hospiz".

The way to the summit offered no difficulties. The strong dry Tibetan wind had carried away all the loose snow from the bad weather period, and the sun transformed the steep, 1,500-foot wall into good firn. We could climb it like the top part of the

Brenva face or the Peuterey ridge, only much more freely. At one's back stood the highest mountain in the world. The incomparable lines of Pumori, this mountain without a blemish, seemed to lift themselves up above the earth.

On May 17, 1962, shortly after 11 a.m., we stood at the edge of the summit triangle and stepped onto the highest point. The gale swept across it and tried to hurl us down. We knelt and turned our gaze over the sea of mountains. The few happy seconds of fulfilment, though fleeting, were the reward of our efforts.

The summit hour was over and we went briskly down over the steep track. Two-and-a-half hours later we were back at the Hospiz. The sun sank behind the summit and it became cold, but we had a quiet night. The weather held and everything went well until we were back at Camp III. Then the first brown cloud showed up out of the south, the same clouds that robbed the Indians on Everest of success.

On the second day after the summit we reached the camps below the mountain. The dangers had been overcome. On May 24th, on our way back over the highest summer meadow (Lobuche), I found the first primulas and the tender grasses. We laid our faces on the warm spring moss and enjoyed our good fortune.

PEAK OF COMMUNISM

By Malcolm Slesser

"We train on the walls of a former Czarist Palace and by cross-country skiing at the week-ends", explained Eugene Gippenreiter of the Foreign Relations commission of the USSR Ministry of Sport, and an eager mountaineer. And by these means do the enthusiasts of western Russia, dwelling in the greatest extent of flat land in Europe, maintain form. They go further still. For months prior to a serious expedition they forego smoking and liquor. They train as the serious sportsmen they are, and on the mountain it pays off handsomely.

As Gippenreiter knew from personal experience, in Britain it is different. Though our mountains may be small, they are never far off, and we climb throughout the year, giving scant attention to any muscle not at once associated with pinch grips or pull-ups. Many of us succumb weekly to a national predilection for beer and social communion. That two such differing groups should elect to join forces in an expedition to the highest mountains of the Soviet Union, the Pamirs, is therefore full of interest.

Some members of the Alpine Club and Climbers Club in England, and quite independently, the Scottish Mountaineering Club in Scotland, had been angling for permission to climb in the high mountains of Soviet Asia ever since the first successful sortie of Sir John Hunt's party to the Caucasus in 1958. Moscow, in an impish frame of mind, finally assented, provided the English and the Scots joined forces in a single expedition, an improbable coalescence never hitherto attempted, which as John Hunt, who led the expedition, once jocularly voiced, aroused considerable dismay in the breasts of the Alpine Club. The real disadvantage, of course, was that we should be a relatively large party of twelve, to which would be added six Soviet alpinists, in all a perilously large number of individualists to gather together at one time.

Our permission was for the Garmo-Gando Glacier area, embracing Pik Kommunisma (Peak of Communism, and until recently Peak Stalin) and its western approaches. The Pamirs, together with the Tien Shan and the Altai, form the high mountains in the USSR. Being the only outlet for Soviet high-altitude climbers they had been fairly fully explored. All the seven-thousand-metre peaks had been climbed, and most of the six-thousanders. In the Garmo-Gando region only peaks of less than six thousand still remained virgin. Pik Kommunisma, 24,590 feet, had first been

133

ascended in 1933 by Gorbonov and Eugene Abalakov from the eastern or Fedshenko Glacier side. After the war a succession of skilled and tough Soviet expeditions followed the route of the German climber Rickmer-Rickmers into the Garmo area and between 1957 and 1961 climbed the mountain by no less than three new routes, so that today it must be one of the best known of high mountains.

There remained one well-defined line to tackle: the south face. This remarkable wall is 8,000 feet high, most of it at an angle of 70°, and rises from 17,000 feet. At the time of planning, ignorant of these impressive statistics, we suggested it to the Russians. It was kind of them not to take us too seriously, though in self-defence it may be said that one of the hardest things in planning this expedition was to get detailed information of the area. At no time did we ever get a close-up view of one of the better maps of the area, and worked largely from annotated photographs sent to us.

During a week's visit to Moscow in 1961, I was charged with making the detailed expedition arrangements with the Russians. We would fly by jet to Dushanbe, capital of Tajikistan, and thence by charter to Tavil Dara, a small township on the Obichingou river, some 150 miles distant. The expedition stores and most of the personnel would be ferried by helicopter to a base camp at Avodara, a few miles above the Garmo snout at 11,000 feet. Others would take a horse caravan along the ten-day overland route, said to be hazardous on account of many torrents, but desirable because full of orchards. This caravan would furnish us with meat on the hoof, and fruit, would deliver mail and ultimately help us to walk out. As a plan it had two snags.

Firstly, British mountaineers depend on the walk into the mountains to make them fit. Secondly, in this remote corner of the Soviet Union, while entrepreneurs had been banished and capitalism discredited as elsewhere, when it came to hiring horses nothing had evolved in its place. My Soviet colleagues treated me to an engaging picture of expedition forays to remote collective farms to buy horses at whatever price could be bargained. The early summer, I gathered, was a seller's market, and local custom was to pay by the kilogram. But in the autumn, horses attract few buyers outside the sausage factories, who would understandably offer low prices for the overworked, debilitated beasts we should have to offer. I had visions of seeing the expedition's overdraft in the form of several hundred kilos of live horse being inexorably sucked into the swirling milk-grey waters of one of the "hazardous torrents".

Thus, however irritating it was to forego the joy and very considerable interest of journeying to and fro up the Obichingou valley, the fact that the Tajikistan authorities failed to implement the Moscow decision to let us go out on foot did make life simpler.

We met, the eighteen of us, one hot scented evening under the floodlights of

134

Dushanbe airport. We introduced ourselves in a welter of firm handshakes and friendly grins, high-lighted by the flash guns of the local press. Eugene Gippenreiter, the man who, along with A. Kaspin of the USSR Federation of Mountaineers, had done so much to help us to get to the Pamirs and make our stay agreeable; he spoke faultless English. Tolia Ovchinikov, the leader of the Russian group, had frank blue eyes and a sympathetic face that belied his reputation as an "iron man". Anatole Sevastianov was tall, with dashing good looks. Kolia Shalaev, small, gnarled and as tough as he looked, had his face perpetually creased in a leathery grin. These three were all Masters of Sport, indicating a very high degree of competence, and more; the freedom to pick and choose climbs. Younger, around thirty, were Kolia Alchutov and Vladimir Malachov, who required only two more 5B (the hardest category) peaks of over 6,000 metres to gain a Mastership themselves. All came from Moscow, a matter of some bitterness to Leningrad climbers we had met.

The immediate pleasure of getting together was blunted by the news that we were not to be allowed to penetrate the Pamir valley of the Obichingou, nor even travel as far as Tavil Dara. Our kit would be handled by our Russian colleagues, while we were to be sent by some other air route. It is typical of the Soviet system that these changes were visited upon us without any explanation or excuse, and that it fell to our unfortunate Russian companions to bring us the news and bear our ill grace.

On the other hand, expeditioning to the Soviet Union was in some respects idyllic. The USSR Federation of Mountaineers handled everything for us, saw it expeditiously across the overland route to Dushanbe, and stored it for us, once there. Not so much as a single crampon strap was missing, no niggling customs officials, not a penny of duty to pay. Those familiar with Himalayan expeditions may have been nostalgic for the drawn out hagglings of Bombay and Karachi, but if so they never mentioned it.

Our equipment caused no little astonishment amongst our Russian comrades. Geared as it was to deal with the ultimate problems, such as the south face, it resembled the lavish scale of some national sortie. They saw little use for our sacks of pitons, mile of fixed rope, and endless chains of karabiners, and were appalled at the abundance of our tentage. Thus it seemed, either the mountains were easy or they and we had different ideas on how to climb high mountains.

Chiefly, I think they were disturbed by the weight that all this represented, for we would have no porters. Employing another man to bear your burden has no place in Marxist philosophy. We did not relish the sheer drudgery of man-packing that lay ahead of us, and though we had yet to discover it, the absence of horses was to add much to our load-carrying activities.

While our Russian comrades departed to the forbidden pastures of Tavil Dara with all our kit, we assumed the guise of tourists. On the morning of July 6th, having been rudely awakened from sleep by an earthquake tremor, we flew some two hundred

135

miles to the upland town of Jirgital at 6,000 feet, a fascinating flight that kept low in the valleys, and breasted mountain passes with little to spare. Beneath us the incredible Pamir highway worked its way into the mountains, coiled upon itself like a fankled rope.

The use of helicopters was a new venture not only for us, but for the Russians. They are not cheap, and we could each have taken an excursion air ticket round the world for the price of flying the expedition in. In one hour we covered the ten-day journey on foot.

Gaining height over upland pastures, peopled largely by wild horses, we crossed a pass at 12,000 feet and plummeted like an eagle to the upper Obichingou valley. Here there are many mountain villages, all abandoned. Flying at 9,000 feet, the Garmo valley slowly came up to meet us, till we were close enough to see the buckthorn lying along the river bank of the broad U-shaped valley. Turning sharply over the Garmo snout, the usual moraine wilderness, we got a fleeting glimpse of the 21,800-foot Pik Garmo, its flanks burnished by the early afternoon sun.

This was to be base camp, two miles below the snout, in a walnut grove. With a sinking feeling in our stomachs, we realized that we were some 15,000 feet below our mountain, and separated from it by twenty-five miles of porterless glacier. Pik Kommunisma was not visible. The immediate hills seemed in an advanced state of disrepair, with minor peaks dropping dismally into gullies and other inscrutable corrugations. Snow lay at the 13,000-foot contour. It was a late season.

Avodara, our projected base camp, lay at 11,000 feet, seven miles up the Garmo glacier. Lacking horses, we started on the painful business of carrying there, and made it Camp I. Out of that painful week emerged the truth that the Russians were indeed supremely fit and we had a lot to catch up. For the moment, only Robin Smith of Edinburgh, a man who virtually lived in the mountains, was up to their mark. Towards the end of that time, the Spartak expedition arrived to fill our wood. This twenty-eight man party from one of the largest trades union sporting clubs was led by the greatest living Russian climber of them all, Vitale Abalakov, brother of Eugene, who was the first to climb Kommunisma. They were here to participate in the all-Union mountaineering competition for the longest high-altitude traverse and the hardest high-altitude ascent. For the latter they had selected the south face of Kommunisma, and had, we gathered, priority over us. We reserved judgment on Abalakov's offer of a secondary route on this face till we saw it for ourselves.

For the easier routes, the Russian technique is to wait until, as it were, the mountain is looking the other way, then charge up it at a great rate, toting enormous rucksacks. In this way Ovchinikov had once made the summit of Kommunisma in eight days from Avodara. It was soon obvious to Hunt that either we must adopt easy peaks

136

and the Russian tactic, or that some of us be relegated to the role of porters while others climbed something worthwhile.

Neither appealed. Then it became known that the helicopters might be persuaded to make a drop at 13,000 feet, some eighteen miles up the glacier at projected Camp III. This suggestion, which had been roundly scotched during the planning stage, demonstrated the anxiety of the Russians to help us. In this way considerable supplies of equipment and food were ferried painlessly. Unhappily we had no way of protecting our lightweight packs of twelve man-day food boxes, which were badly damaged by these drops. Nevertheless, on balance it was a useful move, and by July 16th we were assembled at Camp III.

Once in the middle reaches of the Garmo, our mountaineering beings took on life anew. Astride our path sat the squatting lion of Pik Patriot, 21,000 feet, its south and west ice aretes linking acutely at the summit. Peeping over its right shoulder, to the south, was the temporarily anonymous Pik 6,878 metres, for convenience dubbed "former Molotov". Leftwards, the last 4,000 feet of the south face rose as a sheer precipice above a nearer bastion, forming a perfect isosceles triangle. Only a little snow held onto the steep face.

From July 17th to 26th Hunt planned an acclimatization period, during which we would divide into three groups with two Russians and four British in each. Wilfrid Noyce and Ovchinikov would have a go at a new route on 21,800 feet Pik Garmo, which dominated the headwall of the Vavilova Glacier. With them would be Anatole Sevastianov, Ted Wrangham and Derek Bull of the Alpine Club, and Robin Smith of the Scottish Mountaineering Club.

My party had been drawn to Pik Patriot, the west ridge of which remained unclimbed and looked a superb challenge, while Sir John decided to go for a 19,000 foot peak in between, so that he could lend support to either side as necessary. With him were Kolia Shalaev and Gippenreiter, Ralph Jones of the Climbers Club, who had been on the 1958 Caucasus expedition, and George Lowe, the well-known New Zealander, and Graeme Nicol of the Scottish Mountaineering Club, the expedition doctor. In the course of a well-planned, hard-hitting ascent, they quickly climbed the mountain, one of the few virgin peaks in the area. It is now called Peak of Concord.

Pik Patriot rose 8,000 feet above Camp III, directly across the Vavilova Glacier. As a 5B peak it appealed to the two Russian aspirants in the party, Malachov and Alchutov, but so keen were they that they even entertained ideas of going on and making the traverse from Patriot to "former Molotov". The mountain had been climbed once in 1959 by the south ridge, and on the descent two Russian climbers had been avalanched, and a further three killed while trying to rescue them.

We had ten days in hand—we being Ian McNaught-Davis, of the Alpine Club, from London, and Joe Brown, a powerful pair who had last joined forces on the

Mustagh Tower, and Ken Bryan of the SMC who had made some fine ascents in Greenland, myself and the two Russians.

Our rather methodical manner of stocking the mountain with food and tents did not appeal to the two Russians, who felt we were cluttering ourselves up with unnecessary weighty gear. The rock proved abominable, like bad teeth, loose in their sockets. Gaining the 16,500-foot col where we placed Camp V was like climbing a set of library shelves using the books as handholds. Pitons would only hold in horizontal cracks, where they were retained by the sheer dead weight of the mountain. Once the British members mooted abandoning the climb because of its intrinsic danger. Finally, on July 23rd, after being pinioned by two days of bad weather at a camp at about 18,000 feet, McNaught-Davis, Brown, Alchutov and Malachov set off for the summit. At that stage we had been under the false impression that the summit was at 20,000 feet. The extra 1,000 feet baulked them of the summit, and, as an added burden, Brown was suffering a common, but painful affliction of mountaineering men. He and McNaught-Davis went down, and by scraping together what food we could find, we mustered four man-days, just enough to let the Russians have another crack at the top, if the rest of us backed down the mountain. On July 24th a note was placed in a cairn near the top noting that Alchutov and Malachov, members of the "English-Soviet Pamir expedition" had arrived there. They are now Masters of Sport too.

We had expected to re-unite with the Garmo and Concord climbers on July 25th, and by the 26th we were getting worried. Late that evening Hunt and Nicol arrived at our camp. Tired men, their faces and hands were cracked and blistered with sun and exposure. Briefly, Hunt told us that Noyce and Smith had fallen to their deaths on Pik Garmo. Words are inadequate to describe the impact of such news on a small group of climbers far from home and deep in the mountains.

The eight of us crowded into a small double-skin tent and heard Hunt's story, told in a simple direct way. After their own successful ascent they had gone over towards Noyce's base camp for Garmo, as promised; it was July 24th. Finding no one, he and Nicol continued upwards beyond the second ice-fall and eventually met four very tired men, Wrangham and Bull and the Anatolis, who gave the news. In the course of a vigorous attack on the mountain, they had placed a camp at over 18,000 feet, and had all set out for the summit, 3,000 or more feet above. They were on the route of the first ascent, the promising buttress being too steep and ice-coated to tackle as an acclimatization ascent. Smith, Noyce, Ovchinikov and Sevastianov made the summit, and about four in the afternoon turned to descend. Smith and Noyce, wearing crampons, continued when the Russians had stopped to put on theirs. Moving together, they swiftly descended snow-covered ice slopes. The Russians from above, and Bull and Wrangham from camp, saw one of the British pair slip, pull the other off his feet. They failed to brake and fell 4,000 feet, coming to rest on an ice ledge, still roped, side by side. It was a mysterious accident to happen to two such able climbers. Noyce, possibly the most experienced high-altitude climber at that time in Britain, and Smith, young, but already one of our most brilliant ice climbers.

Many people had worked hard to bring eastern and western mountaineers together on a venture of this nature. Thus, notwithstanding the enormity of the tragedy and its impact upon us, it was felt that the expedition should continue. Naturally, those intimately involved felt little inclination for further climbing, and Sir John himself decided to go home as well to explain our apparent heartlessness to the world at large. It was not an easy decision for him, and those who returned had to bear the brunt of world publicity.

Amongst those who remained enthusiasm for the south face had waned utterly. We lacked the numbers to support a full-scale assault; we had lost two of our strongest climbers and we were wary of cliffs composed not of rock, but of craggy *wiener-bröd*. On balance we chose to climb the mountain by the 1959 route, found by the Georgian expedition of that year, led by Giginevshi. The route is also entirely of snow and ice, the crux being a 3,300-foot face rising from 17,000 feet and terminating in an unwholesome slot called the Georgian couloir, which now lends its name to the whole face.

A second-hand route can never have quite the thrill of a new one, especially if some of the party have been up it before, as Ovchinikov had, and are making the pace. Barring accidents, the issue seemed beyond doubt, a factor which inevitably dulls one's mountain palate. Thus there seemed everything to be said for tackling the mountain in the swift Soviet way. This we did. Ovchinikov produced a time-table, we modified it, and on August 1st we once again toiled up the barren slopes to Camp I, but this time fit and raring to go. We were ten: six British and four Russians.

We had equipment and food littered over the many lower camps. The Russians worked from Camp II and we from Camp III, and by August 5th we had established ourselves at a new Camp IV at 14,000 feet with enough food for ten days. Behind us were the nasty, rock-scarred corrugations of the Belaev icefall, with its seedy rotten tenements of corroded ice. Above lay the real mountain.

Camp IV was ideal, a belvedere upon which to sun-bathe and armchair mountaineer. The west ridge of Patriot soared gracefully and impressively across the glacier bay. An impenetrable curtain of ice hung between it and the distant "former Molotov". The exit of the Belaev valley was blocked by the headwall joining Molotov to Kommunisma. Towards us and left of Molotov fell glaciated slopes resembling the north side of Monte Disgrazia. From their lowest point, the col at 20,300 feet, ran the Georgian couloir. Left again was the small pyramid of Pik Pravda, then at about 19,600 feet a gentle plateau col from which rose the final 5,000 feet of Kommunisma. Abutting this col and facing us was the south face.

139

From Camp IV we planned a relay to V at 17,000 feet, at the last reasonable camp-site before tackling the Georgian couloir. Bryan had already shown signs of Brown's earlier malady (now cured), and had to abandon his carry to V. I never quite made V, assailed by food poisoning, the cause of which, we believe, lay in some of our dried food which had not stood up to the heat of the journey in a freight truck through the desert of Kyzyl Kum. Next day, August 7th, we all made Camp V, now stocked with everything we needed for the rest of the mountain, including a bottle of oxygen for therapeutic purposes.

Clouds, which had mercifully covered us during the earlier part of the day, now evaporated. The glacier became a vast pan in which we were helplessly roasted by the radiant heat of the Pamir sun; for here the weather is close to a high mountain ideal. Snowfall was uncommon and seldom fell in great quantity. High winds were never personally encountered, though occasionally spume would fly like a banner a quarter of a mile out from Kommunisma's summit.

By the evening of the 7th Bryan was in great pain, and Dr Nicol decided he must return. Coming as it did to an otherwise fit individual, it was a great blow. Since he could not return alone, Jones gave up his chance and offered to be the one to accompany him.

The crux now lay before us. Some 1,300 feet of easy slopes to the foot of the ice face, and a further 2,000 feet to the top of the Georgian couloir. On this whole span no camp site commended itself to us. Indeed the route looked dangerous and had that reputation. There was plenty of evidence of avalanche about. Ovchinikov's advice, which was to climb the face in one day with everything for the upper part of the mountain was obviously sound, but it was going to be a heavy haul. Doing the mountain at this rate, we were carrying only slim reserves of food, and only the party's detailed knowledge of the mountain and the generally favourable Pamir weather made it justifiable. From now on we should be out on a limb. We should leave this camp with five days of food, cine gear, and the minimum of climbing equipment. We carried three days surplus of butane gas canisters.

Bryan woke me before dawn on the 8th to say that Nicol had had a bad night, with sickness and vomiting. The food again. He was quite unable to move. The departure of Bryan and Jones was going to leave us with spare food. Mercifully we could afford to sit out a day and see if Nicol recovered. Ovchinikov elected to go on, make the Georgian couloir, and perhaps tackle an adjacent peak while waiting for us to catch up. Periodically during the ensuing hot day we conned the face for them, till about midday we lost them for good. Nicol had doped himself with anti-biotics and spent the day comatose. It seemed hardly likely he would recover sufficiently to go on.

We were awake before dawn again on the 9th. Astonishingly, Nicol judged himself able to continue. We shouldered heavy packs and trudged through the giant snowballs of a recent avalanche to the roping-up point, from where, across the cwm, we could see the magnificent back drop of the south face, now modelled by snow and oblique sun into its true relief and revealed in its entirety. Mentally we doffed hats to Spartak, who, in their thorough way, were at this moment on the self-same route as us, three days ahead. Their eight best men were making the summit by this *voie normale*, as an acclimatization move. They would excavate an ice-cave on the upper part of the mountain and stock it against the south face party's descent some weeks ahead.[1] Because it had been reported that Spartak had put a fixed rope up the only difficulty on the ice face, we had, at Russian advice, saved weight by leaving much of our rope and ironmongery behind. Thus, on a mere 140-foot rope, the four of us, led by Joe Brown, tramped rope-length by rope-length up the face.

Midday found us at a ledge, which gave a respite for food. We were now in the sun: above us a *rimaye*, a steep snow slope, a second *rimaye*, then the Georgian couloir, a glistening green-blue slab of ice, perhaps 400 to 500 feet high, topped by menacing bulges of glacier sliding off Molotov. And there, too, were four figures, stepping out of the sun into shade. They were our Russian comrades, who, we discovered, had spent the night near our lunching spot.

The ascent of the ice slab, at 60° in the heat of the day, was an unpleasant experience, less for what happened than for the pregnant danger of the place. For Nicol and I, weaker than our two English brethren, it remained a place where at one time we felt at the limit of our strength.

We camped at the col and next day dropped by the back of Pravda to the plateau col of 19,600 feet to the Russian tent, which was empty! But high up, on the south-east flank of Kommunisma, a cluster of dots was moving down quickly. As they came into camp, we saw that Ovchinikov and Misha Khirgianov of Spartak, one of the USSR's greatest climbers, were supporting a deathly pale exhausted being. He was Oleg Abalakov, son of Vitale, suffering from water on the lung. Nicol ministered, but unfortuantely our oxygen had had to be left at Camp V. We waited at this camp, VI, overnight, and by morning he was still alive and the worst past. Five of Spartak had made the summit.

By now only McNaught-Davis seemed to be suffering no readily identifiable physical malaise. The Russians, on a diet of tinned chicken, caviar and kasha (semolina porridge) were eating heartily and none the worse. There is a lesson here. Our climb to the Spartak ice-cave on August 10th nearly finished me, and 500 feet from the top my companions nobly saved the day by carrying some of my load. It was a long dull climb of 2,500 feet up steep insubstantial snow on ice, and Joe Brown, though short in the leg and ill after each meal, was still doggedly in the van.

[1] As it happened, the traditional settled weather of late August never came, and the face was not even attempted.

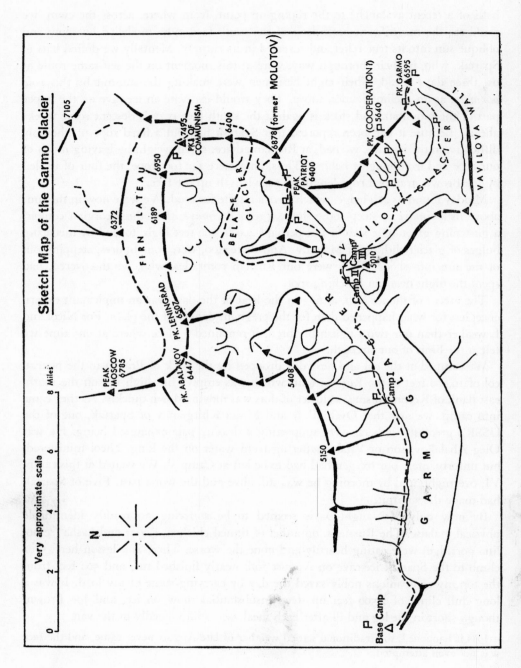

Sketch Map of the Garmo Glacier

Very approximate scale

N

0   2   4   6   8 Miles

△7105

△7495
PK 3 OF COMMUNISM

6400

▲6950

FIRN PLATEAU

6189

6372

PK. LENINGRAD 6507

PEAK
MOSCOW
6705

PK. ABALAKOV
6447

6878 (former MOLOTOV)

BELAEF GLACIER

PEAK
PATRIOT
6400

PK. (COOPERATION?) 5640

PK. GARMO
▲6595

VAVILOVA

V
Camp
III
5010

VILO GLACIER

WALL

Camp II

F
E
R

5408

5150

CampI

G A R M O

Camp

Base Camp

142

Some 500 feet below the east ridge, where the angle lessened, a single red rag on a bamboo marked the cave. Ovchinikov and his men were already there, leaving us the half near the door.

"Welcome to the Spartak ice-cave", said Gippenreiter. "There are two rules. No smoking and no spoiling of the air". McNaught-Davis and Brown took up positions near the entrance, for they smoked. We prayed that restive stomachs might be kept in check. Alas, they were not, and at midnight Gippenreiter heroically bored a second door in our warm cramped and fetid hole and turned it instantly into a through-draught deep freeze.

Ovchinikov was for recovering the lost day by making straight for the summit. Lightly laden, but heavily clothed, we faced the brisk twenty-below wind next morning and headed for the east ridge: four and four, taking it in turns to plough the trail. At 23,000 feet we were above everything. Technically it was easy. The Russians passed through as we entered a level stretch and I was human enough to feel relieved that even the steel-stranded Alchutov seemed a trifle out of puff. In the space of a few minutes I faltered. Nicol was little better. McNaught-Davis and Brown, the experienced high-altitude men of our group, were going as well as ever. They would reach the top. We cut the rope in two, and they went on to join the Russians.

We were at the point where the east ridge abuts the upper and less steep part of the south face and becomes the southeast ridge, a highway of snow bounded by a cornice to the northeast and the convexity of the south face to the left. It was a bald, monotonous slope, and in the minds of tired men there was no knowing how far off the summit lay; ten minutes or ten hours? No feature revealed the scale, save the five red and one blue blobs above us. It was curious that altitude took Nicol and me in different ways. It dulled his mind, it sapped my vitality. Nicol had an unholy determination to make the summit and he took me with him. In a way we made a good team. He provided the determination, I the brains!

On three ropes of mixed English and Russian, the others gained the top, rather flat, free of snow, and composed of shale so soft that crampons pierced it. McNaught-Davis filmed the group, waving Soviet and British flags from ice-axes, a fine effort at that height. It is interesting to note that it was the Russians who brought a Union Jack. We didn't have one. Three-quarters of an hour later Nicol and I joined them. McNaught-Davis was lighting a cigarette and Vladimir Malachov, the wit of the Russian party, observed, "How is it, Mac, that you are so decadent yet climb so well?" It is good to laugh, even in the thin air of 24,590 feet.

[A full account of this expedition by Malcolm Slesser, will be published shortly by Hodder and Stoughton, entitled *Red Peak*.]

WILFRID NOYCE
1917-1962

By A. D. M. Cox

Wilfrid Noyce, who was killed in the Pamirs in July, 1962, at the age of forty-four, was generally recognized as one of the outstanding British mountaineers of the last thirty years. This is not to say, in the phrase used by Sir Arnold Lunn of Geoffrey Winthrop Young, that he was "one of those mountaineers who are tacitly accepted as the most representative climbers of a particular epoch". Perhaps it has in any case become meaningless in more recent periods to speak of any individuals as representative in this way, even of mountaineering in one country; but Noyce's place in British mountaineering—despite the fact that he had something in common with Young—was of a quite different kind. He did not seem to belong to a particular epoch, either as a climber or in his attitude towards mountains. Indeed his distinction partly consisted in just this.

He was already a notable climber in the pre-War period, when British standards both at home and in the Alps were very different from what they are now. When the change came during the 1950's, his own standards did not seem to change and his approach remained what it had always been, yet his stature purely as a mountaineer continued to grow. Some of his greatest climbs were done in the last few years of his life. But his reputation did not rest so much on his achievements as on the attitude of mind which underlay his whole approach to climbing. This it is impossible to summarize in a few words, but it is clearly revealed in his own early book, *Mountains and Men*. When Noyce wrote this book, in 1946, he was still only twenty-eight, but he was one of the leading British rock-climbers, had had two remarkable seasons in the Alps just before the War and, by the good fortune of being posted to India for the last three years of the War, had already done some remarkable things in the Himalayas. *Mountains and Men* could have been written (with much more prospect of selling) as a simple record of achievement; instead, as one reviewer commented at the time, it was written "almost as a private paper", with hardly a hint of the fact that the climbing which it described was out of the ordinary. To the end of his life, Wilfrid Noyce remained a climber who attached no importance to achievement or reputation. He was aware that a great climb gives more satisfaction than an ordinary one, and for this reason alone often climbed hard things. But they did not need to be hard for him

37 THE PIK KOMMUNISMA (24,590 ft.) in the Pamir Range. A camp of the British-Soviet Pamir Expedition of 1962. (Photograph by G. Lowe)

38 MOUNT McKINLEY (20,318 ft.), Alaska. The South Face with the South and North Summits. (Photograph by Bradford Washburn)

to enjoy them, and he looked for many other things in mountaineering than the mere element of struggle and success.

Quite apart from his qualities as a mountaineer, Noyce was a person of unusual talent and character. He was Head of the School at Charterhouse, won an Open Scholarship to King's College, Cambridge, and in 1940, having already obtained a First in Part I of the Classical Tripos, took a First Class degree in Modern Languages. When he left the Army at the end of the War, he took up teaching as a career, at first at Malvern for four years, then, after his marriage in 1950, at Charterhouse. Not very long before his death, he gave up teaching in order to give all his time to writing; he was, of course, already well known in this field, especially as an author of mountain books, and he had published two volumes of poems.

Wilfrid Noyce started rock-climbing in Wales in 1934, when he was sixteen, and first went to the Alps in 1935. My own first season with him was not until 1949, in the Graians. We were both starting again in the Alps, having each been involved in accidents a year or two previously, and it was no part of the programme to do difficult routes. The expeditions which we made were quite ordinary ones, though one or two of them involved long days. It was an ideal district for our purpose, and I remember particularly a day of steamy heat when we traversed the Bec d'Invergnan and the Grande Rousse from a camp by a torrent in the pinewoods of the Val Grisanche. I only mention this holiday because on it I discovered in quite trivial ways how different Wilfrid's standards were from my own. There was a little stretch of dry glacier which had to be crossed to reach a bivouac hut; the ice was perfectly easy, except that it was just steepening to spill over a big cliff a few yards below. Wilfrid walked across it without taking his axe from under his arm, then had to wait while I put on crampons. On a traverse of the Grivola, he drifted on ahead up the south face unroped and only came back from the top when I shouted up to him asking to tie on. This was quite a long day, fifteen or sixteen hours, but next morning he made us walk most of the twenty-five odd miles from Val Savaranche round to Cogne and, a poignant memory, took it for granted when we got back to the tent that, as this had not been a climbing day, only one egg would be enough for the evening meal.

This season in the Graians came a little more than half-way through Noyce's mountaineering career, and in a sense was not typical: most of his seasons in the Alps showed a record of far more ambitious climbs. His guided ascents of 1937 and 1938 (I think the only years when, through the generosity of A. C. Pigou, he climbed with a guide) were made at a time when, as I have said, few British mountaineers were doing major routes in the Alps. The following list is incomplete, but his climbs included: in 1937 (with Hans Brantschen) the Rimpfischhorn traverse, the Younggrat on the Breithorn, the south face of the Weisshorn, the Zmutt ridge, the Viereselsgrat, the east ridge of the Dent d'Hérens (with return to Zermatt by 3 p.m.); in 1938 (again with Brantschen) the Mittellegi ridge of the Eiger, the northeast ridge of the Jung-frau (first ascent since the big rockfall of the previous year), the southeast ridge of the Finsteraarhorn, the north face of the Wetterhorn and (with Armand Charlet) the Mer de Glace face of the Grépon (in 3 ¼ hours), the traverse of the Aiguille Verte from the Charpoua Glacier over the Aiguille sans Nom to the Couvercle (reached at 11.10 a.m.), Mont Blanc by the Old Brenva (in 3 ½ hours from the Col de la Fourche, starting shortly before midday). Twenty years later, Noyce was still doing very fine climbs in the Alps and, in his last Alpine season (1959), with J. R. Sadler and C. J. Mortlock as his companions, he made guideless ascents of the north face of the Dent d'Hérens (Welzenbach route), the Furggen ridge of the Matterhorn, direct, the northeast face of the Lyskamm and the northeast face of the Signalkuppe on Monte Rosa—at least two of these being first British ascents. The paper which he subsequently read to the Alpine Club, "Nordwands for the Ageing", is printed in the *Alpine Journal* and is a characteristic expression of his entirely unvainglorious mountain philosophy.

Wilfrid Noyce had a natural sense of balance which allowed him to move easily, and often unroped, on places where other men might struggle. Climbing with Menlove Edwards two years before the War, he had a serious accident when a turf ledge came away on Scafell East Buttress; the completeness of his recovery from this was remarkable. He had already become one of the best British rock-climbers of that period, and twenty-five years later, despite the fact that he could only visit Wales much less frequently, he was still leading the hard pre-War routes with little apparent effort. He also seemed almost unaffected by tiredness or hunger, and few people can ever have seen him really tired. On the last day but one of an Alpine season, one of many in which he was climbing on Mont Blanc, he and John Hunt were caught in a fierce electric storm and heavy snow three-quarters of the way up the frontier ridge of Mont Maudit. The retreat down the ridge must have been an exhausting business for some hours, as two of us who were on the ordinary route on the Aiguille du Midi could judge; yet when we met up in the late afternoon and were walking down, it was Wilfrid who suggested that we should stay on at the Montenvers so as to snatch a short climb in the morning before we left for home.

Perhaps the outstanding feature of his Himalayan climbing was his exceptional stamina. Leave in wartime was short, and much had to be fitted into it. Noyce's first visit to Garhwal, in 1943, was among relative foothills (16,000–17,000 feet) in the neighbourhood of Trisul. In 1944 he was again in Garhwal, and climbed a 20,000 feet peak, Simsaga, in less than a fortnight from Delhi. Next year, an astonishing performance, he left Delhi on September 8th for Sikkim and reached the summit of Pauhunri (23,385 feet) sixteen days later. On Everest, for which he was an obvious choice, he was, of course, the first, with Annullu, to reach the South Col and went a second time to the Col with a load and, for the last 1,500 feet, without oxygen; John

Hunt has recorded that he could certainly have reached the summit. He narrowly failed to reach the top of Machapuchare in 1957, but all the serious climbing on the mountain up to this point had been led by him. On the 1960 expedition to Trivor, in the Karakorum, he had not intended, as leader, to be in the assault party, but when this plan had to be altered he and Sadler, who was far from well, reached the summit (25,370 feet) in a day of nearly fourteen hours from the highest camp.

These were, of course, exploits; but nothing could be more misleading than to give an impression that toughness or the conscious performance of exploits appealed to him for its own sake. He was reticent about his climbs, and when he wrote or lectured about them he never brought out how remarkable his own share in them often was. It was a personal relationship with the hills that concerned him—his own and other people's. This is most noticeable in all his mountain writing, especially perhaps *Mountains and Men* and *South Col*: and the relationship would have been a false one had any element of the competitive entered into it.

Like Geoffrey Young, he saw mountains as a poet sees them, as is vividly revealed by passages even of his prose. Often he liked to be alone, "for then", he wrote, "the imagined shapes of the hills seem to speak". Yet on such occasions he was seldom just passively contemplative. After a full day he would set out from Pen-y-Gwryd again at 10 p.m. to sleep on the top of Snowdon; twice, on recent Easter holidays, he walked by himself over the fourteen 3,000 feet tops of Wales; and during a fortnight in 1961 in the High Atlas, when his companion's illness left him on his own, he not only had no rest day but more often than not crowded two days' climbing and ridge-wandering into one. There is a wartime entry in the hut book at Helyg, the Climbers' Club hut in North Wales, recording about 4,500 feet of solo rock-climbing, much of it severe or harder, as well as a considerable walk. I doubt whether on days like this he was in any sense driving himself; they were simply days of opportunity fully seized.

Although he enjoyed being alone, it would be entirely wrong to suggest that he was essentially a solitary person. Nobody had more friends, or enjoyed friendships more, although his quiet, almost hesitant, manner made him a difficult person to know well. "The mountain itself and action upon it, companionship and an indefinable sense of greatness": these were the things that he put forward in an attempt to probe his own motives for climbing. He himself was a superb companion in a tent or on a rope: considerate, unassertive, completely tolerant, never disturbed. In the most expert party, without wishing to be so, he might find himself the real leader. One noteworthy recognition of this was his election, in the last year of his life, as President of the Alpine Climbing Group.

Noyce had scholarly and literary tastes but, much more than that, it was probably as necessary to him to write as it was to climb. "I needed to grind into words something of the emotion which was holding me," he wrote of Everest. Most of his pub-

147

lished writing, though not the greater part of his poetry, was concerned either with mountains or with the psychology which underlies active adventure or arduous enterprise. He would have wanted to write if he had not been a mountaineer at all, and it is sad that his death has cut short the wider literary career which, with his retirement from teaching, was only just beginning. It is in fact possible to think of his literary career so far as a period of apprenticeship. His earlier books, along with so much that is good in them, show unevennesses, conscious experiment and signs of a still maturing technique; and they were, of course, written in spare moments snatched from a busy school life. But his best mountain writing is memorable, notably *South Col*; and equally *The Springs of Adventure* and his posthumously published *They Survived* leave no doubt at all of what he had it in him to do. It is worth remembering, incidentally, that although spare time was so important to him for his writing he gave a good deal of what he had to the thankless work of editing climbing guidebooks; between 1947 and 1960 he saw a long succession of the Climbers' Club's Welsh guides through the press, and in the summer of 1962 had produced, as General Editor, the first of the Alpine guidebooks jointly prepared by members of the Alpine Club and the Alpine Climbing Group.

Many people who knew Wilfrid Noyce must have felt that there was a special quality in him, best defined perhaps as a humanity of both intellect and character, which pervaded everything he did. As a climber, he was of a different order from most of us, but it was not this, ultimately, which singled him out. People who climbed with him will remember his technical mastery and the climbs which they would not have done without him to lead them; they will remember him balanced in a step, or disappearing round an edge of red rock. But they will remember also evenings spent with him in a tent, talking; the walk over the tops on which he always insisted after a Welsh rock climb; and, perhaps most vividly, days of tiredness when he went on ahead to look for the hut or when in mist and snow the party plodded down the glacier leaving it to him to find the way.

MOUNT McKINLEY FROM THE SOUTHEAST

By Samuel C. Silverstein
(Summit section by Boyd N. Everett, Jr.)

We sat in the open door of the aeroplane hangar watching rain fall for the fifth consecutive day. Our food and mountaineering equipment lay a few feet away, neatly piled and ready to be loaded into Don Sheldon's light plane. Boredom was the order of the hour as we waited, frustrated by our helplessness before the grey, moisture-laden clouds which scudded in continually from the Gulf of Alaska, 100 miles to the south. The place—Talkeetna, Alaska—two general stores, an ancient hotel, and an airstrip perched on the banks of the Susitna River. Fifty miles to the north, hidden by clouds and locked in storm, stood the summit of North America, 20,320-foot Mt McKinley. We had come 5,000 miles to attempt its unclimbed southeast spur and we waited impatiently for the weather to clear so that we could begin.

Our bush pilot, Don Sheldon, came into the hangar to commiserate with us about the weather. He told us it was a "waitin' country", and strolled out—leaving us waiting!

There were six of us in the hangar that afternoon in early June. Boyd Everett, leader of the expedition, is a twenty-eight-year-old stock analyst, a Wall Street business-man, and an eternal iconoclast, who the year before had led the third ascent of Mt Logan's east ridge. He had conceived and organized the McKinley expedition during the winter months in New York and was largely responsible for our presence in Talkeetna—at that moment a dubious recommendation.

Next to Boyd sat "cheerful" Charley Hollister, the expedition's constant source of stability. Charley, a doctoral candidate at Columbia University, was the only married member of the group. He accepted the miserable weather philosophically, no doubt due to his training as a husband and father. His previous mountaineering experience included climbs in the Alps and the Cascade Range of the Pacific northwest, as well as leading a mountain rescue group in Oregon. His wife, Jalien, had become a member of the expedition *in absentia*. She had laboured many hours over our food lists and had baked the two dozen loaves of a hard, dark bread (Logan bread) which we enjoyed throughout the trip.

Meandering around the hangar, fuming angrily at the storm clouds as though they were a personal affront to his presence, was Chris Wren, writer, story-teller and troubador. His humour sustained us through many hours of storm, and his hunger

149

nearly ate us off the mountain. Through Chris we had arranged to photograph the climb for *Look* magazine.

Sam Cochrane, a telephone repairman, was the silent member of the group. His warm smile and easy-going manner gained him many friends at the Talkeetna inn, and he was a constant source of news about local people. Sam had climbed in Wales, the Alps and South America.

Last to join our expedition and the youngest member of the group was Hank Abrons, a senior at Harvard College and a superb rock and ice climber. Unknown to most of us before we reached Talkeetna, he quickly became an integral part of our expedition. Quiet, competent, and confident, his enthusiasm was infectious and we grew to appreciate his kindness and strength as the expedition progressed.

I had just completed my third year at the Albert Einstein Medical College and served as the expedition's medical officer, a job which happily required no more than passing an occasional aspirin across the tent.

Despite the bad weather I was excited by Alaska, for it is as much a part of the American legend as the wild west. Alaska is still a frontier and I enjoyed the excitement of being a part of it, if only for a short time. But even the excitement of the frontier begins to pall after five days of rain and inactivity; we were all very anxious to be on our way. Each day it became more difficult to keep ourselves occupied. The only sure entertainment was the noon train going north and the 5 p.m. train heading south. Chris enlivened these arrivals by racing wildly toward the railway tracks shouting, "Has my mail order bride come yet?" We were never certain whether we or the bemused passengers enjoyed this act more; but we took part in it daily, consoling Chris as the train left, assuring him that she would surely be on the next train, and that his patience would be rewarded.

Then, on the afternoon of June 6th, the clouds lifted and the peak cleared, allowing Sheldon to fly Boyd into the Ruth Glacier. However, the flat late afternoon light prevented Sheldon from landing near our proposed base camp at 7,700 feet, close to the foot of the southeast spur. Instead, he left Boyd five miles lower, in the great amphitheatre of the Ruth Glacier. Sam Cochrane and Charley followed on the next flight, joining Boyd on the névé just north of Mt Dickey.

Sheldon returned to Talkeetna too late for another flight into the glacier. That night it snowed in the Ruth Amphitheatre and rained in Talkeetna. Not until two days later did the weather again clear enough for another flight. Our division into two groups seemed strange after the seven-day wait at the airfield. We were now strung out across the Alaskan countryside, just beginning to realize how totally dependent we all were on Don Sheldon and his little aeroplanes.

The weather broke again on June 8th and Sheldon flew the rest of us into the Ruth Glacier. The flight was an adventure in itself.

It is only fifty miles from Talkeetna to the amphitheatre of the Ruth Glacier. Yet they bridge the gap between civilization, with all its conveniences, and the barrenness and sterility of the Alaska Range. From the lush, well-watered plain of the Susitna River to the amphitheatre of the Ruth Glacier took three-quarters of an hour in Sheldon's ski-equipped Cessna lightplane, spanning in that time a distance which Belmore Browne in his epic attempt on Mt McKinley in 1910 required thirty-eight days to traverse.

The rise seems gradual as one approaches the mountain. Below are the forests and many small lakes and ponds. Then the snout of the glacier comes into view and abruptly the forest ends, as though besieged by the debris and chaos at the glacial terminus, it has drawn a line of fortification beyond which no trees dare venture. Beyond lies the Great Gorge of the Ruth Glacier. Ever since I had first read of this gorge I had wanted to visit it. Now I was flying through it. On either side of the mile-wide glacial canyon rose vertical rock walls culminating in the summits of the Moose's Tooth, Mts Dickey and Barrille. This gorge is the only outlet of the entire Ruth Glacier. It is through this narrow gap in the containing walls that the glacier slowly pours, like honey out of an enormous barrel. Some ninety square miles of glacier moves steadily toward the "Gateway" and then, as though propelled by a giant hand, smashes through the southern barrier of the McKinley range, piercing five miles of solid granite until it bursts into the fan-like glacier snout. As we flew up the canyon new peaks appeared to the north, and beneath the plane the broken, tumbling glacier crept eternally southward toward the plains. As we rounded the corner of Mt Barrille and circled toward the little yellow tent on the nevé we saw the message our friends had stamped in the snow—"2 INCHES NEW SNOW—OK TO LAND".

In a few minutes I was on the glacier. An hour later Chris and Hank arrived and the expedition was reunited once again. Next there was the problem of transporting our nearly 1,000 pounds of gear to the base of the southeast spur, eight miles further up the glacier. We expected Sheldon to return in the morning with his Piper Super Cub and make every effort to ferry us to our proposed base camp. Despite clear weather, Sheldon did not appear at 4 a.m. as he had promised. As the hours passed we hurled furious epithets at the sky, hoping at the end of each to hear the hum of his plane coming through the Great Gorge. Finally at 2 p.m. he arrived and our carefully constructed rebukes dissolved into a chorus of cheers.

We loaded Boyd and his gear into the plane and watched hopefully as it rose from the glacier, flew around the base of Mt Dan Beard and headed toward the southeast spur. We had arranged to wait an hour and a half. If the plane did not reappear by that time we were to assume the worst and prepare to walk up the glacier to offer what assistance we could.

151

The first hour passed quickly. Then time began to drag. An hour and a quarter; still no sign of Sheldon. An hour and a half—the skies were empty. Then, from around the corner of Dan Beard the hum of the Super Cub echoed across the glacier. Sheldon had found a landing spot after a long search. The spot was far from ideal, but we were lucky that he had been able to land at all. One at a time we climbed into the yellow and red plane, piled our duffel on our laps, closed the hatch door, and

1. *Mt McKinley. (Route from the Southeast.)*

roared down the glacier into the air. Fifteen minutes later we settled onto the glacier once again but now 2,000 feet higher than our take-off point. Sheldon flew eight times from the 5,700 foot depot to our base camp at 7,700 feet; twice with only supplies in the rear seat for company. On the last three trips he had to land without shock absorbers, having damaged them on the glacier landing strip.

By 5 p.m., June 9th, we were reassembled at base camp. A mile across the glacier rose the first bump on the southeast spur. It was our first view of the ridge. We were impressed.

The perpetual twilight of an Alaskan summer evening set in and the snow grew firm in the sunless air. The roar of daytime avalanches had been stilled and we became aware of the silence of the place for the first time. For the next fifteen days we would be climbing at night and sleeping during the day so that we might take advantage of the hard snow and diminished avalanche danger of the evening hours. Later this schedule would seem only natural, but at that moment it seemed strange.

The ridge, which looked so impressively steep during the daylight hours, now seemed a blank wall, an almost overhanging tower in the shadowless dim of evening. Sam Cochrane, Charley and I set off across the glacier at 9.30 p.m. carrying supplies to the foot of the ridge. Half a foot of new snow slowed our progress and obscured the glacial landmarks. Three hours after leaving base camp we began ascending the lower slopes of the Southeast Spur itself. We climbed a few hundred feet to a wide *bergschrund* and there cached our loads. Sam crossed the *'schrund* on a snowbridge and assured us that the route ahead seemed open. Then, tired by our first day on the mountain, we turned towards camp and in a few hours were lying on top of our sleeping bags in the heat of the arctic sun.

The following evening Boyd broke trail through the knee-deep snow for over four hours, until we reached the site of Camp I on the shoulder of the ridge at 9,200 feet. Later that night we carried another load to Camp I and at 5 a.m. completed our second trip. Boyd and Sam Cochrane remained at the ridge camp hoping to break trail on the following evening to a vertical ice wall which we called the "Arrow". Exhausted, the rest of us returned to base camp happy that we had established Camp I. We reached the glacier at 6 a.m. and staggered across a mile of breakable crust like a weaving line of drunks. Too tired to cook, we ate a bit of cold food, crawled into the tent and passed into happy oblivion. It was early evening when we awoke. Clouds had come in from the southwest and light snow was falling. Hank looked at his watch and said "It's 5 o'clock—5 a.m. or 5 p.m.?" We laughed; we had been tired but not that tired.

We broke camp and turned toward the ridge. New snow covered the steps but Boyd had kicked them so evenly on the preceding day that there was no difficulty following them. Five and a half hours later we reached Camp I where we were warmly entertained and gastronomically delighted by Sam and Boyd. It had snowed heavily since early afternoon and a white-out had prevented further progress. For the next three days we sat in the tents watching soggy snow melting on the walls and listening to the steady drip of water onto our sleeping bags. Reading material was in great demand and our small library of paperbacks circulated rapidly. Soon everyone had finished the collections of short stories while the longer novels were still being read. In order to assure universal enjoyment of our dwindling library we tore two of the novels into halves and then into quarters. Thus I completed the middle of *Gone with the Wind* before I set eyes upon its introductory paragraphs.

On our third morning of forced immobilization the wind picked up. Soon it was screaming straight down the ridge and I awoke to the horrible flapping of the tent. The cloth popped and groaned in violent agony. We lowered the pole a foot or so and I sat in my sleeping bag steadying the tent pole with one hand and reading, appropriately enough, *Gone with the Wind*. Suddenly the tent shredded and we were sitting outside in the storm. We scrambled into the adjoining tent and lowered its pole to prevent further damage. Then we dug an emergency snow cave.

Above Camp I the slope curved upward in an ever steepening arc, culminating at about 10,400 feet in the "Arrow", a 70° slope of polished blue ice, overhung along its entire length by a five to twenty-foot cornice. We called it the Arrow because it formed a corner on the ridge, a sharp clean line beckoning upward.

The evening after the tent blew down Sam Cochrane and Boyd set out for the Arrow armed with hardware and fixed rope. The rest followed with supplies. Our route went upward over a 45° snow slope and then traversed beneath an ice wall on the lower lip of a crevasse. Sam and Boyd turned these barriers on the north, but not before Sam dropped waist deep through an unstable snow-bridge. They continued to the base of the Arrow and looked, without success, for a route. Meanwhile, Chris, Hank, Charley and I ferried loads to be cached at the lower lip of the crevasse. Our thought in not continuing to the base of the Arrow was tempered more, perhaps, by our fears of going through the unstable snow-bridge than by logic. Had we joined the others we might have helped them find a route over the Arrow. That the best route should have escaped their ken is in retrospect easily understandable. By the time they reached the base of the Arrow they had climbed a 45° snow slope with 2,500 feet of exposure beneath their feet, fallen halfway through a snowbridge, continued up another 45° wind-slab snow-face, which shook as if about to avalanche, and ended confronted by a 70° wall of blue ice. Surely our cheerful faces and a bit of moral support might have been comforting, even perhaps helpful.

The shadows shortened and the amber morning sunlight crowned the face of the unclimbed Moose's Tooth, ten miles to the east. The slope above us turned the colour of ripe wheat and we were bathed in the warmth of a cloudless morning. We waited at the cache for Sam and Boyd and together descended to Camp I. They had found a way to the Arrow, which they reported to be 150 feet high. We thought that after these 150 feet of hard climbing the greatest difficulties would be passed. As if offering us premonition the sky clouded over and the wind rose. Lightning and thunder followed and Charley's mountain tent flapped as though ready to fly away. We slept fitfully, awakening to the tremendous din outside and wondering how much more punishment the tents could withstand. Another torn tent could end our expedition. In the Logan tent we took down the pole to prevent disaster. Only Hank slept uninterrupted in the quiet of the snow cave.

In the evening the storm subsided. We broke camp and climbed to the base of the

Arrow. Hank located a route over the Arrow and he and Sam Cochrane set out to chop their way up it. Their task was not a simple one since the 70° ice slope was overhung by a five-foot cornice. While the rest of us relayed the remaining supplies to the foot of their operations Sam and Hank cut their way up the Arrow. By 3 a.m. a neat set of "buckets" led up the ice-wall, which was gaily decorated with pitons, karabiners, and fixed rope, to a window in the cornice. Hank led to within ten feet of the cornice where Sam took over the lead. We cheered as Sam tunnelled through the cornice and waited anxiously for news from the other side. The news was unexpected: the slope above dropped steeply into a glacier basin to the south and the southern exposure made the snow soft and rotten. After sunrise the snow became too unstable for climbing, so we dug a tent platform at the foot of the Arrow. Above us stood a wall of ice, broken into many enormous blocks and capped by cornices. The sky was clear and the warm sun lulled us into a sense of security. I wrote in my log, "Camping here goes against all tenets of mountaineering", and went to sleep, hoping that I would not be awakened by the crash of falling ice. Although we did not realize it then, the crux of our route lay immediately above us; it was to the solution of this problem that we devoted the next three days.

The following evening Boyd, Charley and I carried loads over the Arrow and began the ascent of the snow and ice slopes beyond. Boyd led over a crevasse which ran vertically down the "fall-line", and then climbed a steep pitch to gain the edge of the ridge. Following what he felt to be a safe distance below the cornice he slowly kicked steps in the rotten surface while Charley belayed him. Astonished, we heard a muffled cracking and the whole slope shuddered. A section of ridge had disappeared, leaving a gaping hole where a moment before there had been a cornice. Boyd's footsteps traversed within two feet of the fracture line.

After this incident Boyd continued another rope length and brought Charley and me to where he stood. There we cached the supplies in our packs and fixed a line down to where the others waited.

For the next two nights Sam Cochrane and Hank worked with Boyd on the concave snow slope above us. Hank chopped his way up twenty feet of steep ice and Boyd led to a catwalk beneath an ice-wall capping the ridge. From the edge of the wall icicles hung into space, forming a delicate transparent curtain; below, the snow slope plunged in a great arc to the glacier. Boyd, belayed by Sam from the "pulpit" (a seat on the catwalk, so named because it seemingly looked out over all creation), followed the catwalk until it disappeared. He then descended fifteen feet on the snow-face and dug a narrow ramp which slanted upward for fifty feet to join the ridge. Boyd encountered a forty-foot stretch of 55° honeycombed ice. After two more hours of hard climbing he gained the firm snow slope above, where he placed a rappel stake and anchored the fixed rope.

At 4 a.m. on June 18th we were all near the top of the first bump. Charley and I set up Camp III on a protected terrace on the north side of the ridge while the others descended for a second load. After depositing our loads Charley and I walked along the rolling slopes of the upper ridge, and in an hour's time reached the "Fluting", our next obstacle. The Fluting is a narrow corniced portion of the ridge, eroded by the glaciers on both sides until there remains only a series of rock towers, topped by great toadstools of snow, corniced to the north, and sloping precipitously to the south. At the far end of the cornices rose a thirty-foot snow-wall, buttressed by a snow formation resembling a lobster claw. Despite the formidable appearance of this new barrier we were excited as we returned to camp. One more difficulty and then clear sailing to the South Buttress.

On June 19th we packed to the Fluting where we set up Camp IV. From here Sam Cochrane and Hank attempted unsuccessfully to cross the Fluting. The following afternoon Hank and I set out to force a route across the face below. Using Hank's steps of the previous day we descended 200 feet on the north side of the ridge and followed the overhanging *bergschrund* to a fifteen-foot wall, where we crossed to the upper lip. We worked our way up the 50° fluted snow face for some 350 feet until we reached a small crevasse directly beneath the cornices. We then traversed three rotten snow gullies to a firm snow rib, which led upward to a platform on the other side of the Fluting. From here we spotted Sam and Boyd steadily working their way across the cornice tops. We told them that our route would "go" and began descending, placing fixed rope as we returned. We all carried one load to the far side of the Fluting early in the morning. Chris and Charley remained to explore the route beyond. By the time the rest of us returned to Camp IV it was snowing lightly. A foot and a half of snow fell on June 21st and we were unable to rejoin Chris and Charley until the 22nd. Meanwhile, they had broken trail to just below the site of our future Camp V.

As we climbed upwards the weather seemed to break. At sunrise blue clouds churned in the valleys and low clouds, red in the rising sunlight, boiled over the eastern buttress like flames from an enormous cauldron. We ferried the rest of the equipment to a new campsite (V) among the seracs of the ridge while Boyd and Hank placed fixed rope over a 100-foot ice pitch just beyond. From our camp we looked out over the southeast part of the Alaska Range. We enjoyed the view for almost two hours before the morning heat brought clouds out of the valleys and it began to snow. In the next eighteen hours one and one half feet of light powder snow fell, covering everything in an even white blanket.

On June 24th, in a complete white-out, Boyd and I broke trail to the top of the 13,100-foot bump and placed Camp VI on the far side of the bump in the lee of a crevasse wall. The others followed and in two relays we moved our supplies through deep snow to Camp VI.

June 25th and 26th were the most discouraging days of the expedition. In the wind and blowing snow we waded through hip-deep drifts along a technically easy ridge. The snow filled in the trail almost as soon as it was broken and each relay meant breaking trail again. As I hiked through the drifting snow a stanza from Robert Service's poem "The Cremation of Sam McGee" continually ran through my mind.

> "Now Sam McGee was from Tennessee, where the cotton
>   blooms and blows.
>   Why he left his home in the South to roam, 'round
>   the pole God only knows".

By the evening of the 26th we were at Camp VIII at 14,000 feet. The weather cleared completely and we were confident of good weather for a summit attempt. But in the morning we were in the clouds with snow falling. A decision was now at hand. Fuel, food and time were running short. We elected to carry loads for Sam Cochrane and Boyd to the South Buttress at 15,600 feet and leave them as an assault party. The rest of us would follow in support. At 7 p.m. on June 27th we were laughing and celebrating on top of the South Buttress. Leaving Boyd and Sam we wished them good luck, and gave them a small vial with a few grams of earth from New York's Central Park to place at the summit.

In the deepening twilight we descended to Camp VIII. Three hundred feet above camp Hank, who was last on the rope, fell on a steep, snow-covered ice patch, pulling Chris with him. They tumbled and slid for over 100 feet before Charley jammed his ice axe into the slope and stopped them. Chris regained his footing and his composure almost immediately and shouted up to Charley: "Tell me, pretty maid, are there any more at home like you?"

The weather cleared on the 28th and Boyd and Sam advanced to 17,100 feet on the southeast face, where they placed Camp X. The rest of us returned to the South Buttress and the following day continued to the 17,100-foot level. As we climbed on the 29th we could see Sam and Boyd moving steadily upwards and out of sight, disappearing onto the summit plateau at 18,900 feet.

Boyd Everett describes the summit climb below:

"We left Camp X at 7.30 a.m. The weather was clear and warm. Sam and I had expected some difficult rock climbing between 17,000 and 18,300 feet, but the face proved to be broken and easy to climb. By 2.30 p.m. we climbed over the rim of the south face and onto the summit plateau at 18,900 feet. The summit was only a mile away, but what a mile it was to be. A powerful north wind blew directly into our faces as soon as we left the protection of the south face and we were forced to don down jackets and face masks.

157

"For half a mile we followed the rim of the plateau towards Carter Horn, a false eastern summit. As we traversed Carter Horn we turned directly into the wind. Although the slope was not steep, no more than 30°, the hard wind-packed snow and patches of blue ice made travel extremely arduous. Occasionally, when the gusts were particularly powerful, we were forced to crawl with our ice-axes in self-arrest position.

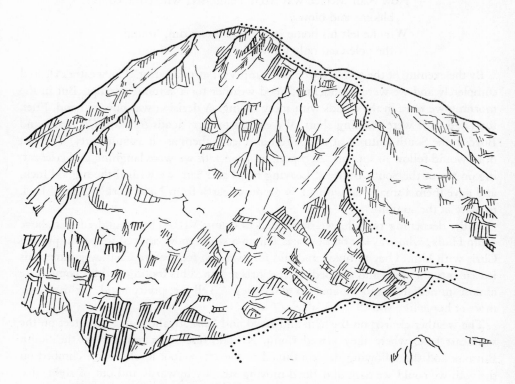

2. *Mt McKinley.* (*Route from the Southeast; upper section.*)

For five hours we battled sixty-mile-an-hour gusts. Then, 300 feet below the summit, a new dilemma presented itself. The blowing snow and failing light made it difficult to see each other; the shadowless shape of the summit became impossible to determine. There were no ridges to follow and no further false summits. In theory we could just wander uphill. But in unknown territory and in a virtual white-out this was particularly unnerving.

"At 7.20 p.m. we came to a pole, and then a few paces further a banner bearing the

158

emblem of the Seattle World's Fair proclaimed the summit. The wind deadened all feeling except that of exhaustion. We did not bother to shake hands. We took three photographs and immediately started down. The wind at our backs acted as a direction indicator and we had no difficulty relocating our route of ascent.

"When we dropped over the rim of the plateau we were able to rest for the first time in seven hours. We were shaking physically from exhaustion. We ate a little food and gulped down some dexedrine tablets. Then, because of our weakened condition, we belayed end-over-end on the steeper sections. At 18,600 feet Sam slipped and fell over 200 feet before my belay stopped him.

"At 1.30 a.m., after an eighteen-hour day, we rejoined the others at Camp X."

In the morning clouds again banked against the south face and a second summit attempt was precluded by our shortage of fuel and supplies. Reluctantly we broke camp and returned in windy but clearing weather to Camp VIII at 14,000 feet. That night a violent windstorm drifted snow against the tents and we were forced to dig them out continually. By the afternoon of July 1st the weather had settled and cleared. The wind-packed slopes made travel easy and by 8 p.m. we had returned to the campsite above the Fluting. We replaced the fixed ropes and on the following evening packed to the first bump where Sam and Boyd cleared the route down the honeycombed ice corner. Across the catwalk, down the rotten snow of the corniced basin, through the window in the cornice, and down the Arrow. The last of the technical difficulties were over. We waded down the soft snow of the lower slopes and gathered the few things we cached at Camp I. Then we continued to the *bergschrund*, anxious to retrieve the "blue box".

The "blue box" is a phenomenon of our expedition which has not yet been mentioned but is certainly deserving of explanation. When we left the 8,200-foot *bergschrund* on the ascent there was one food box, painted blue, which we could not carry. As we got higher on the mountain appetites increased, especially for certain items. Hence, when someone complained about the lack of meat we would reply, "Oh, it's in the blue box". Jam, cereal, cookies, and chocolate were also "remembered" to be in the blue box. Fittingly, the blue box became known as Pandora's Box and we were all anxious to retrieve it for the vast gastronomic delights which its contents would provide. Lucullus could have conjectured no more elaborate feast than that which we imagined to be present in the blue box. But when we reached the *bergschrund* we found that the bridge on which Pandora's Box rested had broken on two sides. The box stood out clearly in the snow, sitting like a frog on a lily pad, surrounded on all sides by seven feet of clear Alaskan air. Pandora's Box it was and Pandora's Box it will forever remain.

We glissaded to the glacier floor and soon were feasting and celebrating at base camp. On July 3rd we snowshoed to the amphitheatre of the Ruth Glacier where we met our bush pilot on July 4th.

We flew down the Great Gorge and out over the plains of Alaska. I was glad to see green trees, brown earth and running water once again. The sun set behind the white bulk of McKinley, covering the peak in a yellow mantle. I reflected momentarily on the enormity of our experience. The expedition was over; but, for me, the warmth of our shared adventure and the friendships it cemented were just beginning.

39 MOUNT McKINLEY (20,318 ft.). The Southeast Face and, in front of it, the Southeast Spur. (Aerial photograph by Bradford Washburn)

40 HANK ABRONS on the ice slope below the "Arrow". (Photo by Silverstein)

THE STAUNING ALPS
OF EASTERN GREENLAND

By Malcolm Slesser

EDITORIAL INTRODUCTION

In the 1953 issue of *The Mountain World* Peter Braun wrote about the first major ascents in the Staunings on the east coast of Greenland. The inauguration of mountaineering in this unique arctic climbing region began with the work of the Danish East Greenland Expeditions of 1950, 1951 and 1954, under the leadership of Dr Lauge Koch.

In the summer of 1950, the Swiss, G. Styger, who was one of a geological team in the region of the Werner Bjaerge, crossed the Skeldal from the west and made a solo ascent of an unnamed peak to the south of the Berserkerbrae. At the end of August 1950 the two Swiss, Braun and Fritz Schwarzenbach, started from the Alpefjord, reconnoitred the Vikingebrae, and in unfavourable weather conditions climbed a peak of about 6,230 feet, which the named "Käthi-Spids".

In the summer of 1951 the Basel geologist, Erdhart Fraenkl, worked on sedimentary deposits in the northern Stauning Alps and in the range of the Syltoppene, which stretches in front of them to the east. During its investigations, this team inspected all the larger glaciers from the Vikingebrae to the Berserkerbrae, establishing fixed camps along the coast by motorboat. In order to cover the extensive area dominated by the Skjoldungebrae, the team set up intermediate camps on the glacier. On August 2, 1951, two of Fraenkl's companions, Braun and Schwarzenbach, climbed from a cirque on the Skjoldungebrae to the summit of the Frihedstinde (8,560 feet). A few days later, after an unsuccessful attempt on the "Pyramid" (Hjörnespids), the two climbers ascended the Elisabethsminde (7,413 feet). Later there followed the ascent of the Birhids Bjaerge (5,937 feet) in the range of the Syltoppene.

That same summer the Elisabethsminde was climbed a second time, by another route, by the Norwegian climbers, Arne Rander Heen, Friis-Bastad and Ø. Røed. As luck would have it, the Norwegian climbing group had left its camp at Cape Petersen a few hours before the arrival of the geological team and could not be informed of the already successful ascent. Apart from the Elisabethsminde, Heen's group climbed two further peaks in the region of the Skjoldungebrae.

The summer of 1954 saw the first mountaineering advances into the Staunings from the Alpefjord. In addition came the first reconnaissances in the region of the Sefstrøm's Glacier.

A climbing party composed of the two Norwegians, A. R. Heen and Ø. Røed, as well as two Danes, E. Jensen and E. Hoff, set up their base camp to the north of the mouth of the Vikingebrae. On August 7th the three members of this party started from a high camp and

M

climbed the third-highest mountain in the Staunings (Norske Tinde, about 9,315 feet, also called Erik Rødes Tinde).

During the same summer a geological party from Dr Koch's Danish East Greenland Expedition covered the crystalline regions of the Staunings. The leader of the party was the Swiss mineralogist and petrographer, John Haller. His two assistants were Wolfgang Diehl and Schwarzenbach. After a long reconnaissance and cartographic flight across the Stauning Alps, this party of three set up a camp on the Alpefjord to the south of Dammen. They explored the Gully Glacier throughout its length, crossing Sefstrøm's Glacier at a height of about 1,500 feet above the great ice-fall. The lowermost ice-fall of the Gully Glacier was circumvented on the south over wintry snow. The further approach and circumvention of the upper ice-falls succeeded on the northern side of the valley. On August 5, 1954, the party of three started from the northern cirque of the Gully Glacier and climbed the Danske Tinde which, at 9,610 feet, forms the highest summit of the Staunings.

After their return from the region of the Gully Glacier, the party resumed its scientific projects in the Sefstrøm's Glacier region. The entire length of the glacier was ascended on skis. Unfavourable weather conditions hindered further ascents.

In pursuance of the geological investigations in the region of the Vikingebrae, Diehl and Schwarzenbach repeated the climb of the Norske Tinde by the same route as those who first climbed it.

In the same summer of 1957, an Austrian party led by Hans Gsellman flew directly into Dammen in a flying boat, thereby establishing themselves much earlier than previous expeditions, for at this time the outer fjords are still unnavigable. In addition to climbing the angular "Eckhorn" at the snout of the Sporregletscher, the party made a sortie to the head of the bleak Fureso and showed that a route existed up the Violin Glacier onto the inland ice.

Their main activities were centred round the head of the Sefstrøm Glacier, now explored for the first time. They made many noteworthy ascents from the upper basin of the glacier, where they made profitable use of skis. The party failed to make their intended exit to Mestersvig through the Gully Glacier, and finally Gsellman canoed round the dangerous coast of Alpefjord, and gained the help of Knud Lauritzen of the Lauritzen shipping line, then holidaying in that area.

THE 1958 EXPEDITION

Reflecting upon a more recent venture, a much-travelled member of the 1958 Scottish East Greenland expedition commented nostalgically that, while entirely harmonious, it had lacked the colour of the 1958 affair. He referred, of course, to the participants, but it was true too of the mountains. We were lucky that amongst our nine widely assorted personalities, no single one dominated, none were submerged. We felt at ease in a country whose wide vistas of mountain and water so closely resembled homeland conditions in bright winter weather.

Out of darkness into light, our chartered plane flew northwards from rain-washed Reykjavik into sun to a 2 a.m. landing at the air strip at Mestersvig, latitude 72°N. In the crisp invigorating air there was that indefinable tang of the "Arctic", which old hands relish so much. There were few to meet us, for a mountaineering expedition is not an attractive liability to the inhabitants of this remote station. We disembowelled the aeroplane onto two enormous lorries and climbed the 700 feet to the lead mining camp, seven miles inland. Perhaps a Celtic quality of romance made us reject the noisy, comfortable civilization of the mine settlement in favour of a camp on the greensward of the Tunnel river, but our Austrian driver could only be persuaded of the point when Smart, in dynamic German, explained that it was the "Fuehrer's wish!"

The expedition had set out with three objectives in addition to its scientific aims; to further the exploration of the fine peaks at the head of Alpefjord, so energetically started by the Austrians, explore the mountains of the south, and make a crossing of the range. To carry out the first two, we must await the fjord ice breaking up, then sail round the coast some seventy miles. The last aim could be conveniently studied from the east, and accordingly we headed for the Bersaerker glacier. This valley was quite untouched, and seemed from aerial pictures to offer great interest and a highway to the core of the Staunings. Judging from the pictures, both Erik Hoff of Copenhagen and ourselves felt that a possible pass lay just to the southeast of the highest peaks.

On the day of arrival (July 10th), Bennet, Paterson, Rose and Bryan departed to seek a route. The Gefion Pass led easily to the Skel Valley, with a mighty river which no less a person than the famous Dr Lauge Koch had declared to be impassable. But they found a point where sandbanks split the river, and in the small hours of the night found that the torrent had subsided enough to let them pass over. To the end of the expedition, however, some members preferred the safer, if tedious route via the Skel Glacier snout.

The sun shone ceaselessly from cloudless skies for ten days. There was no wind. Even at night the freezing line was over 6,000 feet. The party wallowed in deep *gletschersumpf*, to a 5,000-foot pass via the Kishmul Glacier, marvelled at the wonderful peaks, descended into the Bersaerker, and walked back, reporting the main glacier to be gentle, almost crevasse free, but ridden with surface torrents.

By July 14th we were established on the Skel, waging war against the mosquitoes and wearying from lack of sleep, for the ever-shining sun made our tents intolerably hot—yet an essential refuge from the mosquitoes.

Bennet and Bryan, equipped with the expedition's only pairs of skis, squelched their way up the water-logged Skel Glacier and climbed a fine peak of some 6,500 feet, only to find that a Swiss, Steiger, from a survey party, had been there many years before. Indeed, this was one of our problems . . . to know what had been climbed, and to sort out the nomenclature. We had been able to obtain only the sketchiest of maps, and had failed in our efforts to contact the Austrians, though of that party, Erik Hoff, President of the Danish Mountaineering Club, had been most helpful. Many peaks (for example Norske Tinde) had two or more names. We worked with excellent Danish aerial survey photos, and temporarily christened the nameless glaciers with numbers. We were much concerned to provide a system of naming at once dignified and related, yet applicable to every nationality, so that English, Danish and German equivalents would not proliferate. We chose, I think aptly, castles, and all the names given here have been approved by the Greenland authorities.

The peripheral peaks of the Staunings, though handsome in aspect, are composed of shattered rock. At a second attempt, Bryan, Rose and Paterson scaled the tottering gendarmes of Dunvegan Toppene, the expedition's first virgin summit, and had their first exciting glimpse seawards to the immense stretches of the coastal pack ice, inland to the still frozen fjords, and near at hand the bewildering array of appealing summits towards Alpefjord.

Meanwhile, using a higher camp, Smart, Lovat, Cameron, Scott and I penetrated to the head of a fine glacier now named Kishmul, and in the still hours of the arctic summer night scaled the head wall to a col at about 6,000 feet. We had taken eight hours to get there, and it was becoming plain that the stark clear light of this latitude made the scale deceptive. The climbs were a good deal longer than they seemed. We abandoned our goal of climbing Kishmulborg, for we had come unprepared for climbing a strenuous 1,500 feet of blue ice, and the peak remains unclimbed. Instead, we climbed to the west of the col, by an arête of rock so friable, that one gendarme was almost entirely demolished in the process of searching for sound rock holds. This peak, Glamis Borg, presents a noble prospect from the west, not unlike the Weisshorn.

The long glacier approaches were not to everybody's taste, and I do not think Lovat was too disappointed when it fell to him to join Scott in some ornithological work on the lower Skel. They counted twenty-two species and found verdant terrain alive with spring flowers. We separated on the 19th, and by that evening had founded Camp II well up the Bersaerker on the only dry, snow-free place to be seen; a moraine. Above us on a gentle hillside a stream irrigated numerous plant beds, specifically, Hyeracium. It was a superb site. At 2,500 feet it was cooler, enjoyed about six hours shade each evening, and was quite windless and mosquito free. We lived happily in a state of permanent *deshabille*. Facing us were the ice-girt slopes of Kishmulborg and the vast unclimbed face of the Bersaerker Tinde.

All glacier courses were now covered at night. At midnight on the 20th, four men embarked up the Dunnottar Glacier running west from the camp, at whose head lay the Elizabeth Minde, climbed by the Norwegians from the west (Skoldunge) side.

164

Bennet and Smart made a rapid ascent of a fine top of 8,000 feet, named Dunnottar Bjerg, while Cameron and I, across the upper bay of the glacier, enjoyed ourselves in the early morning sun as it beat upon the coarse red granite of the east wall of Achnacarry, the 1,500 feet of slabs and cracks of which were so redolent of a smaller Chamonix aiguille.

These mountain days were of twenty to twenty-four hours. Much could have been saved had we skis for every man, but our plane had only been able to carry a total load of 3,700 pounds, and weight had been something of a problem in an expedition due to last two or more months. On the 22nd, with skis, Bennet and Bryan penetrated to the head of the Bersaerker. Clouds and a light snow-fall lent the mountains a tremendous aura of impossibility. They reported impressive peaks, particularly one resembling the Grande Jorasses, with a northwest face of 5,000 feet. The glacier terminated in a steep sweep of blue ice, about 1,500 feet. It was bounded on the right by a steep buttress, which they forced to reach a col. Now in heavy cloud, they were unable to tell what the prospects were down the far side, or even if it led towards the Gully Glacier and Alpefjord, as we hoped. In their view, the route was too hard for laden men, and we abandoned our attempt at getting a party across the range till the autumn, when conditions would be firmer.

By July 23rd the fjord ice had broken up considerably, and the first boat from Europe had arrived, bearing with it stores and a dinghy for us, lent generously by Knud Lauritzen of the famous Danish shipping line. I had expected to be able to put about a ton of stores and two men into the boat on each journey, and had calculated movements on this basis. Next to the rivers, probably the greatest hazard in these parts are the fjords, subject to fickle katabatic winds which can create quite local storm conditions. A knowledge of sea and boats is vital. We were just plain ignorant. Thus it was that single-mindedly I had the boat loaded with a ton of equipment, Cameron as engineer, Lovat as co-pilot and Scott as observer, and in Lovat's own words, "cast them loose upon the fjord". To do myself justice, Smart and I did sing a farewell hymn, "For those in peril on the sea", as they puttered out of Mestersvig Bay. Alas, we ignored the fact that the freeboard was a mere eight inches, and the crew landlubbers. The boat had a name—appropriately as it turned out—*Tippa Dan*.

Those still in the mountains had two more good climbs, the 8,500 feet Merchiston Bjarege, and the elegant spire of the Lennox Spids. They found Smart and I swanning it at our seaside camp, ostensibly engaged in histological studies of the lemming. Here, Greenland was at her most beautiful, and we revelled in the lingering light of evening and night, the still fjord, and the curved sandy beach, backed by the snow-capped Syl-toppene.

We were, as Smart put it, on the point of rifling their kit, having given them up for lost, when five days later, on the 30th, our worthy crew returned. They had a harrowing tale to tell, were gifted story-tellers, and had rehearsed well. They deserved and expected sympathy. "Farm hands!" we unkindly iterated as they related how within an hour of departure a short choppy sea had caused them to make swiftly for the shore, shipping water at every wave, of how they had abandoned half their pay-load, of icebergs, of high seas in the inner fjord, and of the final dramatic journey through the ice canal, a narrow water-way between the 100-foot high terminal ice cliffs of the Sefstrom and Gully Glacier snouts, leading into the inner sanctuary of Dammen, seeming to them like the eighth wonder of the world.

By the end of another week, August 7th, we were established at Dammen. Bennet and Paterson went first, to get on with the glaciological study of the Sefstrom Glacier. Small boating is so precarious, and timing so much at the whim of local winds, that we decided not to use the boat to carry men. The party walked along the fjord edge, and only at one or two places was the boat used to ferry them past difficult places.

This experience will be remembered by all of us as one of the most pleasurable, for it is the fjord coastline that gives Greenland its character. Alpefjord has lush banks, alive with flowers, almost verdant, and with musk ox occasionally lending a primaeval air to the scene. Into the fjord ran numerous glacier valleys, with the ice never far from the fjord edge. There were flocks of geese, pink-footed and barnacle, a multitude of terns, the less frequent snow-white glaucous gulls and the occasional close groups of eider duck.

Base camp was set up by the fjord edge, 200 feet below the vegetation line, which due to the comparatively recent fall in the level of the Dammen, lay well up the hill-side. Here, surrounded only by the occasional brilliant pink of arctic willow herb, we camped in that homely squalor which has long distinguished the British, and especially the Scottish, climber from his continental counterpart.

At an early stage we decided not to press the exploration of the south Staunings. The only line of weakness to the south, the Sporre Glacier, was reconnoitred and pronounced as too difficult for rapid movement and heavy carrying, and there was a considerable body of opinion in favour of doing a little more climbing, a little less humping around of heavy loads on tediously long glaciers. Nearby was the Sefstrom with its fabulous peaks, most of them unclimbed. We placed our camp at about 3,500 feet on a belvedere overlooking the upper glacier, near last year's Austrian site, directly beneath the superb battlements of the Sefstrom Tinde, the fourth highest of the Staunings.

In a twelve-hour *tour de force*, Bryan and Lovat climbed a fine rock tower from the same col used by the Austrians in their ascent of Kapelle. It was a 1,000 feet of splendid red granite, much of it grade V. About 300 feet from the top they came across a cairn of the Austrian party but there was no sign of anyone having reached the top, so they called it Beaufort Tinde. On the same day, Rose and Cameron ascended a

3,000-foot ice couloir to reach a col between the Sefstrom Tinde and another peak. Thinking the Sefstrom Tinde had been climbed they chose the other peak, which they gained by a fine ice ridge, naming it Ruthven Spids. It is ironic that they did not climb the Sefstrom Tinde, so easily reached from here; but only later did it emerge that what the Austrians had climbed was a peak at the Sefstrom Glacier, and called it Sefstrom Gipfel (*Gipfel*—German = *Tinde*—Danish).

On the 9th Smart and I ascended a fine steep icefall behind the camp, giving exciting climbing and route finding, and gained a high glacier valley, from which a pure ice couloir led to a high col. Here, at midday, we bivouacked for four hours, then climbed a delightful snow and rock ridge to gain Tantallon Spids, 8,400 feet. Our reports of the climb so delighted others that Bennet and Rose repeated the ascent.

On the 11th an attempt was made to climb the Sefstrom Tinde by its southeast flank, a fine rock face and ridge, but with fully 5,500 feet of climbing, much of a very high standard, it had to be abandoned. It would require combined assault with high camps, for which we were not equipped. Meanwhile, Scott and I crossed the Sefstrom Glacier to tackle a high peak on the other side called Attilaborg, 8,700 feet. Steep glacier and icefall led us to a saddle at 6,000 feet, from which a west face rose steeply for a further 2,600 feet. It looked impossible, but a route across 800 feet of ice sheet, so brittle that a piton driven in merely fractured the ice in great cartwheels, which then slipped off, led us to the northwest ridge, which gave a climb about A.D., with several pitches of IV. The route led naturally to the base of the final tower, 100 feet high, which we could not ascend. Descending 300 feet, we could see a route that involved delicate cutting across the west face and then up a couloir. Scott had had no sleep for forty hours, myself for twenty-four. We were too tired to tackle it. This peak presented a supremely fine ridge when seen from the head of the Dammen, offering a magnificent rock climb, fully 6,000 feet.

Clearly the Sefstrom had much to offer. The rock was good, the peaks superb, and delightfully adjacent to base camp, involving the minimum of load carrying. Lovat and Bryan stayed here, and in the subsequent ten days climbed four fine rock peaks of about 6,000 feet.

Their first sortie was to the Krabbe Glacier, which flowed straight into the sea from an impressive cirque of cliffs. They, like succeeding parties, failed to penetrate into that beguiling climbing ground. It would appear that the peaks lying between the Sefstrom Glacier and Dammen lie on the periphery of the main granite intrusion forming the central Staunings. This adds considerably to the diversity of the climbs in the area. The abrupt change is seen in the peak of Eilan Donan as seen from Dammen, where the red gneiss changes to cream-coloured granite in its upper part.

Their climbs were all on fine clean rock, as good as found anywhere, and of con-

167

siderable length, that on Eilan Donan being 5,000 feet, and that on Inverarnan little less.

Smart and I were particularly anxious to see the entirely untrodden grounds of the South Staunings, and so on August 14th, moved by the eye of faith and an unjustified optimism, and aided by our companions, we embarked on our attempt to cross the range from west to east in a southerly direction. It may be that our decision was influenced by the fact that twenty-eight man-days of balanced rations lay dumped half a day's march in the right direction, while at base the diet had been reduced to one of flour, jam and such protein as our diffident marksmanship could pluck from the skies.

It rained dismally. On the second day we had to choose between following the main line of the Sporre Glacier, which climbed for many miles in a southeasterly direction, to terminate in a high col of unknown character on the far side, or to take the left-hand branch, named Duart, to what appeared to be less of a gamble. We played safe, and at the head of the Duart Glacier found a snow plateau over a mile in extent providing excellent landing for a light plane, at a height of 5,500 feet. All around delightful peaks stood about 2,500 to 3,000 feet higher. The main branch has since been traversed by Clarkson's 1961 party.

On the 17th, realizing that we must make better time if we were to reach our goal, we marched for twenty-one hours down the far side, the Roslin Glacier (formerly Ivar Bartsen's), reaching the lush pastures of the Schuichart Valley in the evening. There to our enormous surprise we met Scott. This wily and experienced traveller had also sought the Schuichart Valley. He had sailed back to Mestersvig, and found that the small monoplane associated with the mine would fly him to a glacier strip not far from the Roslin exit. Here he was, fresh, well-equipped with food, intent on exploring the bird life of this valley over the next twelve days. He planned to travel slowly, alone, without tent or stove, relying only on the dry willow scrub for fire. We reached the eskimo summer station on North-west Fjord in a stiff two-day walk, during a period of idyllic weather, the night frosts having killed off the mosquitoes and made outdoor life delightful. Scott, more leisurely and profitably, did the same.

On our recrossing of Roslin-Duart, we paused on August 23rd to make the ascent of Roslin Borg, rising directly north of the watershed. From this view-point it was easy to see how little of the Staunings had yet been explored, and how much interesting mountain country remained untouched. From the 8,500-foot summit we got an excellent view of a group of blunt-topped towers of about 7,000 feet lying south of the Sporre Glacier.

It is a tribute to the ideal climatic conditions here that at our highest camp, which we passed later that day, we found flimsy scraps of paper lying just where we had left them.

168

41 TUNDRA LANDSCAPE of a small island in the King Oskars Fjord, East Greenland. In the foreground, a brooding tern. Behind the withdrawing storm clouds rise the peaks of the Syltoppene, a range of between 5,000 and 6,500 feet, on the eastern side of the Stauning Alps. (Photograph by Tom Weir)

42/43 THE STAUNING ALPS of East Greenland. The two-armed Seitne Glacier shimmers in the light of a day with a Southwind. A late summer snowfall has powdered the steep ridges and flanks of the southwestern Stauning Alps. (Aerial photograph from Dr. Lauge Koch's East Greenland Expedition)

44 THE CENTRAL STAUNING ALPS, whose steep ridges are generously decorated with gendarmes, spires and obelisks. Korsspids and Danske Tinde are seen from the north. (Aerial photograph by Dr. Lauge Koch's East Greenland Expedition)

By the evening of the 24th the entire expedition, save for Scott, was reunited. Food was now becoming a problem. This, together with the increasing cold, decided our return home. One final geographical problem remained. The crossing of the main range to the Bersaerker Glacier, which Bennet, Bryan and Rose were to try. On the day before departure Bennet had suffered a blow from a falling rock. A fractured skull was suspected and he was proclaimed *hors de combat* in spite of his protests.

The crossing party left on the 26th, with myself taking Bennet's place. Lovat and Bryan had already made a route past the lower icefall of the Gully Glacier, along the route taken by Haller in 1954, and that evening we camped above the first fall. Next day was a wonderful experience, and no one could have called the long approach tedious, for around us rose a bewildering mass of unclimbed peaks, Grépons, Ravenels, Réquins, their frail snow crests and serrated granite arêtes untouched and un-named.

At this time we did not know how Haller had handled the third icefall, and though we were as impressed with it as he was, we sought out and made a route up its chaotic centre, and were almost stopped by an enormous crevasse splitting the glacier in two. Beyond this lay a rolling sea of new snow shimmering in the sun. Side glaciers shot off, each yielding lovely peaks. We decided that here was the point to return and make a prolonged stay. Equipped with skis and well provided, a camp here would bring tremendous rewards in climbing pleasure.

By late evening, just as the pink glow was lighting the summits, we breasted the final slope to a col, and found to our joy it was *the* col. We named it Col Major. Immediately above rose the superb trumpet stem of the Hjornespids, and to its left the broader bulk of the highest point, the Dansketinde. Next morning we paused at its top to admire the view east and north; the peaks we had climbed on earlier in the expedition, the low rounded hills by the coast, and distantly the gleam of the pack ice high-lighting the blue of the fjord.

We had brought 400 feet of rope and much ironware for the descent, but as soon as we had embarked on the first few feet, it was clear that the snow of two weeks earlier had consolidated and the couloir was eminently negotiable. It took less than two hours to descend. We abandoned all the surplus gear and there followed a hearty round of mutual back-slapping, for we really felt this to be the greatest success of the expedition. The ease of the couloir, which could obviously be safeguarded with fixed ropes, meant that a simple route to the Gully Glacier existed overland from the east coast.

At Alpefjord our companions gave us sufficient time to turn back and then headed round the coast, leaving a drum of paraffin, a half-bag of flour with a "help yourself" notice to any future comers. We left Greenland well pleased, wishing only that we could continue to live in that timeless, beautiful region.

THE 1960 EXPEDITION

Sir John Hunt's desire to visit Greenland was of long standing and in 1959 there seemed to be a possibility of its fulfilment. Some of us of the 1958 party wished to return to the Gully Glacier, and there was talk of sharing a plane. Then ideas began to develop. Sir John was asked by the National Association of Mixed Clubs whether he would lead an expedition of youths to the Arctic, and so two ideas and three parties became one, and the 1960 Greenland Expedition was born. It was to remain primarily a mountaineering expedition to the Staunings, in which the younger people would participate as fully as they could.

There are always many candidates for a trip to Greenland, and Sir John's party consisted of experienced hands. Tony Streather, George Lowe, I. G. McNaught-Davis, Allan Blackshaw, John Jackson, and Tom Weir are well-known mountaineers. Then there were Dr Iain Smart, Dr David Jones, John Sugden, who came as glaciologist, and Roderick Cameron as boatman. In charge of the youths was Dick Allcock, with two assistants, Frank Gwatkin and Bunny Roach. Sir John had Lady Hunt and his daughter Susan with him; and there were twenty-one younger people. Selection could not be on the more personal basis of seniority, and it was decided to use the Duke of Edinburgh's Award scheme as a criterion. Under this scheme boys are encouraged to acquire skills and show initiative by entering for the various awards of the scheme, which are graded according to age. The ultimate is the Gold Award, for which the participant must go on a three-day expedition in mountainous country, amongst other things, such as showing proficiency in a chosen hobby. The criterion proved a good one, and there was little to complain of in the young men who so enthusiastically dropped their tools and came to Greenland.

Because of the large size of the expedition, it was difficult to make it a long one, and plans were based on a total absence of exactly six weeks. This is little in terms of an expedition, but time could be saved by flying direct from London to Greenland, a flight of only eight hours, and by having an advance party to set the scene.

The expedition's plans embraced both scientific and mountaineering aims. The former involved a continuation of the glaciological and ornithological studies of 1958 and other items. The mountaineering aim was to follow up the discoveries of 1958 and establish camps high on the Berserker and Gully Glacier, and then, during the second half, move south and make a determined effort to explore the southern mountains, still virgin. It was an ambitious programme and depended upon two things: a good large boat and the usual fine weather.

All those of the party who had been there before vouchsafed the weather, though Blackshaw had read somewhere that once in twenty years the weather breaks, and put in a note of caution. The boat was a problem. We could not fly out a large enough boat, and since the conception of the expedition was not approved of by everyone in certain Greenland circles, it was not easy to find means of transporting a boat to Greenland for that summer. Eventually the Danish Ministry of Civil Aviation came to our rescue and offered us the part use of a superannuated cabin cruiser, the *Polyp*, or *Polypen*, long time-server on the Lauge Koch expeditions, which now enjoyed a semi-retirement at Mestersvig, where it was occasionally used for the recreation of the airfield personnel. This, for better or worse, was the solution to the boat problem, or all the solution that seemed probable. Cameron, our boat man and radio operator of 1958, was taken on to manage the *Polypen*. The job called for a man who knew the fjords, knew boats, and was a good engineer and repair man. Cameron was a good engineer and repair man, and he knew the fjords; by the end of the summer he knew a good deal more about boats.

Inevitably, plans were made in the light of previous experience. An ample supply of short summer ski were brought, food supplies were rated at 4,600 K.Cals per man/ day, but even this substantial ration proved inadequate for the more active towards the end. In a country where there is no darkness one tends to go on and on, and often a man's fuel intake is the governor of his effort. After the first fortnight a good many could have stepped up their consumption to 5,500, or even 6,000 cals. All rations were in six man/day boxes, which with packing weighed eighteen pounds each. By having this rather high figure it was possible to provide a most varied diet, while still retaining the essential mobility of the ration pack system.

Advance party

By the time the advance party flew to Reykjavik on July 7th, Sir John Hunt had ironed out most of his problems. He was to fly in with the main party on July 21st, and he sent certain problems ahead to Greenland for solution. In spite of this, I think that the advance party enjoyed some of the most interesting weeks of the whole trip. On the 10th, Weir, Smart, Cameron and myself landed in Greenland. Warning had already been given us of the phenomenally late season, and when we arrived the land was still 95 per cent covered with deep snow, and the only open water was the small lagoons at the point where the bigger rivers flowed into King Oscar's Fjord.

Beautiful though the scene was, it was a blow to the expedition, and much of the succeeding two weeks, which should have been spent in getting glaciological work under way and establishing the expedition's base camp at the sheltered bay of the Menanders Islands, was spent in trying to reach it. Since most of the expedition's work was to be on the west side of the Skel, the base had also to be on that side, thereby avoiding the risks attendant on frequent crossings of the river.

On July 9th we left on ski to pack a collapsible canoe to the mouth of the Skel river. Our intention was to seek to cross this river by the lagoon forming at its mouth, and so reach the projected base camp on the far side. It took six hours to cover a distance

171

normally walked in dry conditions in two-and-a-half; the cause was the deep water-laden snow, melting fast in the brilliant heat of an Arctic Riviera sun. At one point, crossing a poorly drained watershed, it took us an hour to cover 600 yards. Cameron actually lost his skis when at one point he sank to his waist and had moved a few feet before he realized that his skis had parted company.

But the reward was great and we reached the fjord edge as the sun was at its lowest, and revelled in the coral hue that suffused the scene, and marvelled at the enormous thickness of the sea ice which still lay along the shore. A sortie to the Skel mouth set our plans further back. A project to span the river with a 300 feet rope, with a rubber dinghy attached, so making a ferry, proved impracticable; the river was too wide and swift. As for the lagoon, it was divided into three parts, each circumscribed and un-linked. Clearly the time had come to relax for a few days and renew old friendships amongst the local people, for Mestersvig, with its air strip, manned by a handful, its weather station, and inland the intensely vigorous lead mine, created a little pool of Scandinavian civilization in the still sunlit waste of northeast Greenland.

By the 14th the swift thaw was having effect, and we made another attempt and left for the Skel mouth, intending to be away over a week. Cameron was left to help in the preparation of the *Polypen* for the summer's work, and we last saw him bearing a bag of tools and a guitar, both useful materials to his task.

We chose an incredibly lovely promontory for our site and lived the relaxed time-less existence that gives as little thought to meal and bed times as the sun did to night and day. Inevitably the sheer beauty of the night hours kept us about till early in the morning.

On the evening of the 15th the canoe assembled, Smart and I went to try the cross-ing, leaving Weir a watcher—perhaps to record the events. I was a little apprehensive as to the performance of a light canoe, with a wafer-thin skin, in an ice-filled sea. The thawing action leaves the edge of the floes with a surface that is a cross between the cutting properties of broken glass and the abrasive action of an enormous file. Our route necessarily took us across the first lagoon and then upstream, where soon we were swept away and had to leap into the race and haul the boat ashore. Now that our legs were wet, nothing mattered, and we tracked the canoe up stream, walking on an island sandbank, until a branch swept down in the direction we were heading. Leaping into the canoe, we enjoyed an exhilarating schuss into the middle lagoon, nearly capsized on a bar hidden in the opaque waters of the glacier melt river, and landed on a second island spit. Henceforward we enjoyed a superb view to the first bristling peaks of the Staunings at the margin of the Skel glacier. The top of the enormous north face of the Berserker Tinde loomed high and snow free, a possible expedition target. The 'route' had now to be along an ice-covered sand bar. We dragged the canoe, Captain Scott fashion, for an exhausting hundred yards, and then looked at its under-surface. We had done her no good. There followed a relay of contents and canoe, and climbing on to a smallish grounded iceberg, we surveyed a route through a labyrinth of ice floes. Into the water with her, and with Smart in charge, and myself as excited passenger, we twisted and turned, slowly making headway, till barred by two floes adjoining. Here we learned the beauty and ease of the canoe in this sort of condition, and in this and subsequent journeys we evolved a technique. Either one man stood on the floes and with his oar pushed the other floe away—one might push with no effect for minutes, then slowly, and with incredible inertia, it might slide away with the movement of an enormous oiled lock gate—or else, having established the floe was a firm one, one merely climbed on to it, drew the boat over and into the water on the other side and departed. Attempts to hack the floes to pieces were useless. (Though standing a bare inch above the water surface, the ice had considerable thickness).

The final run across the last lagoon was an exquisite experience. Paddling slowly and silently, we drew up on four long-tailed duck, getting a close view before they, equally silently and more swiftly, paddled away. Cold and soaked, but feeling very much alive, we waded with the boat in the last twenty yards to shore. Here it was still winter, and with a sea mist climbing in from the sea, the surface water was freezing. It was just past midnight.

We walked over the Menanders Bay, and there, in place of the bright carpet of flowers with which this lovely bay had greeted us in 1958, was a forlorn beach, largely snow-covered. Neither bird nor beast nor ice floe moved, and only the distant roar, as of city traffic, told of the tempestuous melt water rivers still running.

By the 18th we had established ourselves on the west side, and while Weir and Smart sought out a suitable tern colony, for the study of these birds was to be their summer's work, I made a reconnaissance of the route up the west side of the Skel Glacier to the Berserker Glacier. I was delighted to find it easy going, on lush tundra, barred by one sizeable but not too difficult river, descending from the Sylltoppene. Camp I location I found on a delightful flat fifteen miles up the glen. For me this valley must always have a different memory from that of the rest of the expedition, who saw it only in rain and cloud, and for whom it remained a bleak memory.

The others found their tern colony, but it spoke of the lateness of the season that even by July 22nd there were still few of these birds, and none nesting. However, we were well satisfied with the base camp site. It was sheltered from most winds and had an excellent anchorage, and we had built a jetty and charted hidden rocks. All that remained was to try and get essential fuel and other supplies over before the main party arrived. Meanwhile the weather became colder and cloud frequently obscured the sun. Weir, who on our advice had travelled lightly, was from time to time commenting bitingly upon the matter and fingering my warm sleeping bag. It was interesting to have this man's experience. The most widely travelled of us all, he had never been to the Arctic and found the scarcity of animal and bird life at complete variance with all he had read of sea cliffs bristling with sea birds. As an ornithologist he felt most disappointed, yet in due course he was to see everything he sought except the elusive little arctic redpoll and the arctic phalarope. This last he found on a rubbish dump near his home shortly after he returned from Greenland.

By the 20th we were back at Mestersvig, enjoying again the superb hospitality of Dr and Mrs Washburn, who made us one of the family in their little summer home and laboratory, '*det lile røde hus*'. On the 21st, in spite of the most unpromising conditions, I resolved to try a journey in the *Polypen* to Menanders Bay. At eleven o'clock we left, loaded with 160 gallons of paraffin and other gear. In six hours Sir John Hunt would be leaving London airport with the main party.

All invitations for a free ride were turned down by local personnel, who clearly regarded the journey with misgiving. Only the mine manager's wife, an Englishwoman, accepted, and to her we are grateful for an excellent photographic record, for the rest of us were very busy. In an absorbing five hours we twisted, turned, buffeted, rammed, rode, swept aside, through, past and over ice floes, large and small, until only a hundred yards from the channel leading to the base camp bay we were brought to a halt by an enormous floe bridging the channel. We backed and dumped our supplies close by.

Shortly after heading homewards, I rammed a particularly recalcitrant floe too hard and rode up on it. My first reaction was to put the screw in full speed astern, whereupon the propeller shaft promptly slipped out of the gearbox. We were in dry dock. Mrs Nyholm went below to make tea.

In two hours Cameron had tapped the shaft back, a thousandth of an inch at a time. The rest of us rocked the boat, sawed through the ice, and eventually she slid off. Yet our return was still to have its excitements; a fresh breeze from the sea was sweeping in big floes, one of which trapped us, and it was only a lucky easing that let us shoot through its rapidly tightening noose. By the time we moored at Mestersvig we felt veterans and Mrs Nyholm had had the time of her life.

By now it was a grey lowering evening. We heard that Hunt had landed at Reykjavik. Would he get through to Greenland? He did, and at three in the morning of the 22nd, ten hours from London, the Douglas Skymaster, *Solfaxi* the sun horse, swept in, bearing its youthful cargo.

The next few days were frustrating to a party so short of time as we were. One major breakdown after another beset the *Polypen*. Eventually, in the afternoon of the 22nd, the *Polypen*, sailing through ice-free seas that made our tales of yesterday seem a pure invention, reached the base camp bay, and proudly we brought her to the jetty and unloaded her, and then under the benign influence of Remy Martin cognac we sailed home through the steadily thickening mist that was sweeping in from the sea. It was the beginning of really poor weather that set up local records and lasted until August 3rd.

With attendant breakdowns and occasional hold-ups by heavy seas, Cameron did a round the clock boat-lift, so that by the 24th nearly everything was delivered. By now the jetty was a source of ridicule, for a change in tide movement brought it under water at high tide, and frequent westerly winds brought ice floes from the fjord into our 'safe' anchorage. On the night of the 24th Cameron slept little, frequently having to move his ship. Fortunately, he now had a mate—Mike Holden.

THE EXPEDITION PLANS

On the morning of the 24th John Hunt outlined the plans to the assembled party. Two mountaineering groups of four would penetrate the Berserker Glacier—Gully Glacier group, backed by six lads with one youth leader to each group. Our glaciologist, John Sugden, would leave on the 25th for Alpefjord with Lady Hunt and her daughter and six lads.

Due to delays caused by boat and weather, two days had already been lost. That evening both parties carried material to the first big river, four miles short of projected Camp I. Next day, bearing the residue, and with the help of some of the men left at base, both parties left again. The plan was for the two parties to move on alternate twelve hours, so that the first party would move by night and the other by day. In this way our twelve pairs of short ski would be available to almost everyone.

My party moved first at ten in the evening on the 25th. It consisted of George Lowe, I. G. McNaught-Davis and John Jackson, with Frank Gwatkin looking after the lads. In order not to have to send back for small left-overs, we all carried much more than was comfortable. However, by half an hour after midnight on the 26th we had reached the river and the first dump. Only one man fell in on the crossing, and the amusing spectacle was to be seen of four men racing pell-mell down the banks to the cry of 'boots'. They were recovered. The individual had foolishly taken them off and strung them round his neck.

By the time all gear was across and relayed the four miles to Camp I, it was 6.30 in the morning and everyone was tired. As we turned in it began to rain.

When John Hunt's party arrived at seven that evening they had been travelling in rain all day and were wet through; the lads were exhausted. There were some comments about the 'Arctic Riviera', chiefly directed at my tent. Rain continued off and on for the next few days, and though the snow line was 4,000 feet, plenty was lying high up. It would exclude some of the climbs we had in mind, for at this latitude the snow does not shift quickly after the end of July.

My own group found a common pleasure in bridge, and this utterly absorbed the

175

days when we were not actually moving. It was no longer meaningful to retain the staggered marching hours, and it was Sir John Hunt who forcefully set about the next move up the glacier and established Camp II an hour and a half below the 1958 Sun Valley camp. In a night of raw wind we packed to this camp, almost missing it in the poor light, and sent the lads down to Camp I. We had not been able to carry enough up to maintain them at this distance from base.

By the 30th we were three days behind schedule. Sir John had taken a lightly loaded party on ski, for the glacier was snow-covered from 2,000 feet up to a suitable site for Camp III. This was to have been at the foot of Col Major, but the heavy going and the limited stamina of the younger party restricted the steps possible, and later on the 29th our party established a dump there. Returning on ski, I looked in on the 1958 Sun Valley camp and found some supplies left there still in edible condition.

On the 30th John Hunt resolved not to move forward till things improved, and made a sortie up the side glacier immediately downstream of Camp II. From it, with Streather, Jones and two boys, he gained the peak of Harlech, about 6,500 feet, which offered delightful but not hard climbing on its upper stretches. He had taken Tony Cooper and Brian Mills with him, who were thus of the lads the first to make an ascent, and perhaps the youngest ever to make an ascent in Greenland.

Sir John now had a number of his younger people at Camp II and decided to stay there a while; during the next break, the 31st, he set off for another side glacier, yet again downstream from the Harlech Glacier, making for the prominent highest peak. Near the summit, his party of Streather, Blackshaw and Jones were working up the heavily corniced summit ridge, when in spite of the precaution of keeping below the crest, it cracked, carrying Hunt down the steep southern slope of the mountain. Fortunately, Blackshaw, on a lower line, was able to make the classic defence, and the rope held. The peak, Caerleon, was abandoned, for conditions seemed dangerous. This peak is closely located to one of the peaks climbed by the Norwegians in 1951 from low on the Skeldunge, but it seems unlikely it is the same peak, since that side presents a very steep snow and ice slope.

My own party occupied Camp III on the 31st, building an agreeable little ledge on which to pitch the two tiny orange tents, and there we continued to play bridge, pausing only to admire the magnificent 5,500 feet wall of the Berserker Tinde in occasional lulls in the close weather.

It was during this period that it struck us how curiously silent these mountains were, there being practically no avalanche noise, and even later, when the sun shone strongly, there were few dramatic falls.

At Camp III the mist was thinning as we bedded at two in the morning on the 2nd, and when we rose at midday conditions were brilliant. We walked up the bluff behind, 5,100 feet Tintagel, and gained a superlative viewpoint. My companions had their first view of the Hjørnespids and were as enamoured as I had hoped they would be.

The same day Sir John's party had ascended Elsinore to the northeast of Harlech.

On the 3rd we rested till late afternoon, giving the sun its opportunity to consolidate the snow; then at 5.30 p.m. we skied slowly up to the foot of Col Major. Lovely peaks rose on all sides as the glacier wound its way gently upwards. Beyond the Berserker Tinde, which from below appears as the headwall of the valley, lies a bigger and finer peak, presenting a face having both the dimensions and appearance of the north face of the Grandes Jorasses.

I was most interested to see the reactions of my companions, who, all having considerable Himalayan experience, were finding it hard to get an idea of the scale of these mountains. Opinions of the height of the ice couloir to Col Major varied from 600 to 1,000 feet, and the time required as one to three hours. It is 1,500 feet and takes 4½ hours. Only an actual measurement of the Berserker Tinde would convince us that it presented a face of 5,500 feet.

That night we put a fixed rope up the side of the couloir, which we reached at five in the morning on the 4th, and left a small dump at the top. It was cold and windy, and we were tired after a long trudge in a mixture of bald blue ice and soft avalanching snow. Clearly the time was not yet ripe to try the higher peaks.

The early morning ski run down the glacier to camp was, however, supremely delightful—a six-mile schuss on the gentlest of slopes.

Our leader arrived as we were eating our bed-time meal at nine in the morning. Behind him a red-faced party were doing their best to keep up the exacting pace he always set, for he was undoubtedly the fastest man in the expedition. John Hunt had come to take the place of George Lowe, who had to descend to the valley to obtain ciné film. The bulk of the expedition were to make their way to Alpefjord, and it was planned to adopt the same means as in 1958, namely, allow men to walk along the coast ferrying them over the hurdles in the boat.

The Camp III party had one object, the Hjørnespids, before aiming to reach Alpefjord by traversing Col Major. There was a dateline for the 10th for Alpefjord. Such rigidity, though irritating, was necessary in so large a party where no ready intercommunication with groups was available.

We gave the snow another day to improve, and on the 5th Hunt and Jackson set their sights on a small Matterhorn-shaped peak down the glacier. Going by ski, they soon reached its base, and after a climb up a pleasant airy snow ridge, they traversed round to the foot of the final 800 ft. buttress which gave a climb of grade III. They named it Beaumaris.

Meanwhile, McNaught-Davis and I thought a short day limbering up on some rocks would be pleasant, and we skied up the glacier to a side glacier at the head of which rose a small graceful rock needle. As the hours passed it became clear it was a large rock needle a long way off, and finally resolved itself into a superb climb of 2,000 feet, the last 1,000 feet being consistently hard on faultless rock, giving a route of *difficile* standard and many pitches of grade V. The summit of Berserker Suilen (needle) was a tilted slab upon a vertical pedestal. A tin of tuna fish on an ice piton is the only desecration left. It was late when we got back, and our companions were a little worried, for we had not thought to go so far.

On the 6th Camp III was abandoned and a dump of surplus food and fuel was left there. Meanwhile Camp II was being broken up too; as a final gesture Streather and Blackshaw, with two lads, made the ascent of the prominent peak that stands in the corner of the Berserker and Skel valley. At the request of the boys, they called it Stirling. Thereafter, all the parties retreated to base. It was a blow to our plans, for originally we had intended to move groups over the Skel pass to the big valley in the south, but the delay of poor weather, and the fact that after so much effort we had got established by Col Major, and might then be robbed of a climb from there, caused this change of plan.

HJØRNESPIDS

It was a heavy carry to the foot of Col Major on the 6th, and John Hunt was there well before the rest of us. We departed for the col at nine in the evening, but even at that hour the snow was sodden and dangerous. Even with the fixed rope, we gained the col only after three hours, and we felt very tired. It was now clear that whoever was to make an attempt on the Hjørnespids must rest and set out soon. John Hunt insisted that McNaught-Davis and I should tackle the climb. After due rest, he and Jackson would return to the col for the remainder of the gear.

The Hjørnespids has no easy side or obvious point of weakness. The final rock tower is a trumpet-stem perched upon the tripod of three approach ridges, the southeast, the south and the northwest. Of these the south rises directly from the upper snowfields of the Gully Glacier branch that leads to Col Major. It presents a sweep of steep rock, bristling with steps and pinnacles, just over 3,000 feet high. It is thus the shortest route, for the southeast ridge has a centre section a mile long, featuring fourteen major towers. The northwest ridge had only been clearly seen by the climbers of the Frihedstinde in 1951, and they made no report, but it is short and very steep, and to gain its foot may be most of the problem. Certainly it is well guarded, both to east and west, by enormous ice slopes.

When Jackson saw the Hjørnespids from Col Major, he picked out the south ridge, and pronounced it 'a cake walk'. It was certainly the obvious route, and McNaught-Davis and I were tempted; yet as we mulled over the matter at breakfast at ten o'clock on the 7th we decided against it, for at this juncture our skis were still at the foot of the col, and the approach of over a mile to the foot of the south ridge would involve a most exhausting and wetting journey in deep, soft and sometimes wet snow. By contrast the southeast ridge rose abruptly, thirty yards from our tent. McNaught, whose first love is rock, opted for this, and there was no denying the attraction of that immense sweep of steep orange-brown buttress above us; I agreed.

This climb has been fully narrated elsewhere.

We left just before noon in hot and windless conditions and climbed in shirtsleeves, spent three delightful hours forcing the first buttress, which gave a climb whose pitches were continuous, never less than grade III, and often grade V. We met here in concentrated form the curious black lichen with which even the highest summits are garnished. We called it the Black Death, for when wet or iced, a vibram sole had no adhesison to it, and on that day, with so much snow on the mountain melting in the noonday heat, it had no adherent quality.

An overhanging chimney near the start gave hard climbing and took a precious half hour, but after this we moved steadily, and were much helped by having made the odd, but in many ways wise, decision of leaving both axes and crampon behind. Our first summit at 2410 m gave us a good lunching spot and our last real halt. Now, for the first time, one could gauge the height of some of the surrounding peaks. Ahead, the narrow rock ridge, like a castle rampart posted with watchtowers, soared and plunged, bending slightly to the left to the base of the trumpet stem. That looked a long way off, and it was.

The climbing was pure delight, always on firm rock, much covered with powder snow, and most exposed, with drops of over 5,000 feet to the north, and considerably less to the south to the Gully Glacier. Never once could we move together, and yet the climbing was never slow nor tedious, and the route finding was a constant interest, the route up and down the various towers being often obscure. Towards evening, as we ran out of sunlight, we took a hopeful easier line by skirting some of the towers on the south side, but it is questionable how much we saved ourselves. These towers ran down to the ice slopes, liberally covered with snow which throughout the day was sliding off. The only noise was that of rushing water, for the sun had been strong. I suppose the final tower was the finest, and it nearly baulked us. Several days previously, from another vantage point, we had speculated on passing this by a low traverse on the north wall. Now to reach such a traverse was a major undertaking, and not within the compass of a two-day climb. Clearly the tower would not go direct, and there remained the chance of gaining a point half-way up its acute triangular end-section, then traversing right or left. It was McNaught-Davis' lead and he went right. For a long time the rope was slow to move and often slid back to me. It was cold, windy, and in the north steel blue lenticular clouds lent an ominous atmosphere to the moment. Through the wind was the unmistakable "Tinning" of piton vibrating

179

in rock. When I followed, it was to find a tortuous route leading out on to the extra-ordinarily exposed north face. McNaught-Davis stood huddled in a small sentry box, and the narrow ledge at his feet ran out to the right, ebbing to nothing twenty feet away. Between us lay a re-entrant corner. My unspoken doubts as to the wisdom of this route were terminated when my companion pointed out his inability to reverse the last move, so I crossed to him, with difficulty, and admired the lead. His view on the route was that I should climb up an overhanging crack above his head. I did not try, nor was I keen that he should do so with our flimsy belay. The exit we finally chose was satisfying in its technical qualities, and exciting enough for the moment. At the end of the ledge I got a piton in, rappelled twenty feet, and then attempted to pendulum a further distance to the right to gain a ledge of agreeable dimensions. Here the Black Death stepped in and made the start of the pendulum impossible. Every attempt ended in an undignified roll back. Meanwhile the second man grew colder, for he had little on. It finally had to be climbed free on bare rugosities as holds. The ledge offered no easy exit, but since there was no alternative it had to do, and it was with considerable panting, not purely due to exertion, that I finally pulled myself up on to the ridge of the tower. We were across!

Seen at close quarters, the trumpet-stem looked inviolable. Perhaps semi-darkness, wind and cold lent it such an air. A route seemed possible, by first descending towards the Gully Glacier along the base of the stem, and then a leftwards climbing traverse to bring us to the south ridge. The route was good, not too hard, but becoming so as we neared the south ridge. At midnight we could get no further.

It is interesting that on these arctic climbs, once fit, it is not one's strength that gives out but the sheer desire to sleep. In the previous three days we had had thirteen hours sleep, and now the urge to sleep was getting a hold. My companion was suffering from a creeping torpor and feared he might fall asleep while climbing, and suggested a bivouac; but being no lover of unnecessary hardship I countered with other counsels, saying that once I slept I doubted whether in this cold I should wake up. "Which of us is being the most selfish?" asked McNaught-Davis; and with this cogent statement he emptied his climbing sack, took off his boots and got in.

I gave him half an hour during which, shivering violently, I set a rappel. We had agreed to try a line of McNaught-Davis' up the centre of the south-southeast face. It went very well, offering delightful climbing, enabling us to gain the summit at four in the morning of the 8th. Even the last pitch had been a small crack of grade IV. The summit was as bald as a billiard table and no bigger. As a mark of our visit I left an orange nylon scarf under a stone a few feet on the north side of the summit table.

It was at this stage that we discovered that we had not brought our spare cord for rappel-loops. This was quite a blow, because it was now obvious to us that we could

180

not go back the way we came, on account both of the time and the difficulties on the final tower of the southeast ridge.

In the subsequent long series of rappels on the south ridge we used up all available pieces of cord, from etriers, anorak cord, piton hammer slings, and so on. At one point, having reached so slow a speed as to make us seem the veriest beginners, we called a halt and slept, enjoying the heat from a lukewarm sun.

The final series of rappels down the last 1,000 feet buttress was impressive and exhilarating. Our aim was to reach some rocks as close as possible to the rimaye and this buttress had that virtue. Our last piton was inserted at the lowest rocks, and, using our last nylon loops, McNaught just lowered himself over the rimaye. It was the only time we could have wished for an ice-axe.

By a most happy chance Hunt and Jackson had been laying a small depot down the glacier, and we saw them plodding up, a mile off, and hailed them. They brought along our skis, and we had the luxury of an easy walk back to camp. Only in the arctic could one have carried through so long a route in twenty-nine hours.

The next day, the 9th, we were forced by considerations of time to make for Alpefjord; so, heavily loaded, we set off down the glacier on ski. The pleasure of this occasion was a function of the ability of the skier; it took the fast man a fifth of the time of the slowest. By mid-day we were at the top of the third ice-fall and looking for a way off to the north side to get on to Haller's corridor. Here, during an encounter with seracs, we abandoned our skis, for we already had too much to carry to add their load as well. The corridor was a most simple, and, ignoring the risk of stone-fall, safe route.

On the 10th we moved down the last ice-fall by the southern snow corridor between cliffs and the glacier, and found so much more snow that we encountered only one of the three major impasses of 1958. By early afternoon we were lying, sweat encrusted, naked on the green spur separating the Gully and Sefstrøm glaciers. In Dammen, discernible only by its wake, was the *Polypen*. It looked as if plans were once again going according to schedule, but we were soon to find out this was not so.

Alpefjord

We found the glaciologist's camp at 2,000 feet on a beauitful flower-decked shelf directly beneath the Sefstrøm moraine. The party were away in the *Polypen* examining a kame at the head of Dammen. We were there to greet them as they came in, and then Cameron reported.

Back at Mestersvig considerable anxiety had been expressed by all the local authorities about centring the whole expedition at Dammen, and finally Cameron, who had been our only representative there, felt impelled to report these views to Hunt before the great step was taken. Thus little had been accomplished in bringing men and materials to Alpefjord, but on the other hand Cameron thought that, considering the size of his boat, the party could be rapidly transported direct, without a walk. It seemed as broad as it was long, and nothing had been lost if Hunt did decide to go ahead.

To Hunt there seemed no reason to reconsider the earlier decision, and he requested Cameron to return for the party. Alas, we did not reckon with the *Polypen*; it did not return till the evening of the 13th. Rough weather in the outer fjord had held it stormbound, and there had been mechanical trouble. The plan was now for two parties, one led by Hunt and the other by Lowe, to cross the south Staunings by the Duart-Roslin route, and pick up a dump of food that was to have been flown in to a gravel strip near the snout of the Roslin Glacier. Lowe, with Lady Hunt, Susan Hunt, Streather and four boys, would head south to Syd Kap, to pay a visit to the eskimos there. Meanwhile Hunt, with Blackshaw and Jackson, would investigate the south Staunings; six of the lads went with them.

The whole crux of the south Staunings exploration is—and will be—supplying this remote area. The simple and effective plan had been for the Mestersvig Mine's light plane to fly in food and fuel. Unknown to Hunt while he was up in the mountains, the plane had just crashed, and a relief plane from Europe had crashed in transit. Fortunately, Cameron had taken advantage of a suggestion that supplies could be taken by tracked vehicle to a pilot mine which the Danes were operating on one of the side glaciers at the head of the Schuichart valley, into which all the south Staunings glaciers run. Knowing that I had previously visited this Schuichart, he assumed I was aware of the location of this mine; but when he got to Alpefjord it was found that neither I, nor anyone else, knew this. Hunt therefore had to take the bold step of deciding to cross the range, and set about looking for the mine or the dump. Meanwhile he sent a message via Cameron to Smart, asking him to leave his tern island and with a small party make his way over the mountains from Mestersvig (from where they would learn of the dump's whereabouts), and so come south to meet them.

The morning of the 14th was wet, with low cloud. The crossing parties were ferried to the head of Dammen, with Sugden, Allcock (the youth leader), and six of the lads to help in portering over the icefall of the Spørre glacier. Hunt and Lowe were route finding and reported that they found it quite easy, a change from 1958, and twelve hours later Sugden, coming off, found an alternative route which was even easier. His party, with only a rubber dinghy at their disposal had a tough time making their way round the terribly unconsolidated shores of Dammen, and at one point, where a fast steep glacier comes right into the fjord, they were forced to use a rubber boat to cross, and found it a nasty experience in the prevailing high wind. All night it snowed heavily, and for the crossing party conditions were cold and unpleasant in leaking tents. All were deliberately travelling light. Next day, as they gained height, conditions improved and by evening they were at the top of the pass, the long caravan taking turns in beating out the trail and testing the crevasses. By the 16th they had reached the snout of the Roslin, and next day began to search for the dump. Their food would be exhausted by the morning of the 18th.

After a brief rest, Cameron turned round and headed for Mestersvig for the residue of the food. He took with him McNaught-Davis, who was to make some of our return transport arrangements, and Jones and myself, who were to reconnoitre the fjord coast as a walk-out route in emergency. We were unloaded with canoe at the outer end of the canal, and made our inspection, afterwards returning to Dammen.

Cameron had an uneventful voyage, picking up a reluctant Smart, who with Weir was engrossed in their tern study, then at a most critical stage. Smart, with Roach and two lads, crossed over to the dump, which turned out to be at Sirius Glacier, off the Schuichart Glacier, a hard two-days' march from Mestersvig, and a further very full day from the Roslin snout. It was now the 17th. By this time yet another light plane had been obtained by the mine, and this one had successfully reached Greenland. It landed at the pilot mine, Erzberg, at the same time as Smart's party reached it, and the pilot promptly radioed his base, the Mestersvig mine, asking permission to fly the expedition's stores down to the originally planned landing strip, lying between the Roslin and Lang Glaciers. But it was the morning of the 19th before permission arrived, and the plane departed with stores at once. Meanwhile, Smart was twenty-four hours late for his rendezvous with Hunt, and an increasing anxiety prevailed amongst the crossing party.

Hunt lost no time in casting around for the missing dump, which he rightly supposed to be at the small pilot mine somewhere at the upper end of the Schuichart valley. He had a choice of several glaciers, an area of 120 square miles in which to look for it. A search with binoculars along twenty-five miles of the valley revealed no sign of it. By the late evening of the 18th the search parties returned home empty-handed; all but one, for Streather and Lowe, who forged a crossing of the Schuichart River, did not re-appear. By the morning of the 19th the situation was critical. With no food, it was a case of making a run for Mestersvig; but to add to difficulties, Lowe and Streather were still missing. In the circumstances it was very easy to imagine that they had been drowned in the swirling grey waters of the Schuichart, a not uncommon fate in the Arctic summer. A few hours later they appeared, to the immense relief of all, and were astounded at the warmth of their welcome. They, too, had found nothing useful; but a solution was at hand, had they known it. They scattered again, and while Hunt, Jackson and Blackshaw made a final sortie in the direction of the Sirius Glacier, an aircraft was seen flying down the valley. This plane spotted the tents, landed a mile from them, picked up Lady Hunt, and on a second flight dropped a message to Hunt giving the news that food had already been flown south. In a flash the situation had been retrieved. In due course Smart's party was united with Hunt's. Later, Smart was heard to utter the fine piece of expeditionmanship, "the bird watchers had rescued the mountaineers."

Hunt now resumed his plan, having been delayed forty-eight hours, which severely restricted his programme. One party, under Lowe, headed southwards to the coast of North-West Fjord at Nord Vest Bay to visit the summer hunting station of the Scoresby Sound eskimos. It consists of three huts, and a bigger house and store under the direction of the Greenland Administration. The huts were seen on a remote spit of land sticking into the impressive iceberg-laden North-West Fjord. The party titivated and combed beards in honour of the meeting—only to find the place empty. The shortage of seals in recent years had caused the eskimos to let the place lie fallow.

Hunt's party, comprising Blackshaw, Jackson and the two youth leaders, Roach and Gwatkin, as well as four lads, made their way to the Bjørnebo Glacier snout. Camp I was established on a lovely site above the glacier snout. In bad weather, Hunt, Blackshaw and two lads continued up this great ice-stream, setting up their camp II at midnight on August 20th in the centre of a vast area of ice, at a point where the main glacier is joined by a number of tributaries. The temptation to call it Concordia was not resisted.

Next day, while Hunt and one of the lads, Church, explored a tributary which they named Jupiter, covering twenty-seven miles and getting exciting glimpses of fine peaks, Blackshaw and the other lad, Baber, made an exploratory ascent of Kilmory, 7,650 feet, lying in the junction of the Bjørnebo and Jupiter Glaciers.

The party was greatly elated that evening and was joined by Jackson, who had recovered from an indisposition. On the 22nd, now in glorious weather, Hunt and Blackshaw climbed two peaks lying on the north flank of the main glacier, immediately above their camp. These were named Kilvrough (8,050 feet) and Pevensey (6,500 feet). Meanwhile, Jackson and the younger men made an exploratory journey up a big side glacier on the south side of the Bjørenbo, named Mercury.

All too soon, on the 23rd, the climbers had to return to the support group at Camp I. The loss of forty-eight hours in seeking the dump had almost halved the climbers' time in the area, a tragedy when so much in the way of exciting prospects was being revealed. On the last day the party found time to examine a side glacier and climb a rock peak (Karabiner, 6,900 feet) before leaving the Bjørnebo.

By the 24th both parties were united at the Roslin and returned home to Mestersvig by the 28th.

Meanwhile, on the west side, I was awaiting the arrival of Weir and McNaught-Davis in order to launch an attack on the south ridge of the Sefstrøm Tinde. Everything was prepared for a quick start when they arrived. They never came. By the 20th

45 SNOWCOVERED SLOPES, ice couloirs, and cliffs mark the way to the summits of the Stauning Alps. Peterson on the South Ridge of the Sefstrøms Tinde. (Photograph by Slesser)

46/47 ON THE WEST SIDE OF THE STAUNING ALPS the Sefstrøm Glacier and the Gully Glacier flow together into the Alpefjord. (Aerial photograph from Dr. Lauge Koch's East Greenland Expedition)

48 THE SEFSTRØM GLACIER affords an easy road of access to the summits of the southwestern Stauning Alps. (Aerial photograph from Dr. Lauge Koch's East Greenland Expedition)

food, which had already been reduced to threequarters rations, was clearly going to be reduced even further unless the *Polypen* turned up or the numbers were reduced. The most useful work that could be done was glaciological, and so I decided to walk out with two boys, taking three days' food. In this way, if the boat did not arrive by the 25th, Sugden's party would still have a bare ration to march out themselves. They had a canoe and a rubber boat.

I took the two most able mountaineers among the boys, Duncan and Brooks, and together we set out on the 21st, a day which will long linger with me for its beauty. Unusual fleecy clouds hovered daintily here and there, for there was no wind. Our plan was to make Kap Petersens, at the north point of the land, before our food ran out. Here we were sure there would be something, if only dried fish, at the old trappers' hut.

The crux of the route is not the crossing of the Gully and Sefstrøm Glaciers, difficult though they are, but the stretch of coast beyond the Viking Glacier, where a mountain slope 6,000 feet high, of steep and insubstantial scree, tumbles without a single break into the fjord. Anxious to have the worst behind us, we had a light supper at the Viking snout at seven in the evening, at A. R. Heen's 1954 base site, and went on to tackle this obstacle. The scree soon proved easiest where it enters the sea, for tide action had consolidated and lightly flattened the stones. Once, when faced with a cliff running right into the sea, we managed to skirt round it by wading into the fjord, but at another section this proved too deep and we had the most unpleasant climbs of our lives on utterly shattered rock. But by one in the morning it was all over. It was indeed a credit to the inexperienced young men who were with me that they had been able to concentrate so well as to keep going without once stumbling.

Next day, shortly after starting, we met Weir and McNaught-Davis. A series of mishaps, both political and technical, had befallen the *Polypen*. It had been required by the airfield personnel, whose boat it was. Cameron and McNaught-Davis had then set out with two small boats, including the *Tippa Dan*, the lifeline of the 1958 expedition. Almost at once they tasted excitement, being caught in some big pack ice that was being blown in from the open sea. At one moment Cameron, who stepped on to a small floe to push his boat off, was marooned and was reduced to paddling his own floe, but was ultimately able to reach a boat again. Exhausted by this they slept through what little good weather there was; then it became rough again. With this obvious loss of time, it was decided that Cameron should go back to Mestersvig and there await the *Polypen*, which was the only sound solution. This was done in the next spell of fine weather, and then, though this continued, McNaught-Davis fell ill. Finally, on the 21st, he and Weir set off but were driven ashore by high seas at Kap Petersens. On the 22nd they left early, and when we met them they had just put in to warm their frozen limbs. We ate with them and saw them on their way, two boats, one in tow of the other, piled high with food. They reached Dammen that night exhausted and cold. During the night unusually high seas and tide swept much of their cargo back into the water, and on waking they found the now calm fjord bobbing with strange objects.

We ourselves had ample food now, and we walked in leisurely fashion to Kap Petersens in wonderful Indian summer weather, with only the blood-seeking mosquitos to spoil our delight. Our route took us up the west arm of the Skoldungebrae, the first visitors since 1951. Here we got an excellent view of the white triangle of the Caerleon.

Here we rested from the 23rd to the 26th. The *Polypen* passed on the 25th, without noticing us. She had eventually returned from a trip down King Oscar's Fjord and had badly needed maintenance; finally, that day, Cameron and his mate had been able to put to sea again. However, this was the deadline at Alpefjord, and the party had already evacuated Dammen and were well up Alpefjord by the time Cameron hove into sight. He pressed on to Dammen and collected equipment abandoned there.

On the 27th we reached Mestersvig, proving that the coastal walk is readily possible in four days, five if taken leisurely. The other parties came in on the 28th. A keen awareness of our situation and the knowledge of how to cope with it had brought us all back intact, on time. In the remaining two days we gossiped and cut our hair; some shaved, and the doctor took beard samples for his survey of growth against temperature. It was the relaxing finale to a most happy and varied expedition, not always well favoured by weather or circumstances. But now the sun shone from a brilliant sky. The Arctic Riviera was showing that the summer of 1960 had only been a little fit of pique.

CONCLUSION

These, then, are the hills of the north, and they have much to commend themselves to the mountaineer. Their remoteness itself is an attraction. The northern part, containing many of the finest peaks, is most accessible. The climbing is hard, the routes are long, and there is every variety. The scenery is unrivalled, for where but in the polar regions can one see so vividly the contrast of the white, black and red of snow and rock with the blue and gleam of the fjord. The clarity is that of much higher mountains, the weather giving possibly the best mountaineering climate in the world. The Staunings are little Alps, mature in quality, benevolent in temperament, free from the curse of darkness, and bounded and made accessible by the peaceful highways of the fjords. There is no combination like that of sea and mountain, and there is no lighting quite like the low-angled light of the high latitudes. And vices? The Staunings have their faults, but less of these perhaps than most mountain ranges. Undoubtedly this is a place for holiday mountaineering for the experienced and skilled mountaineer, truly the Alps of the north. Their golden age is about to begin.

186

THE SOUTH STAUNING ALPS IN 1961

By James Clarkson

Why the Stauning Alps again? These mountains, which lie in the Scoresby Land Peninsula of East Greenland at latitude 72° N, have received the attention of a whole series of expeditions since the end of World War II. The reasons are found in the excellent mountain scenery and the easy access to this range. However, our own party waited for the results of Sir John Hunt's 1960 expedition before making a final decision to go ahead. Sir John's party ranged far and wide through Scoresby Land and they were the first mountaineers to explore the glaciers of the southern half of the Stauning Alps. They also climbed four peaks in this area, the first peaks to be climbed, and they came back with some impressive photographs showing hosts of unclimbed peaks. This decided us.

Our party of nine was composed of members of the Junior Mountaineering Club of Scotland. It consisted of Howard Brunton (deputy leader and geologist), Ian Douglas, Gwyn Evans, Michael Fleming, Graham Hendry (geologist), Cyril Levene (doctor), Keith Murray, Raymond Tanton, and myself as leader. The youngest, Keith Murray, was 20, and the oldest, Gwyn Evans at 42, was the only married member of the party. We were a mixed bunch but we were all keen and experienced mountaineers, and our principal objective was to explore and climb the mountains of the south Stauning Alps.

In the early hours of the morning of July 8th we were waiting at Reykjavik airport in Iceland for our chartered plane to take us to Mestersvig on the coast of East Greenland. "Just like Scotland" said Keith as we watched the thick damp clouds drift low overhead, with occasional smatterings of drizzle. We took off at 3.30 a.m. and we were a bit apprehensive as our heavily laden plane lumbered into the air. Soon we were flying smoothly above the clouds in bright early morning sunshine. Two and a half hours later, we dropped down through the clouds and saw glimpses of pack ice on the sea below. Almost before we had realized it, we were flying low over the stark brown hills of the coast of Greenland, and a few minutes later we roared to a stop on a vast gravel runway. What a contrast from Iceland! Here, in Greenland, the air was cold, clear and sharp, and reminded us of the best days of a Scottish winter. The entire journey from Scotland to Greenland had taken me only about ten hours. The previous afternoon, I was still at my post at the Naval Construction Research Establishment in Dunfermline, and it was hard to appreciate that we were actually in Greenland. Such is the accessibility of Scoresby Land: except that it took nine months of intensive preparations which absorbed us for almost our entire spare time.

We unloaded our gear from the plane, for there are no airport porters in Greenland. There were 2,000 pounds of food and equipment for our six weeks stay, all of it packed in army type kit bags, a bag containing twelve man-days of food rations. The idea was that two of these kit bags, plus personal equipment, would make up a man-load, amounting to about eighty pounds, and carried on wooden pack frames. From Mestersvig on the coast, where we had loaded, to the site of our proposed base camp on the Bjornbos Glacier in the south Stauning Alps is a distance of about eighty miles, all of it untracked country, though mainly below the snow line in summer time. To carry all our supplies on our backs was quite out of the question, but we had arranged for a mining company reconnaissance plane to assist with transport to an advance airstrip sixty miles to the south. An unpleasant surprise awaited us at Mestersvig as the mining company plane had not yet been delivered from Europe, and we wondered whether our expedition would fail almost before we had started. However, the Danish authorities at the airfield came to the rescue with a generous drop of stores by parachute, which was effected in the course of an exercise. It was arranged that the bulk of our gear, save that required for the journey in, would be dropped at the site of our proposed base, about halfway up the Bjornbos Glacier.

Next day our party set out on foot, with the exception of Howard and Graham, who accompanied the aircraft dropping our supplies, to ensure that they were dropped on the right glacier. These two would follow us to the south Staunings a day behind the main party. When our loads were made up they worked out heavier than we had anticipated and we started, or perhaps staggered would be a better word, with about eighty-five pounds each, which exceeded the eighty pounds which we had regarded as the absolute limit before leaving Scotland. The first stage of our march was across easy slopes covered with fine moss and flowers, broken by occasional patches of scree. On the second day we began to appreciate the scale of the country. We were skirting the eastern flank of the north Stauning Alps and planned to cross the Skel Col, 4,000 feet high, to the Schuchert Valley away to the south. A snow-covered glacier rose gently towards the col, which appeared to be about five hours distant, but in fact it took us all day, stumbling over boulder-strewn slopes and across ravines, to get on to the glacier, and we camped about three miles up where dry ice gave way to a covering of slushy snow. The weather was none too good, with an overcast sky and intermittent rain or sleet. Next day was spent on skis and we had some bad moments when we slipped backwards and our packs went over our heads. The snow was extremely soft and making the trail in front was a heart-breaking task which required the skis to be lifted out before each step forward. On the final steep slope to the col

188

we were sinking in about eighteen inches, but after six hard hours we reached the top. Once we had started down the south side the sun came out and our spirits rose. We made quick progress to the snow line and camped.

We had now reached the head of the broad Schuichart Valley, which we were to follow southward for the next three days. Around the foot of the glacier we encountered some of the worst terrain I have ever seen, a vast moraine consisting of huge piles of stones and rubble rising to 200 feet or more. We had hours of toiling up and down the sunbaked stones, and in the midst of it was a river of mud several feet deep, flowing slowly down the hillside. I attempted to cross, hopping from boulder to boulder, but found I was being sucked in. With my heavy load I was glad of a pull from Keith Murray to help me out. We eventually crossed at a point where the river ran under the ice of the glacier snout. Much of the Schuichart Valley was covered by a lush carpet of flowers and mosses, and we made easy and pleasant progress across the firm tundra. The weather had become extremely hot, with a relentless sun beating down from an almost cloudless sky, and we preferred to travel in the morning and evening and rest during the middle of the day.

On our second day in the Schuichart we came to the Lang River, where a large tributary flows in from the glaciers of the Central Staunings. We made several attempts to cross, using the climbing ropes for safety, but each time found the current was too strong. Not only was the water waist deep and icy cold but the whole bed of the river, consisting of big boulders, was on the move. We retired battered and bruised, to wait for the night when we hoped the flow would be considerably reduced. At 3.30 a.m. the next day, we made our second attempt. The river dropped a foot but the current still looked formidable. Ray Tanton and I made the first attempt, advancing sideways to the current and holding a ski-stick between us to give stability. The stream was still almost waist deep, but we kept a footing and, after eighty feet or so, reached an ice shelf on the far side. I cut some steps in the ice on the bank and we were out. We made a belay on the ice, then the rest of the party made two crossings each to ferry the loads across. Meanwhile, we sat shivering, taking in or playing out the rope. When Gwyn Evans had made his second crossing, we found to our horror that the current had ripped off one of his boots. The water had been so numbing that he had never noticed this happening and now his boot was lost for ever. We wondered how to meet this tragedy, but not Gwyn, who immediately made an improvised boot from a plimsoll, some nylon cord and an old kit bag. After a few days of travel his toe nails became black with the cold and damp and we wondered whether they would fall off, but he never complained and always insisted on carrying his full share of the loads.

Excitement came in a different way on the seventh day, when we cut across a spur of hillside on the west side of the valley and first looked up the Bjornbos Glacier into

189

the south Stauning Alps. The glacier was at least twenty miles long. On its south bank was a fantastic skyline of rock aiguilles, with bigger snow peaks rising behind. We immediately named the highest point of the aiguilles, which towered above all its neighbours, the Citadel. Perhaps this peak would become one of the main objectives of the expedition. Below us was the snout of the glacier and it was another short day's march to cover the eight miles or so to our proposed base near the junction of several branches of the glacier, a place named Concordia by Sir John Hunt. The going was over almost level dry ice, though in part badly rutted and, as the glacier was about one and a half miles wide, we seemed to make very slow progress.

As we approached Concordia I became more and more anxious about finding the supplies which should have been dropped. The glacier was very wide and very large. To my surprise I soon noticed some small specks on the snow at the foot of some impressive vertical rock buttresses. Too near the rock face, I told myself, so they must be boulders. However, we walked towards them and they took shape and colour. They were the yellow parachutes. It took a full hour to reach the site of the drop and we were very relieved to find that it had been successful. All eight parachutes were in a neat line, perhaps 500 feet long, and our kit bags had survived the drop extremely well, with the food hardly damaged at all. Then we examined the crate of paraffin cans and found a horrible mass of battered and buckled cans. On investigation it appeared that this one parachute had failed to open and only six and a half gallons of our original twenty gallons had survived. We would have to manage somehow.

Our base camp, which we pitched about half a mile out on the glacier, consisted of a large bell tent and two small mountain tents. We were about 2,700 feet above sea level and still just below the snow line. Immediately to the south, behind our tents, were the vertical rock spires of the Citadel range rising to peaks 5,000 to 6,000 feet high, and quite as impressive as the aiguilles of Chamonix. Across the glacier, to the north and west, were bigger but more compromising mountains perhaps 7,000 feet high. Almost all of them were unclimbed. Howard and Graham, who had accompanied the air drop, arrived safely at base a day later. They too had had their adventures at the Lang River, Howard receiving a ducking.

With our party complete, perfect weather and plentiful supplies of food, we were now very well established for three weeks of mountain climbing and exploration. We planned to spend a week climbing directly from base camp, then to form two separate parties. A group of four, led by Howard Brunton, would attempt the first crossing of the range to Alpefjord in the northwest. Meanwhile, the rest of us would move to a camp on the Mercury Glacier, a southern tributary of the Bjornbos. Then the entire party would spend a week climbing the peaks of the Jupiter Glacier, which is another large tributary further southwest, where we expected to find the finest and highest peaks of the south Staunings.

190

The mountains of the south Staunings usually involved a long but easy and fairly level glacier approach, then a climb of anything between 2,500 and 4,500 feet. The scale was very similar to that encountered in the Alps of Europe when climbing from huts, and we usually climbed in parties of either two or four. My first climb was with Ian, Ray and Cyril. We chose a peak, which we subsequently named Hermitage, rising from the Mars Glacier and situated about six miles to the north. We left camp at 8 a.m. and at 10.30 a.m. had reached the foot of our peak. The proposed route of ascent was by a steep buttress of granite to the southeast ridge, thereafter following this to the summit. The buttress started off quite easy, then we came to a belt of bulging slabs, which we climbed by an oblique open chimney with a definite lack of positive holds. The climbing continued to be interesting, on sound rock for a while, then our buttress degenerated into a broken and tottering arête. All this time the sun had been bearing down on us and we became very dehydrated and lethargic. It was an effort to carry on at all, and difficult to force ourselves to eat any food. We were learning our first lesson about the mountains of Greenland, for in fine weather it is far too hot to climb around the middle of the day! We persevered with our climb and eventually reached the southeast ridge. There was a slight breeze and the ridge was easy enough to climb unroped. First we plodded up a broad shoulder covered by slushy snow, then it was a pleasant scramble along a shattered rock arête for about and hour and a half. We reached the summit at 6.20 p.m. and our altimeter indicated 6,700 feet. After a brief rest we descended by the same route and regained camp at 12.30 a.m., a sixteen and a half hour day.

After our lesson in the glaring midday sunshine on Hermitage, we devised a new time schedule which was rather novel for alpine climbing. Instead of starting in the morning with the almost certain knowledge that the noon sun would catch us up, we started in the afternoon, reaching the foot of our peak anytime between three and five o'clock. Then we climbed in the cool of the evening and reached the summit towards midnight. There is no darkness in Greenland in midsummer, and a very late return would be followed by a long lie-in next morning. Breakfast and lunch would often be one and the same meal, and one of my happiest memories of Greenland is of long, lazy mornings at the camp-site, relaxing under a hot sun.

During our week at base we accomplished a number of successful climbs, including Kilroy, the Bastille and Pisa, all of which are steep rock peaks, outliers of the Citadel range. We climbed these peaks by their steep and, in some places, vertical north faces, and encountered some hard rock climbing on excellent granite. Pisa, which resembled a big leaning tower, included one very severe pitch which occupied us over an hour, and the entire 1,800-foot-high face took six and a half hours. To our great surprise, there was always an easy route of descent, usually on the hidden southeast face. A contrast to these mountains was Sentinel, a big 7,200-foot peak guarding the route to the upper reaches of the Bjornbos Glacier. The approach took three and a half hours but, once on the mountain itself, we were engaged in pleasant scrambling, first up a rocky spur then a delightful arête of mixed rock and snow, taking a further four hours. From Sentinel we had our first view across the range towards Alpefjord and the inland ice cap, and also to the magnificent ice-covered mountains around the head of the Jupiter Glacier. We were all exceptionally fit and keen, and the time had now arrived to move further afield and explore the inner fastnesses of the range.

Next day was a busy one, packing supplies for the coming week, and towards evening Howard's party started very heavily laden for their journey to Alpefjord. The rest of us had a much shorter trip to the Mercury Glacier, taking only a few hours. This glacier involved a steady uphill grind with our ninety-pound loads, and eventually Gwyn's foot with the missing boot was giving him considerable pain. We were right at the edge of the snow line and about 700 feet higher than base, at a point on the north side of the glacier, directly below the summit of the Citadel. We immediately pitched camp and turned in. Next morning we woke to feel the sun beating down from a cloudless sky. Whereas at base we had often felt the penetrating chill of a breeze flowing down from the head of the glacier, here we were completely sheltered in a veritable suntrap. The lowest slopes of the Citadel, only a few hundred feet away, were covered with arctic poppies and saxifrage, and there was only an occasional rumble from the moraine to disturb our peace. This was the arctic riviera of which we had longingly read. Late that afternoon we skied up the glacier to a fine cone-shaped snow peak and climbed it by its northeast ridge. First a rock buttress, then a steep snow slope with some unpleasantly large crevasses and very dubious slushy snow. We were lucky, and all the snow-bridges held, although we sent down a few minor snow avalanches. The final plod up the ridge was hard work, with thigh-deep snow in places, but we reached the summit without incident at exactly midnight. We named it the Midnight Peak. When we had regained our skis, the glacier snow was freezing and we had an exhilarating run back to camp.

The fine weather continued unbroken and our next climb was the Citadel itself. To our great surprise, the south face contained a broad and quite easy rock buttress which took us straight to the western summit in only three and a half hours from camp. We were even able to sunbathe at the summit, the air was so still; then we traversed to the eastern top by a very exposed ridge taking about one and a half hours. In places our ridge actually overhung the grim ice-glazed cliffs of the north face. Then we descended by the easy south face.

Next day we attempted a rock peak on the south side of the glacier, but half way up we encountered a belt of impregnable bulging slabs capped by an overhang which was virtually devoid of holds and we had to retreat. All our other climbs around the Mercury were successful. MacLear and Hermes were both mainly rock peaks and quite easy, whereas Aries included a beautiful snow arête, followed by a fine exposed crest of granite which was very difficult at the summit tower. All these peaks were about 6,400 feet high and on Aries, our last climb, the snow was firm and frozen and we wore crampons for the first time. This was an excellent omen for our projected snow and ice climbs around the Jupiter Glacier for the final week, and we felt highly optimistic as we returned to base, to await the return of the boys from Alpefjord. When we arrived back we found a possibly unique spectacle. The two tents which we had left pitched had become raised above the surrounding ice, and there was ice almost to the roof inside! The ice of the glacier had melted down by about thirty inches during our week away and, of course, the shade from the tents had protected their base.

Next afternoon the Alpefjord party came into view. We all rushed out with cameras to greet them and they were in great spirit after a most successful trip, though not an uneventful one. After a short march to the snow line below Sentinel they had a long though easy day on skis to the head of the Bjornbos Glacier. There was a choice of several cols but, after consulting some aerial photographs, they rather optimistically floundered up the easiest one. The general angle was no more than 55° and, after a two hour struggle up thigh-deep snow, they reached the top at over 6,000 feet. On the other side, instead of a steep or impossible face, there was a beautiful gentle snow slope dropping to the north. They fixed their skis and covered the first six miles in about forty-five minutes before camping. Next day they encountered a badly crevassed area and had a trying time on their skis as a roped-up party. Eventually they were forced to the side of the glacier and crossed a spur to the Duart Glacier. Here Howard dropped into a hidden crevasse and only his pack saved him from falling a long way. The rest were able to pull him out. Once on the Duart they had gained the route followed by previous expeditions, between Alpefjord and the Lang Glacier, but this year the lower icefall of the Spaerre was in a chaotic condition and Howard's party was forced into a vile ablation valley at the side of the glacier, filled with ice, mud and scree. One stretch of only a mile took five and a half hours and it was a tired party which reached Dammen at the head of Alpefjord five days after leaving base. Near the fjord they were astonished to find an apparently fresh vibram print on the moraine; on closer inspection it was found to contain a layer of moss and it must have been made by a member of Sir John Hunt's 1960 expedition. After a brief rest at Alpefjord the return to base was made by the same route, the whole trip taking ten days.

After a day's rest at base, we packed again and moved camp to the Jupiter Glacier. We were all going well and, to my surprise, it took only three hours to reach the snow line at about 3,600 feet, shortly before a large tributary glacier called the Orion. Although we were still about five miles short of the icefall below the head of the glacier, there seemed little point in camping higher as we were centrally situated and would cover the approaches to the more distant peaks quite quickly on our skis. So we pitched camp midway between two delightful glacier pools.

It was now August and the midnight sunshine was at an end. This meant better climbing for us and the snow became firm and frozen, except on south-facing slopes. Perhaps my most pleasant day's climbing was a long traverse of a snow and ice ridge on the south side of the glacier. We climbed by razor-sharp arêtes of snow which would not have been possible except for the perfect conditions. Then the ridge opened out and a steepish bosse of ice brought us to a minor summit. There was a steep rock descent beyond, involving a very difficult pitch, then we continued by ice arêtes, made tricky by the afternoon sunshine, to the first main summit, which was perfectly symmetrical at the junction of three ridges. We named it Culross, after the Fifeshire village near my home. We had made good time and so decided to continue to the next summit a mile further on. We were able to traverse under the cornice, on the northeast side of the ridge, and made rapid progress, using crampons, turning several rock gendarmes en route. The final summit tower was capped by a slender needle of granite 25 feet high which we surmounted using some rounded horizontal cracks on its north side. The climb from the glacier had taken seven hours, and after a brief rest we returned to Culross, then descended to the glacier by its south face, an easy route, though we sank waist deep in slushy snow just above the glacier.

What we took to be the highest peak of the south Staunings, subsequently named Prometheus, was situated about eight miles distant, up the Orion Glacier. The face overlooking the glacier was composed of steep rock ribs, but its south face, which extended in a spur towards the Jupiter, consisted of a hanging glacier merging into the summit ice dome. We hoped this would form a feasible route to the top and, in customary casual fashion, Ray, Michael, Cyril and Graham set out at 4.15 one afternoon. The glacier approach, on skis, took over three hours but, once on to the peak, the climb went well. They quickly reached the hanging glacier by an easy rock buttress 1,200 feet high and strapped on crampons. The glacier was quite steep, but provided no real obstacles as they threaded a way through its icefall to the upper snowfields. Higher up the angle lessened, but the climb went on and on and there was a feeling of being on a big peak. At 10.40 p.m. they reached the level summit and consulted the altimeter. It recorded 8,600 feet and the air was extremely cold. All the other summits were dwarfed, even the big peaks around the head of the Jupiter, and many photographic panoramas were taken before fingers became numbed. The descent went quickly and the party regained camp at 2.40 a.m.

During the early days around the Mercury Glacier we had noticed twin peaks, apparently higher than any others, lying near the head of the Jupiter. The easterly one was a rock peak capped by a neat gable of snow, and we immediately named it the Tent Peak. The westerly mountain was bolder in outline, a stark crest of rock glazed by slabs of ice, and I insisted that we should name this the Wedge Peak. Keith thought I lacked any literary imagination and suggested some alternatives, but somehow this mountain was always the Wedge Peak to us. From our camp on the Jupiter, the Tent and Wedge peaks were hidden by an intervening ridge, and only their summits showed above, so the secrets of their northern slopes were hidden until we had threaded our way through the dangerous crevasses of the Jupiter icefall to its upper basin. The appearance of these peaks did not disappoint us. Each was a huge rock face, and between the two was a stoneswept couloir of grey ice rising 1,500 feet to the skyline. The Wedge Peak soared above this, a vast rock tower. Keith and Michael, who attempted the climb, had thought of ascending by the ice couloir but, on reaching the face, they found it swept by stonefalls, so they tackled the vertical rock face to its right, not very hopeful of success. Right from the start the climbing was severe up a series of vertical chimneys separated by short traverses over ribs and slabs. About 350 feet up they reached a scree-covered ledge, but above this the face appeared hopeless. They managed to climb about 100 feet up the line of a crack, but this petered out and it looked like being a retreat. However, Mike succeeded in crossing a bulging rib on the left, a desperate move, and he was into another crack. This was the crux, and the angle then eased a little. The climb went on, pitch after pitch, up incredibly deep chimneys. Now the technical difficulty was no more than severe and they rested awhile to watch the midnight sun dropping towards the spires of the north Staunings. But they had forgotten it was late in the season and the sun disappeared completely for a few hours. The rock which had been pink and warm became, in an instant, cold and hostile, and they were more conscious of the tongues of ice at the back of every chimney. They continued and, after many hours, gained the main west ridge 200 feet from the summit. One more hard pitch and they were at the top. It was 4.30 a.m. and they had been eleven and a half hours on the face.

Hoping that the cold would have stopped the stonefalls in the couloir they decided to attempt to descend by this route, but they soon came on to a sickening 70° slope of brittle ice which broke into great flakes and was hopeless for taking ice pitons. Eventually they managed to cross to a rock rib on the face of the Tent Peak opposite and quickly descended this to the glacier. Very tired, they arrived back at camp at midday after being away for twenty-four hours. We were very relieved to see them and eager to hear the news of their climb.

After a week at the Jupiter camp our time was up. Altogether we had climbed twenty-four peaks of the south Staunings, and the weather had remained fine throughout. Now the season was drawing to a close and, on our last afternoon, a cold ground mist drifted up the glacier. The peaks around the Bjornbos were completely obscured, but there were glimpses of the Jupiter tops from time to time. We struck camp, a little regretfully; for we all knew, we should never have another such holiday again. All that remained was to carry our gear and belongings back to the mining company airstrip in the Schuichart Valley, then to make our own way on foot to Mestersvig. This was the end of the expedition and very soon we were in the air again, flying home.

THE CAULLARAJU SYSTEM OF THE CORDILLERA BLANCA

By Domingo Giobbi

GENERAL

Geographical Description

The Caullaraju[1] system consists of a group of mountains and glaciers which, with the Rajutuna, dominates the plateau called the Pampa de Lampas and constitutes the southernmost group of the whole Cordillera Blanca. From these mountains there is an excellent close view of the impressive Huayhuash system which is dominated by the mass of the Yerupajà and the summit of the Jirishanca — another characteristic feature — stands out conspicuously among the other peaks.

From the glaciers of these mountains the first streams descend — the Rio Tucu, Rio Queullish and others — which are headwaters of the Rio Santa. This river, rising close by in the Conococha tarn, 4,020 m below the col of the same name, descends in an SSE–NNW direction, dividing the Cordillera Blanca to the east from the Cordillera Negra to the west. Having passed the village of Huallanca, almost at the end of the two Cordilleras, the Rio Santa turns westward and discharges itself into the Pacific north of Chimbote.

Much has been written already about the Cordillera Blanca; none the less it may be mentioned that it is about 112 miles long and runs between the latitudes of 10° and 8° 40′ south, parallel to the Cordillera Negra and to the coast.

It may be noted that although the Cordillera Negra has several peaks of about 5,000 m, it has no glaciers, to which fact it owes its name.

To reach the Cordillera Blanca from the south, by motor road, a drive of about 200 miles from Lima is necessary. For the first 125 miles northwards the route is along the coast, on the Carretea Panamericana (Pan-American Highway) which is asphalted throughout; then for the remaining seventy-five miles it turns inland and ascends through arid steep valleys to the Conococha Pass, 4,080 m. Here the first mountains of this chain — those, in fact, which are the subject of this article — come into view. From the Conococha Pass the road ascends to Huaraz (about fifty miles) and beyond, skirting the Rio Santa, in a valley commonly called "the Callejon de Huayla."

Besides Huaraz, chief town of the department of Ancash, other important small places in the "Callejon" are Carhuàs, Yungay — right opposite the Huascaran,

[1] *Caulla* is the Quechua name of a bird found in those regions; *raju* means snow or glacier.

6,768 m, the highest peak in Peru—and Caràs, which is connected with Lima by a direct weekly flight.

These little towns are surrounded by green valleys with a rich agriculture, especially in cereals. This gives the whole valley of the Rio Santa a verdant aspect almost like that of the Alpine valleys, in contrast to the coast, nearly all of which is arid. For this reason the "Callejon" is called the "Peruvian Switzerland". Good hostels offer the climber delicious days of rest before and after his expeditions.

Topographical and geological characteristics

The mountains of the Caullaraju group have almost the same characteristics as the other three groups into which the mountains of the southern part of the Cordillera Blanca fall, namely the Pongos group, the Raria group, the Tucu group and the Rajatuna massif (Nevado Paulista).[1] In fact these different groups are separated from one another by wide ice-free zones overlooking, especially those more to the south, green plateaux where cattle-breeding and sheep-rearing is widespread.

The Caullaraju group is composed of various peaks and ridges which enclose different valleys or *quebradas*. It is separated from the Tucu group by the Quebrada of Huicsu to the northeast and from the Rajutuna by the Quebrada of Tucu to the southeast, while on its western slopes lie a series of quebradas, of which that of Queullish is the most beautiful and offers the most difficult ascents.

The system may be considered to be divided into four distinct groups:

Western Caullaraju, which includes four summits of 5,603 m, 5,588 m, 5,500 m and 5,460 m, and which from its configuration is called by the local inhabitants Cruz de Plata (Silver Cross.)

Eastern Caullaraju, which includes the highest peak in the system, 5,686 m and four others of 5,353 m, 5,295 m, 5,147 m and 5,127 m, not to mention a peak which stands on the ridge that joins peaks 5,636 m (see below) and 5,686 m and the height of which is not known.

Northern Caullaraju, with two peaks of 5,420 m and 5,180 m.

Central Caullaraju, consisting of one mountain which has the largest glacier formations and is 5,636 m in height.

It should be noted that all these heights, except one or two in the Western Caullaraju which are not marked on it, are taken from the 1:100,000 topographical map of H. Kinzl and E. Schneider, to whom I offer my heartiest thanks. I am sure that in doing so I express the opinion of all alpinists and andinists, for this map is the *vademecum* of all expeditions in the Cordillera Blanca. In fact, the little map published in this volume is based on it, with the addition of the cols, peaks and more important geographical features which did not appear in the original map.

[1] *Nevado* means in Spanish a snow mountain.

198

Of these peaks only two (5,180 m and 5,127 m) are not covered with ice and snow, on the others there are many large glaciers, where seracs, crevasses and cornices combine to form fantastic mountain scenery. The line of eternal snow is about 5,000 m.

As for geology, Drs V. Cordani and A. C. Rocha Campos of the 1961 expedition, which made a geological survey of an area of about forty-five square miles, penetrating into all the valleys of the system, write:

"The Caullaraju region is one of the most interesting geologically, both for the variety of rocks present and for the structures found. It is an anticline formed of rocks of the Cretaceous system—sandstone and schist and limestone—on the limbs of which are slightly reversed faults more or less following the stratification. The nucleus of this structure is a bathylith of light-coloured granodiorite, the intrusion of which was responsible for the presence of signs of thermal metamorphism in the sediments. (The granodiorite of the Caullaraju corresponds to the 'leucogranodiorite of Cohup' of Egeler and De Booy, who give a detailed mineralogical and chemical description of the igneous rocks of a large area situated to the north of the system.) Volcanic rocks are also found in the region, superimposed on or intercolated with the cretaceous rocks; they are principally agglomerates, lavas and tufts which speaking generally form the highest 'peaks of the system'."

Fauna

As already mentioned, on the plateau below the group stock-breeding is carried on, and sheep especially are reared, but also cows and horses. Llamas are not seen here, as they are in the other regions of the Peruvian-Bolivian plateau (Cuzco, Lake Titicaca, etc.) but only vicuñas and alpacas, not to speak of the venado or deer. There is an abundance of trout in the morainic tarns on the mountain slopes and in the torrents. It is interesting to note that everywhere on the plateau horses, mules, donkeys and even pigs have long hair, allotted to them by the wisdom of Nature to protect them against the cold. Nor, lastly, should the presence of the condor in these regions be forgotten.

Climate

As is known, the period of fine weather in the Cordillera Blanca (as in the whole of the Peruvian-Bolivian plateau) is roughly from May to September and corresponds to the climbing season. Although this chain of mountains is in the southern hemisphere, so that the above-mentioned period corresponds to the geographical winter, these months, thanks to the dryness and the clear atmosphere, are the *verano* (summer) of the plateau; but this is not so on the coast, where we have the real winter and Lima is gloomy, cold and damp. For the other months, October–April, the opposite is the case, and we have the *invierno* (winter) on the plateau, where it is the rainy season.

It may be noted that in the Cordillera days and nights are almost always equal in length (twelve hours) all the year round, and the sun sets very quickly; climbers should not forget this.

According to observations made at a little meteorological station on the Pampa de Lampas plateau—to be quite exact, at the Vivienda Shiquicancha, ca. 4,080 m.—the rainfall during the period July 1961–June 1962—showed a minimum of nil for more than two months and a maximum of 207.8 mm (ca. 8 in.) for the month of March 1962.

The shade temperature during the same period showed a maximum of 15° C. and a mimimum of −8 C., while in the mountains the minimum temperature can be −20 C. and lower. The wind generally begins to blow at 10 a.m. and goes on till 4.30 or 5 p.m. with a maximum force of 8 to 15 m per sec. From May to July the prevailing winds are easterly and from August to May southerly. At this same observatory the lowest humidity noted in summer, at 1 p.m. and with a wind blowing, was about 18 per cent.

There are no such great storms or very high winds as are met with in the Andes of Argentina and Chile: in the climbing season the days are hot and bright, though large cumulus clouds can appear in the afternoon.

Folklore

In regard to folklore, the Callejon de Huayla is less striking than, for example, the province of Cuzco, owing to a higher standard of civilization and an approximation to modern life, especially among the young people. The language used among the Indians and "Cholos" is the Quechua.

Final Considerations

After having made four expeditions in the Andes of Argentina (Zone Aconcagua–Tupungato) and having visited other groups of the Bolivian-Peruvian plateau, I can affirm that for the beauty and boldness of its icy mountains, for the mildness of the climate in the mountaineering season (I have never heard of a case of congelation, of which there are many in the Argentinian and Chilean Andes), for the ease with which supplies can be obtained and porters engaged in the little towns of the valley, for easy access from Lima both by road and by air, the Caullaraju system, and especially the more important mountains to the north of the Cordillera Blanca, are of all the Cordilleras of the Andes the chain which offers most to the mountaineer.

Now that all the summits in the Caullaraju system have been reached by the most natural and easy routes, there still remain unclimbed the intermediary peak between the Nevado Brasil and the Eastern Caullaraju, as well as peaks 5,295 m and 5,127 m, of secondary importance, in the Eastern Caullaraju.

49 CAULLARAJU EAST (18,655 ft.) in the Peruvian Andes, seen from the ascent to Queñuaracra chico. It is the highest summit of the entire massif. (Photograph by Giobbi)

50/51 top: THE VIEW FROM THE NEVADO VINCI (18,045 ft.). From left to right: Nevado Caullaraju West or Cruz de Plata (18,380 ft.), Nevado Shumakrasu (18,310 ft.), Nevado Brasil (18,490 ft.), an unnamed summit, Caullaraju East (18,655 ft.). They form the icy amphitheatre of the Quebrada Queullish. (Photograph by Giobbi)

bottom: View from the summit of the Nevado Queñuaracra (17,562 ft.). From left to right: Nevado Caullaraju East (18,655 ft.), a nameless summit on the ridge between Caullaraju East and Brasil, Nevado Brasil (18,490 ft.)

52 NEVADO QUENUARACRA (5353 ft.) seen from the rock ridge of Caullaraju East. (Photograph by Giobbi)

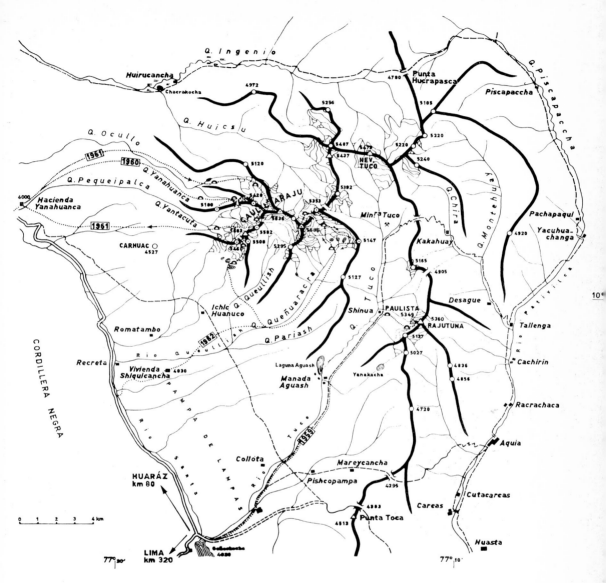

CORDILLERA BLANCA SOUTH (Peru). Routes and camps of the Brazilian Expedition. (By D. Giobbi)

Most interesting from a mountaineering point of view, and very difficult on account of their sheer rock faces and their cornices, are the walls which form the Queullish amphitheatre, viz. the southeastern face of the Shumakraju, the southern face of the Brasil and the southwestern face of the Eastern Caullaraju.

The Caullaraju system also offers several ascents of moderate difficulty, on walls as well as on slopes and ridges, which can fully satisfy the lover of mountains.

1959. NEVADO PAULISTA
Rajutuna massif, 5,349 m. 1st ascent.

The beauty of the Cordillera Blanca, known to me from various publications, had excited my imagination for a long time before I talked of it with the famous French alpinist Lionel Terray, my dearest friend. He was passing through São Paulo and told me of his ascents of the Nevados Pongos, Huantsan and Chacraraju.

So, when I founded the Club Alpino Paulista (C.A.P.) in 1959, taking advantage of the presence in São Paulo of other European mountaineers, I wanted to find at once in the Cordillera Blanca a group of mountains whence a systematic exploration could be made. In Brazil, where there are no mountains, I wished to form a mountaineering outlook and technique in the boys of my club, whose instructor I was, and at the same time to awaken the interest of scientists in mountain exploration. With this intention I set out for Lima on September 11th, and after ten days of exploration in the Cordilleras of Vilcanota and Uriebamba, in the province of Cuzco, I started at last for my longed-for goal, the Cordillera Blanca.

I arrived at Huaraz from Lima by motor bus and at once introduced myself to the Club Alpinista Cordillera Blanca, which brings together the best climbers and Peruvian porters. We were in the good season, so we quickly organized a light expedition consisting of myself, Apollonio Yanac, a well-known Peruvian andinist, and Eugenio and Macario Angeles, excellent fellows, who had already taken part in European and North American expeditions, as well as porters. After two days spent on preparations, we returned south, to the Pampa de Lampas. Austrian climbers from Innsbruck[1] had been in the Caullaraju and Raria groups in the same year and I knew that they had made some ascents, but none of the local shepherds could say exactly which. Meanwhile Apollonio assured me that the isolated mountain farther south was still virgin; we must attack it at once, as the weather was uncertain and great masses of black cloud announced that the rainy season was imminent.

We proceeded, therefore, by the track which leads to the Tucu mine and on September 20th fixed our base camp at about 4,200 m. The same day, ascending by

[1] Members of the Tiroler Kordilleren Expedition 1959, led by Heeresbergführer Hannes Gasser.

tiring *acarreos* (cones of detritus), we established a high camp above the shoulder of the mountain in the middle of the glacier, at 4,900 m. On the 26th we tackled the last part of the mountain, crossing crevasses and reaching a point below the peak, from which we were separated by an overhanging wall of ice about 40 m high. Fortunately a large fissure enabled us to penetrate into this icy mass: we scaled the western wall and reached the western summit at 11 a.m.

While we were descending it was very hot and we sank into the muddy snow almost up to our waists. We had hardly reached the base camp when the rain which had been threatening for days made an impetuous appearance, announcing the end of the climbing season.

This mountain, which at first we thought to be the Tucu, not having Kinzl and Schneider's map with us, was actually the Rajutuna, and the conquered peak was christened "Nevado Paulista." It was indeed still a virgin peak, since only a lower peak of 5,137 m had previously been reached by Peruvians.[1]

1960. CERRO YANAHUANCA
5,180 m, 1st ascent.

NEVADO CAULLARAJU NORTE
5,420 m, 1st repeat ascent.

Following the observations of the Caullaraju system made in the previous year, from the Pampa de Lampas as well as from the Nevado Paulista, I decided that this would be the group of mountains chosen by me for systematic survey.

Accordingly I returned to Huaraz in July 1960, and set up a base camp in the Hacienda Yanahuanca, on the edge of the Huaraz-Conococha road, 9½ miles from the Conococha Pass and at a height of about 4,000 m. I had with me Eugenio Angeles, now my inseparable rope-mate, and the porters Vitaliano Alvaron, Demetrio Natividad and Donats Solano. The last-named had been with the Austrians the year before and so was able to point out to us the peaks conquered by them—Western Caullaraju or Cruz de Plata, 5,603 m, and Northern Caullaraju, 5,420 m.

On July 13th, crossing the pampa which lies to the north of Carhuac, we entered the Quebrada of Ocullo along the side of it which turns south (this we christened Yanahuanca) and there established a base camp at about 4,400 m. Next day, overcoming the moraines and the *acarreos* (see above), we reached the col which separated the dark rocky ridge from the glaciers of the Northern Caullaraju. The same day, scaling walls with pitches of the 2nd or 3rd degree, Eugenio and I reached a summit which we christened Yanahuanca (meaning in Quechua dark or black stone). From this peak the view over the whole Caullaraju system was impressive, and from it we

[1] See editorial note on page 86 of the *Revista Peruana di Andinismo*, No. 5/1960–61.

studied the possible routes for the mountains which were still unclimbed. The next day, July 15th, Eugenio and I made a repeat ascent of the Northern Caullaraju (5,420 m), conquered the year before by the Austrians H. Gasser and H. Pattis, with D. Solano.

From the col between the Yanahuanca and Northern Caullaraju, and also from the ridge of the Yanahuanca, I took a series of photographs which were to show later on that the Eastern Caullaraju, i.e. the highest summit of the system which Vinci thought he had reached on the Pan-Andine Expedition of 1952, was in fact still virgin. The Peruvian experts, comparing my photographs with those published by Vinci in his book *Cordigliera*,[1] arrived at this conclusion. In fact Vinci photographed the Western Caullaraju group looking towards the southeast and round the col between the Yanahuanca and Northern Caullaraju, and declared that the highest peak of the system was visible to the right of the central peak. This is not correct, for the ascent of the Eastern Caullaraju from the west, from which side Vinci started, cannot be accomplished in a single day, especially in the rainy season. Vinci did reach a summit and, as he himself writes, it is possible that the mist prevented him from seeing that the highest summit of the system lay farther east, beyond the Quebrada of Queullish.[2]

1961. NEVADO BRASIL
5,636 m, 1st ascent.

NEVADO SHUMAKRAJU
5,582 m, 1st ascent.

Authorized by the União Brasileira de Excursionismo, and possessing the data of the two previous expeditions, I organized and directed the first scientific Brazilian mountaineering expedition, which was christened at birth "Expedicão Brasileira aos Andes Peruanos." I chose as mountaineers Michel Le Bret, Peter Slavec and Jair Laguna of the Club Alpino Paulista, and as geologists Umberto Cordani and Antonio Carlos Rocha Campos, members of the staff of the Geological Faculty of São Paulo University.

The equipment which I had obtained in Italy and France was already waiting for us at Lima when we arrived there in the first days of July. We were received, as always, with the traditional Peruvian hospitality, by directors and local Andinists, especially Señor Cesar Morales Arnao, and then started for Huaraz, 2,900 m. After

[1] The Innsbruck guide Hannes Gasser (see above), whom I visited in Austria, fully confirmed what I say here.

[2] See editorial note on page 86 and photographs published in the *Revista Peruana di Andinismo*, No. 5/1960–61.

passing a couple of days there we turned southwards again and, as in the previous year, fixed our base camp in the Hacienda Yanahuanca.

On the 15th and 16th we pitched Camp I close to a tarn which lies at the head of the Quebrada of Ocullo at about 4,800 m. From this camp Michel, being unwell, went down to the base camp and then to Huaraz. My programme was to cross the glacier of Central Caullaraju, 5,636 m, from north to south, and emerge from it by the *quebrada* which separates Western Caullaraju from the Yanahuanca. This *quebrada* is called by the natives Yantacasta.[1]

On the 17th we started on our climb, I roped to Eugenio. We marked the route across the glacier with little red flags, because the snow which was falling would cover our tracks. The other Brazilian climbers and Macario followed us about an hour later. At point 5,100 m Jair and Peter, with the porters Eustaquio Henostroga and Octaviano Zuñiga, descended to Camp I, while Macario and Eugenio remained with me. The weather was very bad, a strange thing at this season, and while we were pitching Camp II at 5,280 m, on the northern shoulder of the lovely mountain which is the centre of the whole system, a heavy fall of snow surprised us.

On June 18th, rounding a few seracs and then proceeding by easy slopes, Eugenio, Macario and I reached the summit of this colossus, on the southern slope of which is a wall 700 m high, falling almost vertically to the Quebrada of Queullish. We christened this summit, which is marked 5,636 m on Kinzl's map, Nevado Brasil. From here we could see the highest peak of the system (5,686 m) and realized that to tackle it by the ridge joining it to the peak where we were at that moment would be a very long business, inasmuch as the ridge falls, then rises again towards an inter-mediary peak, then falls again and rises again towards Eastern Caullaraju. Moreover, this route is very dangerous on account of the great cornices that run all along the ridge. I therefore came to the definite decision that Eastern Caullaraju is more easily approached from the eastern slope, i.e. from the Quebrada of Queñuaraera.

When we had taken various panoramic photographs, we descended towards the Western Caullaraju or Cruz de Plata group to study the crossing of the Nevado Brasil glacier. On the 19th we effected this crossing by means of breaks in the crevasses and snowbridges and established Camp III at 5,200 m in the col which separates the Brasil from the group and also divides the Quebrada of Queullish from the Quebrada of Yantacuta. Still with Macario and Eugenio, I climbed on the 20th the most beauti-ful peak situated above this col—it is marked 5,582 m and is on the eastern side of the Cruz de Plata—and christened it Shumakraju (in Quechua, "Beautiful Moun-tain") on account of its slender pyramidal shape. During this ascent the southern walls of the Nevado Brasil and the southwestern walls of the Eastern Caullaraju came in sight, both almost perpendicular and at times quite sheer, with glaciers hanging

[1] In Quechua *yanta* means wood and *cuta* nook, in Spanish *rincon*.

from them, and their peaks terminating in most beautiful cornices. These two walls, together with the wall southeast of Shumakraju, form the great ice amphitheatre of the Quebrada of Queullish.

We descended the same day and arrived in the night at the camp which Jair, Peter and Michel—who had returned from Huaraz quite well again—had pitched for our reception in the Quebrado of Yantacuta, at 4,600 m. We embraced and celebrated the Brazilian–Peruvian victories. Next day they ascended with Macario to Camp III, at 5,200 m, for the last practice climb. Then, while the geologists were continuing their scientific survey, we climbers returned to Brazil. I was satisfied both with the result and with the technique acquired by my pupils and colleagues. Though not accustomed to great heights, which do not exist in Brazil, they are today physically and technically ready to take part in mountaineering expeditions, which was the object of the directors of the Club Alpino Paulista.[1]

1962. NEVADO QUEÑUARACRA

5,353 m, 1st ascent.

NEVADO CAULLARAJU EST

5,686 m, 1st ascent.

NEVADO QUEÑUARACRA CHICO (LESSER)

5,147 m, 1st ascent.

NEVADO CARIOCA

5,460 m, 1st ascent.

NEVADO VINCI

5,500 m, 1st repetition.

I now knew all the mountaineering problems which still had to be solved in order to reach the peaks as yet unclimbed. With Eugenio and Macario Angeles again as my companions, I pitched our first camp on July 7th, 1962, in the ice amphitheatre of the Quebrada of Queñuaracra at about 4,400 m. On July 7th Eugenio and I made the ascent of the nevado which lies right in the centre of the amphitheatre, 5,353 m high, and christened it Nevado Queñuaracra. Next day we moved camp on to the glacier, beyond the rocky ridge which descends from the Eastern Caullaraju towards the Quebrada of Queñuaracra, at about 5,200 m. This is the glacier which descends towards the Quebrada of Huicsu and which faces north.

Finally, on July 14th, we began to ascend the snowfield of *penitente* of the Caullaraju (*penitente* are not very common in that region): the weather was cold and

<hr>

[1] The geological survey carried out by Drs Cordani and Rocha Campos was published in the bulletin of the Brazilian Geological Society, Vol. xi, No. 1, May 1962.

fortunately none of the little *penitente* moved under our weight. We crossed several crevasses and soon the final pyramid lay just ahead, separated from us by the terminal crevasse, which lay right along its base. We skirted this almost as far as the ridge which leads to the Nevado Brasil, and here a snowbridge enabled us to cross it. The snow of the final pyramid was very hard, and the steep slope compelled us to zigzag. At about 11.30 we were on the highest summit of the whole system. Well secured by Eugenio, I approached the cornice which stands above the Quebrada of Quellish and so was able to get a view of the fearful wall which descends into this valley.

Full of joy, Eugenio, Macario and I planned the conquest of the few remaining peaks of the system. I took various panoramic photographs. The day was clear, and we could see all the groups to the northward: Raria, Pongos, then the Huantsan, the mountains of Huaraz, with the Huascaran beyond—in fact, almost all the Cordillera Blanca. And in the southeast, marvellous to behold, the Huayhuash chain. On the 16th, with Macario, I climbed the peak which forms the eastern boundary of the system and we christened it Queñuaracra Chico (the lesser). Its height is 5,147 m.

Then we left this valley to set up another base camp southwest of the Western Caullaraju, between the Quebrada of Queullish and Carhuac, at about 4,300 m. On the 18th we established a high camp at 5,100 m, and finally on the 19th, still with the Angeles brothers, I climbed the nevado reported by Vinci in his book *Cordigliera*, a very high peak, and another, the farthest westward of the Western Caullaraju; this we named Nevado Carioca as a tribute to the Rio mountaineers. These last two peaks are beside the Cruz de Plata, 5,603 m, and their heights are not given on Kinzl and Schneider's map. The measurements taken with our altimeters were 5,500 m for the Nevado Vinci and 5,460 m for the Nevado Carioca. These will be corrected by topographical measurements.

ASCENTS IN THE CAULLARAJU SYSTEM

Mountain	Height in metres	Group	1st Ascent	1st Repeat	Mountaineers
Nev. Vinci	5,500	C. West	16.3.52		A. Vinci, G. Verganni, F. Anzio
Nev. Cruz de Plata	5,603	,,	24.6.59		H. Gasser, H. Pattis, K. Kepliner, U. Staulacher
Nev. Caull. N.	5,420	C. North	26.6.59		H. Gasser, H. Pattis, D. Solano
Cerro Yanahuanca	5,180	,,	14.7.60		D. Giobbi, E. Angeles
Nev. Caull. N.	5,420	,,		15.7.60	D. Giobbi, E. Angeles
Nev. Brasil	5,636	C. Central	18.7.61		D. Giobbi, E. Angeles, M. Angeles
Nev. Shumakraju	5,582	C. West	20.7.61		D. Giobbi, E. Angeles, M. Angeles
Nev. Quenuaracra	5,353	C. East	12.7.62		D. Giobbi, E. Angeles
Nev. Caull. E.	5,686	,,	14.7.62		D. Giobbi, E. Angeles, M. Angeles
Nev. Quenuaracra Chico	5,147	,,	16.7.62		D. Giobbi, M. Angeles
Nev. Carioca	5,460	C. West	19.7.62		D. Giobbi, E. Angeles, M. Angeles
Nev. Vinci	5,500	,,		19.7.62	D. Giobbi, E. Angeles, M. Angeles

THE ANDES OF VENEZUELA

By Douglas Busk

The Andes of Venezuela were last briefly described for the readers of *Berge der Welt* as long ago as 1948, and later climbs should now be mentioned, even though by the standards of other parts of the Andean chain the Sierra Nevada de Mérida is lower in altitude and infinitely less difficult technically. Even if difficulty is deliberately sought, all routes are very short. Altitude apart—and this is a serious matter—the climber from the British Isles is more apt to make comparisons with Wales or Scotland than with the more glaciated and exacting Alps.

This group possesses, however, the immense advantage that it is now extremely easy of access. It is, for instance, possible to reach a base camp at 4,500 m within seventy-two hours from Europe, providing of course that the trip has been meticulously planned in advance—not easy unless one is living in Venezuela, speaks the language and knows the best methods; often not easy even then.

A note is attached on bibliography and it is assumed that any prospective visitor will have consulted these sources—in particular Gunther's and my articles in the *Alpine Journal*. The latter has an appendix dealing with equipment.

Swiss readers in particular will derive enjoyment from Dr M. Blumenthal's article in the *Jahrbuch des Schweizer Alpenclub* 1922.[1] His journey of forty years ago brings out even more than Gunther's the immense changes that have taken place in Venezuela. In Blumenthal's day it would have required at least three weeks from Caracas to reach our own base in the mountains; let us say six weeks in all from Europe, compared with the seventy-two hours mentioned above. From Valera on the outskirts of the range he had three very long days' mule riding to Mérida; nowadays one drives in four hours over the 4,048 m Mucuchies pass. Now there are at reasonable intervals good hotels; then nought but primitive inns, where animals had to be displaced before the traveller could extend his weary body.

It was on such tracks, over such lofty passes and in much the same conditions that Simón Bolívar led whole armies at the beginning of the last century in his long campaign to free the whole of the north of South America from the Spanish yoke. When

---

[1] I recently found myself in correspondence with the author about a very different range of mountains in Africa and am most grateful to him for sending me an off-print of his earlier article, to which I should not otherwise have had access in Caracas.

53 KERGUELEN. An island group in the southern Indian Ocean. The main island has mountains and glaciers. Toward the east it extends into a glacial landscape with many lakes and deep fjords. In the foreground is the South Face of Mont Ross (6,250 ft.) with three hanging glaciers. (Photograph by Albert
Baur, TAAF)

54 THE SUMMIT OF MONT ROSS (6,250 ft.), the highest point of the Kerguelen islands. The ridge forms the edge of an enormous crater. In the distance is the ice mass of the Cook Glacier. (Photograph by Albert Baur, TAAF)

55 THE MAIN ISLAND of the Kerguelen Archipelago with the Bay of Morbihan. In the foreground is seaweed flora typical of the island. On the rocks are cormorants. (Photograph by Albert Baur, TAAF)

one recalls that his indomitable spirit carried him in such conditions not only through Venezuela but to what are now Colombia, Ecuador, Peru and Bolivia, one can only marvel at the endurance of the *Libertador*, his staunch companions and the gallant men[1] who followed his flaming example.

In other respects, too, Blumenthal's article is a corrective to any modern conceit. We arrived completely equipped by modern standards at our camp; Gunther twenty years earlier had at least ropes, ice axes and tried companions; Blumenthal, travelling alone, had no more than a "rusty garden hoe" for an ice axe and to keep out the piercing cold padded his garments with newspapers. In earlier days in the Alps and Pyrenees I myself found the daily press very comforting in bivouacs, but I am now old enough to prefer *duvets*.

Despite such handicaps Blumenthal made impressive first ascents of outlying peaks and his article contains an instructive passage on humanity in Venezuela that is as true today as it was then; here it suffices to say that he rejoiced, as we still do, in travelling with the courteous and efficient *Andino* of the uplands.

Another disadvantage suffered by earlier travellers was lack of reliable and fairly large-scale maps. Even now there are only sketch maps on a scale of 1:100,000 of the Sierra Nevada de Mérida.

The main and, given the general conditions in Venezuela, almost fantastic novelty since earlier days is the construction of a funicular[2] from Mérida (1,630 m) to the neighbourhood of Pico Espejo (4,765 m) within a kilometre of the culminating summit of the group, Pico Bolívar (5,007 m).[3] This funicular permits the ascent from or descent to Mérida in anything from one to two hours, depending on the pressure of crowds. The management are, one is happy to record, very favourably inclined to mountaineers and thus, while the "trains" normally only run on Saturdays, Sundays

[1] The feats of the British Legion at the decisive battle of Carabobo (1820) are still remembered with pride in Venezuela, where British troops alone among foreign forces are permitted to march with fixed bayonets through Caracas and the other cities.

[2] Work on this funicular was started in 1956 during the days of a grandiose dictator. When the present democratic government assumed power in Venezuela in 1958 it was rightly felt that such expensive and unproductive projects should be scrapped and the money devoted to better ends. Though it is difficult to stop a funicular when it has hewed and crept half way up a mountain, the Company were agreeable to compromise. It is said that the Mexican Government were interested in a funicular up Popocatepetl (5,442 m) and could have used some of the material and skill there. It was found, however, that the deep layers of volcanic ash precluded the construction of solidly based pylons. Popocatepetl therefore remains inviolate and the mountaineer in Venezuela is provided with an insidiously easy method of ascent.

[3] On various maps Pico Bolívar varies from 5,002 m to 5,007 m. I have no particularly good reason for selecting the latter.

and holidays, they will produce a "special train" for real enthusiasts at any reasonable hour. (Workmen, still in 1962 constructing the top station buildings, have to be continually on the move).

The rapid ascent, though highly agreeable to those with flabby muscles, brings penalties with it. One is reminded of these by a thoughtful management, who instal portable oxygen cylinders and masks in each car and station, just as is done in unpressurized aircraft. There is no doubt that the rapid transition is extremely severe, even to those in good training or capable of it.

We had originally intended to travel from Mérida in the old and agreeable fashion by mule, taking three days to camp and thus, we hoped, acclimatizing on the way. Time did not permit and all suffered from lack of acclimatization in consequence, as has been told in the story of our trip in the *Alpine Journal*, Vol. LXVII. What is much worse was that we were deprived to some extent of the chance to meet local inhabitants slowly in their own true environment. Instead we rushed along like any tourists and it was only through the courtesy of our porters, Cupertino Zerpa and Desiderio Castillo that we learned anything. They were both splendid companions. Cupertino is incidentally the *Jefe de Aldea*[1] or mayor of the village of Los Nevados, through which we had hoped to pass on our mule trip. We were flattered that his friendship with Franco Anzil induced him to join us. The major part he played is set out at greater length in my article in the *Alpine Journal*.

As always, seasons should be discussed before the details of mountaineering exploits. The Venezuelan Andes have not yet reached the advance stage of civilization where one must climb a spectacular route on a dangerous mountain at the wrong season of year in order to achieve publicity in the cheaper press.

From April or thereabouts until October or thereabouts rain below and snow above must be counted on. It is not a time for agreeable mountaineering. However, another sport is then possible—trout fishing in the innumerable streams and small lakes of the Venezuelan Andes. Be warned, however, that the more accessible waters are overfished. You must be prepared to walk far, if necessary in the rain, to grass a good catch.

In what Europeans call the autumn—there are no seasons in the tropics as we understand them—comes the splendid interlude of the upland flowers. The mountaineer, even if not climbing, can then enjoy views of the peaks at their best, the foreground above 10,000 feet bedight with the curious *frailejones* of the high Andes. Below about 6,500 feet flowering trees or shrubs, the great glory of Venezuela, are

---

[1] Strictly speaking the form of address is simply *Aldea*, e.g. "How are you, Village, this morning?" or "I should be grateful, Village, if you would repair the bridge."

always in blossom throughout the year—not, of course, all at once, but in a mysterious and breath-taking succession.

Meanwhile in the "winter" (the European summer) there are ski-ing possibilities, but it must be frankly admitted that these are meagre. Under an equatorial sun these peaks are too low to provide sufficient snow in accessible spots. Heroic efforts are made to boost Mérida as a ski resort from August to October. Even before the construction of the funicular, races were held and there is now an annual "Ski Week". The slope used for races cannot be much longer than 500 yards with a total drop of perhaps 300 feet. It starts from the upper station of the funicular close to Pico Espejo. The competitors are, of course, hoisted aloft from Mérida *par la ficelle*. Skilled or unskilled they can just manage a breathless slalom descent and a slow plod back to the starting point, their skis borne up by Andino porters. All honour to those who try to familiarize a splendid sport in such conditions.

Not until December does the wise mountaineer raise his eyes to the heights. He can then at least hope for three months of excellent weather. Being a wise mountaineer he will know that no weather anywhere in the mountain world is predictable and he will be neither infuriated nor downcast if in the middle of the "fine season" he strikes a bad patch, In particular he will soon realize that, while peaks may be clear at dawn, they are likely to cloud over exasperatingly by, say, 11 a.m. and remain shrouded until shortly before sunset. He will also appreciate that even on sunny days he may have to face bitter winds (at altitudes higher than Mont Blanc) and extremes of heat and cold exceeding those of the Alps during the European summer climbing season.

One of the nicest things a mountaineer encounters when he visits Mérida is the enthusiasm of those who have set their eyes on the peaks and without much technical experience or knowledge of modern equipment still contrive to climb the mountains of their choice. It was a pleasure to meet some of these enthusiasts, from whom, in turn, we learnt much about local conditions of travel. The Club Andino is limited in scope by lack of recruits, but as long as Franco Anzil, an Italian resident in Mérida, is able to move as deftly as he does among these mountains, guidance and enthusiasm will be available. No better organizer or companion could be expected. Local climbing records are not easy to assemble and one must rely for the most part on the written word (see Bibliography). Even here caution must be exercised. It would, for instance, be unwise for all but the most daring foreigner to express himself publicly on who made the first ascent of Pico Bolívar.

In these pages it will suffice to say that by the time we made our trip in 1962 all the main summits had been climbed: El Leon and El Toro—the Lion and the Bull—to the west; Pico Bolívar and the peak now known as El Abanico[1]—the Fan—in the

[1] Previously known as "Columna South Peak".

211

central Columna group; La Concha—the Shell; and both peaks of the eastern Corona group, Humboldt and Bonpland. There remained only minor but worthy virgin summits. Of these our party made the ascent of two, El Vértigo, a short but serious rock climb and a prominent peaklet for which the name Pico Jahn has now been adopted.

The former (c 4,950 m) was the principle objective of our expedition. It is unquestionably the most difficult, though minor, *peak* in the Venezuelan Andes (though, of course, other *routes* of high standard remain to be forced). It is very little lower than the culminating summit, Pico Bolívar, and from some viewpoints is easily confused with it. The climb is very short, but it is a measure of the severity (Standard V) that for many years it successfully defied attempts by such fine mountaineers as Weiss and Vinci. After a reconnaissance pushed to within 100 feet of the summit it was finally led on February 28th, 1962, by George Band, who took one-and-a-half hours to master the last twenty feet. Pitons were used as safeguards, but not for artificial climbing; all were removed. His companions were J. A. UZCATEGUI[1] Salas, of Mérida, and David Nott, a British journalist resident in Caracas and an experienced rock climber.

Pico Jahn (c 4,850 m) merits a separate name at least as much as some of the minor Chamonix aiguilles. It was bestowed in honour of the distinguished Venezuelan scientist and explorer, who made the first ascent of Pico Humboldt as far back as 1911. This was the first major summit of the Venezuelan Andes to be climbed—Pico Bolívar was not ascended until 1936, which gives some indication of the neglect of the range by trained mountaineers.

Pico Jahn (standard III) is conveniently accessible from the Col Bourgoin. Its vanquishers were G. Band and D. Nott.

They also made a fine new route up the southwest face of El Abanico (standard III, though it looked much more difficult).

In addition another ascent was made of El Abanico from the Col Bourgoin (G. Band and N. Davis) and two ascents of Pico Bolívar by the ordinary, or Weiss, route. This involves little difficulty save for the exposed traverse below the summit and the final chimney. Minor climbs were also accomplished (including the Shell, the Lion and the Bull by Davis and Cupertino) and much equipment was tested.

The base camp for all these climbs was pitched on a levelled platform below the tongue of the Timoncito Glacier at about 4,500 m. This gives a very short ascent to all peaks, which was most welcome owing to the very sudden rise in altitude by

[1] In Spain and some Latin American countries the last name is often the mother's and not the father's name. Sometimes an initial is used for the former. Here and elsewhere I have used capital letters for the patronymic by which a person is addressed.

funicular and consequent lack of acclimatization. No early starts were necessary though, as already mentioned, it is better to aim at completing climbs by noon, since the mountains are later often veiled in cloud. The camp site can be reached in a couple of hours of easy descent from the highest station of the funicular. Contiguous to the platform is a ruined hut, still however sufficiently weatherproof to be usable by those without tents. It served for the two excellent Andino porters whom we retained throughout. Other porters were employed only for the carry from the Pico Espejo top station to the camp and, nine days later, for the return.

We were lucky to be favoured by almost perfect weather throughout.[1]

In February, 1963, another expedition was made to the Sierra Nevada de Mérida. This time it was designed not so much for exploration, but as a training exercise, and Venezuelan students were invited to attend. A suitable spot was found close to camp where rock-climbing instruction could take place, and rappels be practised. Later the team were taken on to the glacier for instruction in ice work.

Subsequently several climbs were effected, including Pico Bolivar by ordinary route, and by the more difficult route from the Col of Bourgoin. The team enjoyed excellent weather, and it is hoped that the experience can be repeated in a later year so that the students at the University of the Andes in Mérida can acquire familiarity with their own mountains and cope with the difficulties successfully.

In general the Andes of Venezuela should not be regarded as a serious challenge in comparison with those, say, of Peru. They remain, however, a magnificent and very easily accessible climbing centre. If these pleasant mountains were situated in the British Isles or in the Alps every face and ridge would be criss-crossed with routes and every pinnacle named—as in the Lakes, Chamonix or the Engelhörner.

There are even "north faces" and these, though diminishingly so, are glaciated. They can arouse as much controversy as in Europe. Those who read Italian and Spanish can digest the accounts of the first ascent of Pico Bolívar from the north given by Vinci and Chalbaud not only with amusement but profit. In this contentious world no one will be surprised that jealousies are aroused as much in mountaineering as in international affairs, though all will regret that we are afflicted by such spiteful tendencies. In Venezuela, at least, matters were in the end settled amicably. The party that had made the "disputed" first ascent of the north face of Pico Bolívar returned indignantly to Mérida from Caracas and repeated it—insisting that witnesses watch throughout and accompany if they could. That well-known emolient champagne concluded the strife.

[1] For a fuller record see *Alpine Journal* Vol. LXVII, p. 280. The party consisted of F. Anzil (Italy), G. Band (U.K.), D. Busk (U.K.), N. Davis (U.S.A.), D. Nott (U.K.), J. A. Uzcátegui (Venezuela); and porters D. Castillo and C. Zerpa.

To quote Chalbaud, "And in the intimacy of firelight round the hearth the climbers of Mérida showed their esteem and closer became the bonds that will always unite Andinists and Alpinists".[1]

Let us hope that such a pleasant atmosphere will always exist between mountaineers of all nations.

BIBLIOGRAPHY

For earlier years it is best to refer to the excellent bibliographies of Gunther in his articles in the *Alpine Journal* Vols. LII p. 70 and LIII p. 127.

Additions are mentioned in my article in the *Alpine Journal*. For convenience of reference these are reprinted below:

1. *Berge der Welt* (Vol. III (1948) p. 341 (one illustration).
2. *Expediciones a la Sierra Nevada de Mérida.*
   Dr Carlos CHALBAUD Cardona (Caracas and Madrid, 1959, illustrated and pictorial map).

This is a Venezuelan history of climbing in the main group. The first attempts at ski-ing are also mentioned.

3. *Cordigliera*, Alfonso Vinci, (Bari 1959, in Italian).

This book deals not only with the Venezuelan Andes and other links in the chain west and south, but also with travels among Indian tribes in the jungles of the Orinoco (illustrated). Vinci is a very competent mountaineer and a traveller who combines knowledge with cheerfulness.

4. *Itinerarios Turisticos—Alpinisticos en la Sierra Nevada de Mérida*. Carlos Lacruz and Franco Anzil (Mérida, 1961).

This roneoed brochure was produced for a convention on Tourism. No illustrations, no map. The better known climbs, walks, very limited ski-ing possibilities and trout fishing lakes and streams are dealt with in detail. It is very valuable to any visitor.

---

[1] I have translated freely from the charming Spanish: "*Y a la lumbre de la chimenea se hicieron más tangibles las demostraciones de aprecio de los excursionistas merideños y más estrechos lazos fraternales que siempre unirán a los andinistas y alpinistas.*"

KERGUELEN ISLAND

By Albert Bauer

Vasco da Gama opened the route to the Indies in 1494 by rounding the Cape of Good Hope, the most southerly point of Africa. Ferdinand Magellan, a Portuguese in Spanish service, passed through the straits which bear his name and made the first crossing of the Pacific Ocean in 1519. Between these two dates of capital importance for the discovery of the southern hemisphere lie the strange adventures of the French navigator Binot Paulmier, Sieur de Gonneville.

Captain de Gonneville sailed from Honfleur in January 1503 in command of *L'Espois*, hoping no doubt to bring back incalculable wealth from the wonderful East Indies. But a storm which fell upon him in the South Atlantic cost him his navigator and his route. After drifting about for a long time he came to an earthly paradise inhabited by a most hospitable population, whom he took to be the inhabitants of the most northerly point of the southern continent. On his return voyage he was captured by pirates off Jersey, all his documents disappeared, and nothing was left to posterity but the legend of this "parrakeet land" in the southern continent on the route to the Indies – a legend which haunted all the navigators of the South Seas for three centuries.

These cold seas, in which fearful storms prevail all the year round, which sailors called the "roaring forties", remained long unexplored, from their extent and the difficulty of navigating them. Not till 1738 did Bouvet du Lozier make his voyage, to be followed in 1766 by the unfortunate Bougainville, while 1768 saw the first voyage of the famous Captain Cook, who between 1772 and 1775 circumnavigated the Antarctic continent. At that time trading ships and whalers opened up the routes through the South Seas, thus realizing in part the dreams of Captain de Gonneville.

The Compagnie des Indes, reduced to a moribund state by the disastrous Treaty of Paris in 1763, and also the Pouvoirs Publics, decided to rediscover Gonneville's famous southern continent. The Crozet archipelago was discovered in 1772 by Marion Dufresne of Saint Malo and his second in command Captain Crozet of Lorient. At the same moment Yves de Kerguelen was discovering the island which still bears his name.

The Chevalier de Kerguelen, a member of the famous Brest Academy, submitted to Terray, Minister of Marine, a project for the exploration of the southern continent.

This project received the King's consent. Captain de Kerguelen sailed from the Ile de France (Ile Maurice) in January 1772, kept well clear of Bourbon (La Réunion) and followed a southerly course with the two cargo vessels *La Fortune* and *Le Gros Ventre*, commanded by M de Saint Allouarn. The goal of his voyage was the *Terra australis incognita*. The look-out of *La Fortune* reported land in sight in February, but Kerguelen, cut-off from *Le Gros Ventre* by a storm, did not know what had become of his escort, nor did he know that M de Boisguehenneuc had succeeded in taking possession in the King's name of the country he was seeking. As the storm continued, Kerguelen put back to the Ile de France and thence returned to France without news of his escort. He was presented to Louis XV, promoted *capitaine de vaisseau*, and received the Cross of St Louis. He was now entrusted with a further mission, to look for *Le Gros Ventre* and at the same time carry out a full exploration of the "France Australe" which he had described in its most paradisal aspect.

Kerguelen sailed from Brest in March 1773. He had shown scanty regard for regulations in shipping trashy goods for himself and his crew, and a pretty girl called Louise Seguin for his own pleasure. By eighteenth-century standards these were only minor offences, and would have been regarded as such if it had not been for the resentment of the surviving officers and men of *Le Gros Ventre*, whom he found on the Ile de France, at seeing the commander who had abandoned them returning covered with honours and glory.

The fair Louise was shipped back to France, and Kerguelen set off again southward with the frigate *L'Oiseau*, the corvette *La Dauphine* and the escort vessel *Le Roland*. The voyage was not so successful as the first one. After a fresh landing in the Baie de l'Oiseau, in the north of what Kerguelen now thought to be an island and not the tip of a continent, cold, continual storms and the scurvy which was killing off his crew compelled Kerguelen to put back quickly towards Madagascar. Then he returned to France, disillusioned as to the climate and resources of an unfriendly desolate country which he had scarcely seen, a painful contrast to his earlier boasting. An unjust trial condemned him to loss of rank, removal from the Navy list and six years' imprisonment in a fortress. After his release he rejoined the Navy and became a rear-admiral under the Revolution. His account of his two voyages contains a very brief summary of the north-west coast of the island, a description of the mountains and glaciers he had hardly seen, and remarks on the climate.

Captain Cook, on his third voyage round the world, landed in the north of Kerguelen Island at Christmas 1776. Ross's two ships the *Erebus* and *Terror* followed in 1840. The *Challenger*, commanded by Captain Nares, explored part of the island in 1874 on her oceanographical cruise. In the same year Germany, Great Britain and the United States sent scientific missions to observe the transit of Venus across the sun. The *Arcona* under Captain von Reibnitz prepared the way for the despatch of the

216

57 ANTARCTIC. The American expeditionary column of the "Byrd Traverse Party" at the foot of the Horlick Range. (Photograph by Emil Schulthess)

58 MOUNT GLOSSOPTERIS in the Horlick Range (Antarctic). About half way up the 10,000 foot mountain the first fossil shells and snails were found, and higher up were found the leaf-impressions of the Glossopteris Flora which gave the mountain its name. (Photograph by Emil Schulthess)

59 top: FOSSIL SITES at the foot of Mount Glossopteris.
bottom: GEOLOGICAL SPECIMENS from Mount Glossopteris: leaf prints in sandstone stratum; coal (lower left), and fossilized wood fragments of tree trunks of the Glossopteris flora. (Photograph by Emil Schulthess)

60 ANTARCTIC. The endless ice plain of the White Continent with the silhouette of the American expeditionary column. In the sky is a halo, a phenomenon of the refraction and reflection of sunlight. (Photograph by Emil Schulthess)

Gazelle, commanded by Captain von Schleinitz. The British mission was brought out in the *Volage* and returned in 1875 in the *Supply*. The American mission established itself in the south of the Courbet peninsula.

The *Valdivia* (German Deep Sea Expedition) touched at Kerguelen Island at the end of 1898. The *Gauss*, of the German South Polar expedition under Dr Drygalski, on her way to the Antarctic, landed three scientists and an assistant in Baie de l'Observatoire in January 1902. One of them, Dr Enzensperger, died in the course of the year, and the others were taken home in the *Stassfurt* next year.

The brothers Henri and Raymond Rallier du Baty, on board a 45-tons sailing vessel, the *J. B. Charcot* – so named in honour of the celebrated explorer with whom Raymond spent the winter of 1904 in the Antarctic on board the *Français* – stayed for fifteen months on Kerguelen Island in 1908–9. Besides exploring the coasts and carrying out important hydrographic work, they hunted the sea elephants and boiled down their fat with lignite found in the island to extract the oil and so defray the expense of the voyage. Their book, *Fifteen thousand miles in a Ketch*, published in English by Nelson in 1912, remains a classic of exploration. Raymond Rallier du Baty was able to complete the work on the official expedition of *La Curieuse*, a sailing vessel of 32 tons. The current map of Kerguelen Island is based on the surveys carried out by his mission in 1913–14.

All these undertakings brought home important scientific material. But the main exploratory work dates from 1923–24 (Etienne Peau expeditions) and from 1928–1929–1931 (Edgar Aubert de la Rue expeditions).

In addition to the scientific interest of this remote island in the southern Indian Ocean, it has been of great economic interest. From 1800 to 1930 this consisted in whaling and the hunting of sea elephants, enormous seals which formerly existed in hundreds of thousands on the coasts of the Australasian islands. The hunters in these regions were mainly Norwegians, and Americans. What called attention to their campaigns was more than anything a number of spectacular shipwrecks. An English sailor named John Nunn lived at Port du Tonnerre, on the west coast, from 1825 to 1829 as a survivor of the wreck of the sealer *Favorit*. The American Captain Fuller spent a year in the Baie Accessible about 1850 after the *Rosswell King* had been wrecked on the Roches du Desespoir. The Ile du Cimetière is known for its ancient tombs, and on all the coasts remains are still to be found which bear witness to wrecks and chance landings.

In 1894 the brothers Henri and René Bossière obtained a concession for the exploitation of Kerguelen Island. Various attempts at colonization were made, but none were successful. An attempt at sheep-breeding at Port Couvreux made by Pierre Decouz and the Valais guide Valérien Culet, and the occupation of the same station after the Great War, came to nothing. The "Kerguelen Whaling and Sealing Co."

set up the important station of Port Jeanne d'Arc in 1908. It ceased its activities about 1929, as did all concerns similarly engaged, in consequence of the economic crisis. Today the only whaling in these inhospitable waters is done by large cold storage vessels surrounded by modern Japanese and Soviet Russian whaling ships, and not for the oil or the hard strips, but for the whale-meat.

It may be noted that the German scientific cruising ships were followed, in the two world wars, by raiders. In the last war it was from Kerguelen Island that the *Atlantis*, *Pinguin* and most notably the famous *Komet* set out on their raids in the southern seas and down to the borders of the Antarctic.

French sovereignty, reaffirmed in 1893 by the visit of the sloop *Eure*, was renewed by the visits of the *Antare*'s in 1931 and the *Bougainville* in 1939.

Before describing the recent period from 1949 onwards, let us describe this curious island.

Kerguelen Island, consisting of a principal island and a multitude of islets, all volcanic, is a little smaller than Corsica, with an area of about 2,800 square miles. It is deeply indented by valleys and fjords. The coasts are wild and inhospitable. The mountain-tops, many of which are over 3,000 feet high, are almost always covered by cloud. This is true of the highest mountain in the island, Mont Ross, which is over 6,000 feet high and awaits a party of intrepid climbers to conquer its summit. Mont Ross is covered with ice, as is more than a sixth of the island. The Cook Glacier is a strange ice-cap with an area of 280 square miles and rising only to about 3,600 feet. These contrasts are due to the climate of the island, a consequence of its geographical position.

Nineteen hundred miles from Africa and Australia, and 1,250 miles from the Antarctic, Kerguelen Island is a speck in the middle of the South Indian Ocean, at a latitude the same as that of France. But if these latitudes, between 40° and 50° South, are called by navigators the "roaring forties", it is because they are subject all the year round to the passage of depressions bringing cold air from the Antarctic. Moreover, in this latitude we are already south of the sub-Antarctic convergence, which means that the sea water is already cold, with an annual mean temperature of 4°C: hence rain, fog and continual low cloud.

The climate is maritime with a heavy rainfall, the winter is mild (minimum temp. − 10°C) and the summer not hot (maximum 20°C). The annual mean temperature is 4°C, so that the water and the soil are never completely frozen in winter, and in summer it can snow one day and be hot the next. It is the country of wind and wing-less flies. The annual mean wind force can be estimated at 22 m.p.h. A severe gale passes over Kerguelen roughly every three days. In January 1963, i.e. in the middle of the Australian summer, there were twenty-nine days with winds of over 37 m.p.h., twenty days with winds of over 56 m.p.h., and a maximum wind force of 137 m.p.h.

It is easy to understand that today there is not a single tree on Kerguelen Island. In consequence of the barometric instability the depressions often lower the temperature and torrents of rain fall, in the form of snow or hail on the high ground. The rainfall is an much as 40 inches in the east and 120 inches in the west, so that the glaciers and ice-fields receive substantial nourishment. Nonetheless the glaciers are receding markedly, about a mile and a quarter since the end of the last century.

The plains and low slopes are carpeted with a curious umbelliferous plant — *Azorella selago* — and a creeping rosaceous plant — *Acæna adscendus*. The peculiar Kerguelen cabbage (*Pringlea antiscorbutica*), which is disappearing, should also be mentioned. It hardly exists now except in the west and in certain islands not yet reached by the rabbit. An English captain introduced the rabbit in 1874 with the object of assuring the substenance of shipwrecked mariners, and now it abounds to such an extent that everything is being destroyed. An attempt to introduce myxomatosis failed for want of carriers of the disease, namely lice; it has not yet been possible to introduce these parasites to make war on the rabbits.

Apart from all this, the place is truly the isle of desolation which the navigator Cook called it. Marine life, however, is intense, with huge seaweeds and plankton in great density. This explains the aspect of a natural zoo which the island bears, if only at certain privileged spots: seabirds of all kinds, penguins and sea elephants, whales, grampus and dolphins, rare fur seals and sea leopards.

The penguins, assembled in vast colonies, are the curiosity of the island. Two species predominate. First there is the macaroni penguin (*Eudyptes Chrysolophus*), a comical, lively little penguin whose head is adorned with magnificent yellow feathers which give it a humorous expression. The penguinries on the northern coast of the Courbet peninsula, spread in several compact groups over a distance of fifteen miles, contain about 500,000 birds. An equal number inhabit the immense penguinry on the south-west point of the island. There are also the King Penguins (*Aptenodytes patagonicus*) which are as much as 3 feet tall. Grave and dignified in their white and blue-grey dress, their necks adorned with a princely yellow, they are assembled in one great penguinry and two small ones on the east coast of the island. Their total number is estimated at 33,000.

At the present time, about a quarter of the world's whaling (about 300 vessels) is carried on in the waters of Kerguelen Island. The numbers of the sea elephants (*Mircunga leoniad*) were sadly reduced by bloody assaults between 1800 and 1930. They have been hunted for their fat, from which oil has been extracted, and in 1929 alone 40,000 were killed on the coasts of Kerguelen Island. Since then their numbers have increased again, and it is estimated that about 250,000 appear on the coasts between September and November of each year. As for the sea lions, exploited for their fur in ancient times, they disappeared long ago.

A new period began at the end of 1949, when the first French Overseas Mission, headed by Pierre Sicaud, landed on Kerguelen Island. The base, Port-aux-Français, was set up in the Baie du Morbihan. The island has really come into its own through the development of scientific research in connection with the International Geophysical Year. Today, under the direction of an administrator of the Territoire des Terres Australes et Antarctiques Françaises, about eighty research workers and technicians, in a year's stay in the island, carry out meteorological observations, measurements of cosmic rays, atmospherics, ozone, auroras, ionospheric soundings, the registering of slow and swift magnetism, and seismological activity. In the course of the annual relief, thirty additional scientists and technicians, in the short summer campaign, carry out biological, geological and glaciological observations.

Through the employment of Alouette helicopters, used for the first time in 1962, the whole of the island, still unknown in detail, has been reconnoitred. A triangulation has been effected, and in 1963 the first vertical photographs were taken. It seems, therefore, that an exact map of the island will at last be available. The season of exploration has definitely closed with the summit of Mont Ross still inviolate.

It should be noted that a permanent base exists at New Amsterdam, and that after two reconnaissances a similar base will be established at the end of 1963 on the Ile de la Possession (Crozet Archipelago.)

If exploration is completed, adventure still exists. The cruise of the 29-ton cutter *Mischief* is a testimony to this. Colonel H. W. Tilman, former pilot of a Bristol aeroplane constructed in 1906, and well-known to climbers and explorers, sailed from England in the *Mischief* with three companions at the end of July 1959, and reached the Ile de la Possession at the beginning of January 1960. He explored the mountains of this island for the first time and landed on Kerguelen Island at the end of the month. With one of his companions, Colonel Tilman journeyed for twelve miles to reach the centre of the Cook Glacier, the great ice-cap which covers the western part of the island. After this achievement and a visit to the Port-aux-Français base, the *Mischief* reached England again at the end of June 1960, having thus repeated the navigation feat of the brothers Rallier du Baty in 1908. Nor did Colonel Tilman, as a perfect sportsman, fail to transmit to his senior, Raymond Rallier du Baty, who lives on the Lorient roadstead from which the ships of the Compagnie des Indes used to sail, a message of remembrance from the Australasian islands.

INVESTIGATIONS OF THE OHIO RANGE, ANTARCTICA

By William E. Long

EDITORIAL FOREWORD

In October 1962 the Swiss, Emil Schulthess, was informed by Washington that the "U.S. Board on Geographic Names" had given Point 84° 47′ south by 115° west in the Ohio Range (Antarctic) the name *Schulthess Buttress*.

In 1958 Emil Schulthess had been invited by the U.S. Navy to take part as photographer in the "Operations Deep Freeze IV" which formed part of the Antarctic exploratory work during the International Geophysical Year.[1] In the course of his stay of several months in the Antarctic he accompanied the "Byrd Traverse Party" for some weeks. This party, consisting of six American scientists under the leadership of Dr Charles R. Bentley, had the task of carrying out geological, glaciological, meteorological, seismological and carto-graphical investigations for three months on a route planned in advance in the hitherto unvisited regions of Marie Byrd Land. The "Byrd Traverse Party", consisting of three tracked vehicles (Snow-cats) towing transport sledges, were visited by an aeroplane every seven to ten days during this journey and supplied with the necessary fuel and other material. The supply plane was four times compelled to turn back by engine troubles, failure of wireless communications and a particularly bad patch of weather, which made it impossible to find and visit the Byrd Traverse Party. Fuel for the vehicles ran out, the heating system in the Snow-cats, connected with the engines, had to be rationed, and a stop had to be made at Camp 414. Camp 414 lay only two miles from the northern foot of the Horlick Mountains, so that for the first time the party pitched camp in the immediate neighbourhood of a mountain. It used the compulsory halt to make a first ascent of the mountain situated opposite the camp (now called Mt Glossopteris). The leader of the expedition was William E. Long, geologist and glaciologist at the Institute of Polar Studies of the Ohio State University, who is the author of the following report. The party brought back with them geological finds of the greatest scientific value.

After the return of the "Byrd Traverse Party" the authoritative institutions determined to explore the Horlick Mountains (now the Ohio Range) more thoroughly in the course of two further Polar summers with William E. Long as leader.

Prior to the International Geophysical Year, the Horlick Mountains were shown on

---

[1] The photographs taken by him in this capacity have been published in the collection of pictures entitled *Antarctica* (Collins, London, and Simon & Schuster, New York.)

the maps of Antarctica only as a broad and poorly defined area. One of the important tasks of the 1958–59 Byrd Land oversnow exploration programme was to map and make preliminary geological studies of the Horlick Mountains.

In October of 1958 a reconnaissance plane, carrying as passengers Major Dawson, Dr Charles Bentley, traverse leader, William E. Long, glaciologist–geologist, and Emil Schulthess, Swiss photographer, approached the individual ranges of the Horlick Mountains. No one had ever seen these mountains that closely before. Even from the aeroplane the layered nature of the rocks of one of the ranges (later called the Ohio Range) indicated that several thousand feet of sedimentary rocks were present. Sedimentary rocks are particularly valuable for interpretation of geological history.

Two months after the reconnaissance flight the 1958–59 Byrd Traverse party approached the Ohio Range on the surface. The traverse party consisted of Dr C. R. Bentley, seismologist and leader, Leonard LeShack, assistant seismologist, Jack Long, mechanic, Emil Schulthess, photographer, William Chapman, cartographer, William E. Long, glaciologist–geologist, and Fred Darling, assistant glaciologist. In December the three Snow-cat vehicles established Camp 414 within two miles of the cliffs which form the northern escarpment of the Ohio Range. A portion of these cliffs in the centre of the range is now known as the Schulthess Escarpment.

Time was limited, so that only one geological collecting trip was made in 1958. During this trip four men ascended the mountain which is now called Mt Glossopteris (named for the fossil leaves which were found in shales about 3,000 feet above the foot of the mountain). Although the party ascended the mountain only once, several scientifically valuable discoveries resulted. The discoveries made that day included:

1. The first marine Lower Devonian fossils and rocks known in Antarctica.
2. A thick tillite sequence.
3. Thick coal beds and profuse fossil leaves and wood.

These discoveries kindled a driving desire to study the details of the geology of this range of mountains. From this initial reconnaissance there was only enough material gathered to give a very general idea of the types of rocks which were present and their relationship to each other. Much time would be needed to work out the details of the geology.

The Marie Byrd Land oversnow traverse later departed from the Ohio Range to continue with the more routine studies of glaciology and seismology.

The 1960–61 and 1961–62 Seasons

In 1960 a party of four men from the Ohio State University Institute of Polar Studies formed a geological expedition and spent the Antarctic summer doing field work in the Ohio Range and during the 1961–62 season a five to eight man party was in the field to continue the study. Food, equipment and men reached the Ohio Range on ski-equipped aircraft. A small Jamesway hut was built on a plateau called the Buckeye Table at an elevation of 2,400 metres and was called Camp Ohio. From Camp Ohio the party travelled on motor toboggans to reach the mountain slopes where rocks were exposed.

In the 1960–61 season nearly all the effort in the field was concentrated on the eastern end of the range, and during the 1961–62 season the entire range was studied. The results of these two season's field investigations are nearing completion and will be published by the United States Antarctic Programs office of the National Science Foundation late in 1963.

The field geologic studies during two years of investigation have shown that the Ohio Range is probably a faulted-block mountain which is composed of nearly flat sedimentary rock strata lying on a granitic basement complex. The relief of the range is greater than 1,250 metres, from a plateau-level of about 1,500 metres on the north to the summit of Mt Schopf which is 2,990 metres high. The range is about 40 km long and 8 km wide and is surrounded by a nearly flat surface of inland ice. The polar plateau is to the south and the Marie Byrd Land Plateau to the north.

About 1,200 metres of nearly horizontal sedimentary rocks have been divided into four geologic formations. (Formations are mappable units of rock.) The sedimentary formations rest upon an ancient erosion surface which was cut into the gigantic rocks. These old granites are referred to now as basement rocks.

The lowermost sedimentary rock formation is called the Horlick formation and it contains sandstones and shales with several beds of fossils. The fossils are marine shell-fish and indicate that this was a beach area at the time the fossils were living. The fossils populated this beach during the Lower Devonian period, or about 380 million years ago.

A very interesting formation called the Buckeye tillite lies above the Horlick formation. The contact between the two units is a smooth pavement which deeply cuts the Horlick formation and indicates glacial erosion. The tillite is the result of glacial deposition and is up to 300 metres thick. Thin layers of sandstone within the Buckeye tillite were formed during glacial recessions. This tillite indicates that glacial conditions existed at the site which is now the Ohio Range, but the time which the glaciers were present is uncertain due to the absence of fossil material. A clue to the age of the Buckeye tillite was found by Dr J. M. Schopf of the U.S. Geological Survey, who has identified spores and pollen grains of Permian age (or about 250 million years ago) from shales associated with the tillite.

Over the Buckeye tillite rests a 200-metre-thick unit of black shales which is called the Discovery Ridge formation. As yet no definitive fossil material has been found

223

in the Discovery Ridge formation, although numerous tracks are found in some of the platy shales.

The highest and youngest sedimentary rock unit of the Ohio Range is called the Mt Glossopteris formation. The Mt Glossopteris formation is composed of about 650 metres of interbedded sandstone, shales and coals. Fossil wood is commonly found in sandstones and may be in an upright position, indicating that trees grew in the area. The fossil leaf *Glossopteris* is very abundant in many of the shale beds. Other fossil stems and leaves are also present. Fossil evidence indicates that the Mt Glossopteris formation was deposited during middle to late Permian time (or about 230–250 million years ago).

Coal beds are common in the Mt Glossopteris formation and range from a few cm to 36.5 cm in thickness. The coal is a semi-anthracite with a high ash or impurity content. In order to obtain a less-weathered sample of coal, the Ohio State University party dug the "Dirty Diamond Coal Mine" during the 1961–62 season.

The conditions under which profuse *Glossopteris* grew and coal-forming peat bogs existed were greatly different from the cold, glacial times indicated by the Buckeye tillite below.

The youngest rock in the Ohio Range is a diabasic igneous rock which was injected as a molten magma between sedimentary rock layers. This intrusion of diabasic material probably occurred during lower Jurassic time or about 150 million years ago. Diabase is a hard, resistant rock and today forms the flat summit area of Mt Schopf. Erosion during the last million years or more has removed all higher and younger rocks from the Ohio Range so evidence for geologic history later than the diabase sills is absent.

The geologic history indicated by the rocks of the Ohio Range starts with the granitic basement rocks. They were uplifted to form part of a continental area. A long period of erosion gradually reduced the granitic continental area to a low, rolling surface. During Lower Devonian time seas began to invade the region of the Ohio Range leaving the sands and shales of the Horlick formation. After the time of the Lower Devonian seas a gap in the geologic record exists up to the time of glaciation. Glacial erosion removed the sedimentary strata which used to be above the Horlick formation.

Glaciers covered the area probably during early Permian time. The ice fluctuated in a manner which may be similar to ice advance and retreat of Pleistocene time. Following glaciation the area was again submerged and the shales of the Discovery Ridge formation were deposited.

General lowering of sea level or uplift of the continent followed and the Mt Glossopteris sandstones, shales and coals were deposited. During this time (Permian) the area was above sea level and streams deposited much of the sand and shale while plant material accumulated in peat bogs. The duration of plant-growing and coal-forming conditions is not known, but it probably continued into Triassic time (225 million years ago).

The geology of the Ohio Range tells the history of the earth's crust for only one small area in Antarctica, but this little range of mountains has provided a large amount of geologic data. When one compares the geology of the Ohio Range with the geology of other localities in Antarctica some regional relationships can be identified.

Coal measures, which are represented in the Ohio Range by the Mt Glossopteris formation, have been found at many widely separated localities in Antarctica. The coal measures of Permian age appear to be one of the most widespread sedimentary rock units. They are recognized all along the Transantarctic Mountains which extend from the west side of the Ross Sea to the east side of the Weddell Sea.

Prior to the discovery of tillite in the Ohio Range, no tillite was known on the continent. Since 1961, however, a few other tillites have been located in Antarctica and at least one of these newer discoveries is of about the same age as the Buckeye tillite.

Upper Devonian fossils have been found elsewhere in Antarctica but no other area on the continent with Lower Devonian fossils is known. This indicates that the Lower Devonian unit may be of restricted extent.

Diabase sills are common throughout the Transantarctic Mountains and elsewhere in Antarctica.

The whole sequence of sedimentary strata are remarkably similar to stratigraphic sequences in other continents of the southern hemisphere. Perhaps the best known of the southern continents is South Africa. Rock and fossil similarities between the Ohio Range specimens and those of South Africa are striking. Such similarities between Australia, India, Madagascar, and parts of South America have given strength to arguments that the southern continents once were joined in a single large continent called Gondwana. This continent fractured and the pieces drifted apart to form the pattern present today.

Because Antarctica is one of the important continents involved in this theory, the stratigraphic successions have added interest and meaning to the geologists of the world. When geologists have worked out relationships for the rocks of this single continent they can then use their findings to understand larger, more world-wide, geologic questions such as the continental drift hypothesis.

CHRONOLOGY OF HIMALAYAN EXPEDITIONS
1960-62

By Anders Bolinder

The chronology is arranged geographically for each year, in fact from southeast to northwest (including, for the time being, the Pamirs and Hindukush).

Hints and further information will be gratefully received. I am especially grateful to Professor G. O. Dyhrenfurth for his much valued help in the work so far.

Abbreviations: AAJ = *The American Alpine Journal*
                  AJ = *The Alpine Journal*
                  Alpen = *Die Alpen*, monthly journal of the Swiss Alpine Club
                  Alpen-Q = *Die Alpen*, quarterly journal of the Swiss Alpine Club
                  Bergsteiger = *Der Bergsteiger*, journal of the Austrian Alpine Club
                  BK = *Der Bergkamerad*, München
                  BW = *Berge der Welt*
                  HC = *The Himalayan Club*
                  HJ = *The Himalayan Journal*
                  Mitt. DAV = *Mitteilungen des Deutschen Alpenvereins*
                                              (German Alpine Club)
                  Montagne = *La Montagne*, journal of the French Alpine Club
                  MM = *Montagnes du Monde*
                  MW = *The Mountain World*
                  NG = *National Geographic*, journal of the National Geographic Society
                  NZZ = *Neue Zürcher Zeitung*
                  ÖAZ = *Österreichische Alpenzeitung*
                  RM = *Revista Mensile* del CAI (Italian Alpine Club)
                  Sangaku = *Sangaku*, journal of the Japanese Alpine Club
                  Taternik = *Taternik*, journal of the Polish Climbing Club

N = north, E = east, S = south, W = west, Gl. = glacier
P. = point (summital), m = metre, ′ = feet, 1′ = 0·305m
1 m = 3·281′
C = Camp

Italics denote new explorations and ascents (with heights)

Date	Expedition Leader	Region or Massif	Principal Results	Source
1960 IX–X	H. V. R. Iengar	Sikkim NE	Kangchengyao (6890m); Reconnaissance and attempt from the NE 6250m	HJ, XXII (1959–60), 75–83
III–V	Gyan Singh (First Indian Everest Exp.)	Nepal E Chomolungma	Mount Everest (8848m) via Khumbu and South Col—8625m	HJ, XXII (1959–60), 3–12 AJ, May 1961, 15–27 Singh: *The Lure of Everest*
III–V	Shih Chan-Chun (Chinese Mountaineering Exp.)	Nepal E Chomolungma	Mount Everest (8848m) from the N via Rongphu and Chang La-ca. 850m (certain height); *Climb by night to 8848m*	AJ, May 1961, 28–41; Nov 1961, 313–15; Nov 1962, 310–12; May 1963, 48–51; HJ, XXIII (1961), 151–68; Alpen 1961, 42–46, 142–43
IX–XII	Hillary & Pugh (Himalayan Scientific and Mountaineering Exp.)	Nepal E Rolwaling & Khumbu Himal	*Yeti-search:* unsuccessful track and scalp investigation. *Erection of the "Green Hut"* (5300m) *and "Silver Hut"* (5723m) *in the Mingbo Valley.* P.ca. 6100m E Ngojumba-Gl.; *Pumo Dablam* (6375m)	HJ, XXII (1959–60), 141–45; AJ, Nov 1961, 343–64; National Geographic, Oct 1962, 503–47; Hillary-Doig: *High in the Thin Cold Air*
X	R. Sandoz (French Exp.)	Nepal E Rolwaling Himal	Pigferago (6620m); Reconnaissance of Chobutse (6665m); Pimu (6348m), Singkar (6288m) and Parchamo (6318m), 2nd ascent	Montagne 1961, 130–36
IV–VI	P. J. Wallace	Nepal C Ganesh Himal	*Ganesh Peak E (ca. 7390m)*	HJ, XXII (1959–60), 113–17
IV–V	J. Yamada (Keoi University Exp.)	Nepal C Gurkha Himal	*Himal Chuli (7864m)*	HC-Newsletter 17; AJ, Nov 1960, 246

Date	Expedition Leader	Region or Massif	Principal Results	Source
III–V	J. O. M. Roberts (British–Indian–Nepalese Services' Himalayan Exp.)	Nepal C	Annapurna II (7937m); Annapurna IV (7524m), 3rd & 4th ascents	HJ, XXII (1959–60), 22–30; AJ, Nov 1960, 143–50; Grant: Annapurna II
IV–V	Max Eiselin (Swiss Exp.)	Nepal W	Dhaulagiri (8222m) via NE-Spur, 1st & 2nd ascent; Dapa Peak (ca. 5980m)	Alpen 1961, 42–49; ÖAZ 1961, 64–75; BW, XIII, 128–38: HJ, XXII, 38–50; Eiselin: Erfolg am Dhaulagiri; AJ, Nov 1961, 396–99
IV–V	Y. Tsuda (Kyoto University Exp.)	Nepal W	Api (7132m); First definite ascent	HC–Newsletter 17
VI	Gurdial Singh (Indian Exp.)	Garhwal E	Devistan (6678m)–5500m	HJ, XXIII (1961), 138–47
V–VI	S. Kersnic (Jugoslavian Exp.)	Garhwal E	Trisul II (6690m); Trisul III (6140m); Baroltoli (5275m), 2nd ascent	HJ, XXII (1959–60), 70–74; Mitt. DAV, 1960, 178–79; BK, 1959/60, 644
	Calcutta Exp.	Garhwal E	Nanda Ghunti (6309m), 2nd ascent	HJ, XXII (1959–60), 175; HC–Newsletter 18
IX	S. Hosokawa (Japan Ladies' AC Exp.)	Punjab (Kulu)	Deo Tibba (6001m), 4th ascent	HC–Newsletter 18; Sangaku 1961, 9–10
	Calcutta University Exp.	Punjab (Lahul)	Gangstang (6163m)—reconnaissance	HJ, XXII (1959–60), 175; HC–Newsletter 18
V–VIII	P. J. Stephenson (Saltoro Exp.)	Karakorum (Saltoro range)	Exploration and topography between Bilafond and Lower Siachen–Gl.; reconnaissance and attempt K-12 (7468m)–7000m; Topography Chumik & Gyong-Gl.	AJ, May 1961, 147–50; HJ, XXIII (1961), 71–79

Date	Expedition Leader	Region or Massif	Principal Results	Source
VIII–IX	Michael Anderl (International Kondus Exp.)	Karakorum (Saltoro range)	*"Mount Depak"* (ca. 7150m); *Silver Throne* (ca. 6900m)	BK, 1959/60, 715–16, 824; 1961/62, 161;
VI–VIII	W. D. Hackett (German–American KK-Exp.)	Karakorum (Baltoro)	K-2 (8611m)–7260m	Mitt. DAV, 1960, 168–69; BK, 1959/60, 456–57, 825–26
V–VII	G. I. Bell (American–Pakistan KK-Exp.)	Karakorum (Baltoro)	*Masherbrum* (7821m)	HJ, XXII (1959–60), 51–69
V–VI	W. Stefan (Austrian KK-Exp.)	Karakorum (Hispar)	*Distaghil Sar* (7885m)	ÖAZ, 1961, 44–63; HJ, XXII (1959–60), 122–33; BK, 1961/62, 435–40
VII–VIII	Wilfrid Noyce (Anglo–American KK-Exp.)	Karakorum (Hispar)	*Trivor* (7733m)	HJ, XXII (1959–60), 134–40; AJ, May 1961, 9–15; Noyce: *To the Unknown Mountain*; BW XIII, 139–55
VII	Durrani & Khurshid	Karakorum (Hunza)	Dobani (6143m)–5200m	AJ, May 1962, 42; Nov 1962, 38r
X	E. J. E. Mills	Hindukush E (Swat Kohistan)	Reconnaissance Falak Sar (5918m) from the SW & Paloga Pass	AJ, May 1962, 42–44
VII–IX	Y. Sakato (Academic AC of Kyoto Exp.)	Hindukush NE	*Noshaq* (7492m); biological and geological research	HJ, XXII (1959–60), 153–57; BK, 1960/61, 466; AAJ, 1961, 277–88
VII–IX	B. Chwaściński (First Polish HK-Exp.)	Hindukush NE	Noshaq (7492m), 2nd ascent; *Asp-e-Safed* (ca. 6450m); *Khor-pusht-e-Yakhi* (5698m); *Rach-e-Daros* (ca. 5695m); Gunbaz-e-Safed (ca. 6800m), attempt to 6300m; mapping	AJ, Nov 1961, 235–49; Taternik 1962, 87–171; RM, 1961, 282–89

Date	Expedition Leader	Region or Massif	Principal Results	Source
VIII–X	Deutsche HK–Kundfahrt (Sekt. Berlin, DAV)	Hindukush C (Badakhshan)	*Koh-i-Bandakor (6660m)*; 7 summits over 5000m in the upper Pagar valley, Anjuman region; geographical research	BK, 1960/61, 407–11; 1962/63, 387, 449; Mitt. DAV, 1961, 7–9; Bergsteiger 1960/61, 146–53
VIII–IX	Abinger (Afghanistan Exp.)	Hindukush C (Nuristan)	Mir Samir (6060m)–5000m	AJ, May 1961, 139–40
V–VI	Pai Chin–Hsiao (Peking Geological Inst. Exp.)	Chishih Shan (Tsinghai, West China)	*Amne Machin (7160m)*	AJ, Nov 1961, 274–83
1961				
IX–X	Sonam Gyatso (Indian Exp.)	Sikkim NE	*Yulhekang (6429m)*; *Chombu (6362m)*; Kangchengyao (6889m), 2nd ascent	HJ, XXIII (1961), 169–70
III–IV	R. O. Lee	Sikkim W	Talung (7349m), reconnaissance	Alpen-Q 1962, 107
I–VI	Pugh, Ward & Hillary (Himalayan Scientific & Mountaineering Exp.)	Nepal E Khumbu Himal	High level physiological research up to 7770m; photogrammatric map of the upper Mingbo valley and Ama Dablam; *Ama Dablam (6856m), SW ridge*; Makalu (8481m), attempt without oxygen to 8350m!	HJ, XXIII (1961), 30–46; AJ, Nov 1961, 343–04; May 1963, 11–19 & 151–53; NG, Oct 1962, 503–47; Hillary–Doig; *High in the Thin Cold Air*
XI–XII	J. S. Keen (British Army Exp.)	Nepal E Khumbu Himal	Mingbo Peak (ca. 6100m), attempt as far as *ca. 5950m*	HJ, XXIII (1961), 133–37
IV–V	J. Walmsley (British Exp.)	Nepal E Chomolungma	*Nuptse (7879m)*	HJ, XXIII (1961), 3–15; AJ, Nov 1961, 209–34

231

Date	Expedition Leader	Region or Massif	Principal Results	Source
XII/60 –II	Erwin Schneider (Nepal Him. Research Scheme)	Nepal E	Preliminary cartographic work S Rolwaling Himal	Mitt. DAV, 1960, 203–204; BK, 1959/60, 825
	H. Janetschek (Nepal Him. Research Scheme)	Nepal E	Biological investigations S Chomolungma–Massif (Taboche–Dudh Kosi–Ama Dablam section)	Mitt. DAV, 1961, 186–87; BK, 1961/62, 61–62
IV–VII IX–I/62	Erwin Schneider (Nepal Him. Research Scheme)	Nepal E	Photogrammetric survey of the whole Khumbu region	Mitt. DAV, 1961, 186–87; BK, 1961/62, 61–62, 204–05
XI–XII	Gert Mehl (Film-Exp.)	Nepal E Chomolungma	Film of Sherpa work at great heights	BK, 1961/62, 278 & 422
IX–X	Jan Boon (with 2 Sherpas)	Nepal E Khumbu Himal	Fixing of a memorial tablet (Cho Oyu Women's Exp. 1959) on the ridge summit ca. 5800m east of Cho Oyu (8189m)	BK, 1961/62, 211 & 707; Alpen 1962, 45
IV–V	Jan Boon (alone)	Nepal E & C	Five months in the Nepal–Tibet frontier region: ethnological studies (Sherpa life) and climbing.	BK, 1961/62, 707
IV–V	T. Kajimoto (Japanese Exp.)	Nepal E Jugal Himal	Lönpo Gang (7083m)–7050m; = "Big White Peak"	HJ, XXIII (1961), 192
IV–V	K. Morimoto † (Osaka City University Exp.)	Nepal E Langtrang Himal	Gangchhen Ledrub (7245m)–6200m; avalanche disaster C III: † Gyaltsen Norbu (HC Nr. 145)	HC–Newsletter 18; HJ, XXIII (1961), 192; NZZ, 23 May 1961
IV–V	G. Shinoda (Osaka University Exp.)	Nepal C Gurkha Himal	Peak 29 "Dakura" (7835m), re-connaissance and attempt	HC–Newsletter 18; HJ, XXIII (1961), 192

61 SCHULTHESS BUTTRESS in the Ohio Ranges, earlier known as the Horlick Mountains, in the Antarctic. The cliffs, which drop off to the north, border the southern Polar Plateau. The plateau has an average elevation of 10,000 feet. The distance to the South Pole is about 350 miles. (Photograph courtesy of the U.S. Navy)

62/63 FOUR MEN OF THE AMERICAN "BYRD TRAVERSE PARTY" on their ascent to the Schulthess Buttress.
In the rear right is Mount Glossopteris. (Photograph by William E. Long)

64 top: FOSSIL SHELLS from Mount Glossopteris. From the occurrence of these shells one can conclude that the Devonian Sea once covered this part of the antarctic continent.

bottom: A PART OF A FOSSILIZED TREE TRUNK from the Glossopteris flora with plainly visible annual rings. (Photographs by Emil Schulthess)

Date	Expedition Leader	Region or Massif	Principal Results	Source
IV–V	M. S. Kohli (Indian Services Exp.)	Nepal C Annapurna Himal	*Annapurna III (7577m)*	HC–Newsletter 18; HJ, XXIII (1961), 192
	F. Stammberger (alone)	Nepal C Annapurna Himal	Annapurna I (8078m)–6000m	BK, 1961/62, 318
IV–VI	J. B. Tyson (Kanjiroba Himal Exp.)	Nepal W Patrasi & Sisne Himal	*Topographical survey of Jagdula Khola; Matathumba (ca. 6100m), E "Pasang Peak"; Jagdula Lekh; P. ca. 6400m in Sisne Himal*	AJ, May 1962, 120–129; HJ, XXIII (1961), 89–99
V–VI	Gurdial Singh (Indian Exp.)	Garhwal E	Nanda Devi (7816m)–6700m; Devistan I (6678m); Maiktoli (6802m), 2nd ascent	AJ, Nov 1961, 390;
X	P. Chaudhuri (Indian Exp.)	Garhwal E	*Nanda Khat (6611m)*	HC–Newsletter 18
	J. Nanavati (Indian Exp.)	Garhwal E	Nilgiri Parbat (6474m), attempt to 5950m	HJ, XXIII (1961), 193
VIII–IX	B. Biswas (Calcutta Exp.)	Garhwal E	Mana (7273m)–7100m	HJ, XXIII (1961), 148–50
V–VI	N. Kumar (Indian Exp.)	Garhwal E	*Nilkanta (6596m)* ?	HC–Newsletter 18; AJ, May 1963, 139–41
V–VI	P. Consiglio (Sez. Roma, CAI)	Punjab (Kulu)	*Kulu Makalu "Lal Qila" (6349m)*	RM, 1961, 242; 1962, 333–49; BK, 1961/62, 70
VI–VII	R. Pettigrew (Derbyshire Himalayan Exp.)	Punjab (Kulu)	*Topography Kulu/Bara Shigri;* Deo Tibba (6001m), 5th ascent; Indrasan (6221m)–5975m; "White Sail" or Dharmsura (6446m), 2nd ascent	HJ, XXIII (1961), 110–32; AJ, Nov 1962, 323–31; May 1963, 52–60; BK, 1961/62, 70

Date	Expedition Leader	Region or Massif	Principal Results	Source
VIII–IX	J. P. O'F. Lynam (British Exp.)	Punjab (Lahul)	"Shigri Parbat" (ca. 6645m); cartography of the upper Shigri-Gl.	HJ, XXIII (1961), 56–61
IX–X	Women's Kulu Exp.	Punjab (Lahul)	"Central Peak" (6285m); "Lion" (ca. 6100m); P.20495' (= 6247m)–6230m; topography Bara Shigri E–Gl	HJ, XXIII (1961), 63–70
V–VI	Herrligkoffer (German Exp.)	Kashmir	Nanga Parbat (8125m), attempt on the Diamir Flank–7150m	Bergsteiger 1961/62, 457–61; BK, 1960/61, 267–71, 724–27
IV–VI	E. Waschak (Austrian KK-Exp.)	Karakorum Saltoro range	Mount Ghent (7400m); Silver Throne (ca. 6900m), 2nd ascent	HJ, XXIII (1961), 47–55
VII–VIII	A. J. M. Smyth (R.A.F. KK-Exp.)	Karakorum (Hushi valley)	K–6 (7280m), reconnaissance from the SW–6100m; exploration Aling–Gl; "Hunchback," "Atwa Peak" (6550m) and (6400m)	HJ, XXIII (1961), 80–88
—	F. Knauth (American Exp.)	Karakorum (Baltoro)	Reconnaissance of Paiju (6600m)	HC–Newsletter 18
VII–VIII	W. P. Gamble (Cambridge Exp.)	Karakorum (Hunza)	Glaciological & botanical exploration of the Minapin–Gl.	HJ, XXIII (1961), 16–20
I	E. J. E. Mills	Hindukush (Swat Kohistan)	Khan Shai (ca. 5700m), 2nd ascent (?)	AJ, May 1962, 42–53
—	W. Bartlett (Anglo–American Exp.)	Hindukush (Swat Kohistan)	Attempt on Falak Sar (5918m)	HC–Newsletter 18; HJ, XXIII (1961), 194

Date	Expedition Leader	Region or Massif	Principal Results	Source
VII–VIII	Josef Ruf (Bremer (DAV) HK–Kundfahrt)	Hindukush C (Badakhshan)	*Koh-i-Chrebek (ca. 6250m); P.5230m, 4850m and 4600m in the Chrebek valley, S Munjan Pass*	Alpen–Q 1962, 168–79; BK, 1961/62, 100; 1962/63, 388 & 449
VIII–IX	Traunsteiner (DAV) HK–Kundfahrt	Hindukush C (Badakhshan)	*Koh-i-Marchech (ca. 6060m); Shakh-i-Kabud (ca. 6150m); 12 summits over 5000m in the Deh Ambi– and Sharan valley region, Baba-i-Dewana range*	BK, 1961/62, 62 & 274–76; 1962/63, 388–89 & 449; Taternik 1962, 75 & 80
VII–X	A. Desio (Italian Afghanistan Exp.)	Hindukush W Koh-i-Baba E	*"Koh-i-Kol" (5010m); "Koh-i-Shuksi" (ca. 4800m), in the Korkhu valley, NE Afghanistan*	RM, 1962, 54–55; HJ, XXIII (1961), 194
—	Prof. Tamm (Moscow Mountain Club Exp.)	Pamir NW	Peak of Communism (7495m); discovery of documents concerning Kassin's solo ascent in 1959	BK, 1962/63, 450
—	Yuan-yang (Chinese–Tibetan Women's Exp.)	Pamir E (Prov. Sinkiang, China)	Kungur I (7595m), 2nd ascent	RM, 1961, 244; BK, 1961/62, 98
1962 IV	K. S. Rana (Indian Army Himalayan Exp.)	Sikkim SW	*Koktang (6147m)*	HC–Newsletter 18; HJ, XXIII (1961), 195
III–V	Lionel Terray (French Exp.)	Nepal E	*Jannu (7710m)*	Montagne 1962, 267–87; HC–Newsletter 19; BK, 1962/63, 471–72
V–VI	Sasuke Nakao (Osaka University Exp.)	Nepal E	*Nupchu (7028m)*	HC–Newsletter 19

Date	Expedition Leader	Region or Massif	Principal Results	Source
X/61–III	Ingles (British Museum Scientific Exp.)	Nepal E	Botanical research in the Taplejung region	HJ, XXIII (1961), 194
V–VI	Seiki Nakano (Hokkaido University Exp.)	Nepal E	*Chamlang (7317m)*	HC-Newsletter 19
III–VI	John Dias (Second Indian Everest Exp.)	Nepal E Chomolungma	Mount Everest (8848m) via Khumbu and South Col—8720m	AJ, May 1963, 1–10; HC-Newsletter 19
IV–VI	W. W. Sayre	Nepal E Chomolungma	Mount Everest (8848m) via Nup La, Rongphu E and Chang La—7500m (?)	Alpen 1963, 63–64; LIFE–International, 1963, March 25, p. 74–86; Bergsteiger 1962/63, 612–13
III–V	Gerhard Lenser (German–Swiss Nep.–Him. Exp.)	Nepal E	*Pumo Ri (7145m)*; Pumori La (6150m) *from the SSE*	Alpen 1962, 177–78; BK, 1961/62, 708–10; Lenser: *Pumo Ri*
III–X	Diesselhorst (Nepal Him. Research Scheme)	Nepal E	Biological research in the Terai up to 5000–6000m in Khumbu	Bergsteiger 1961/62, 597–600
X–XII	Erwin Schneider (Nepal Him. Research Scheme)	Nepal E	Cartography in the Rolwaling–Khumbu–Barun and southern valleys	Bergsteiger 1962/63, 454–55; HC-Newsletter 19
—	Sthapit & Bahadur (Nepalese Exp.)	Nepal E	P.21000' = ca. 6400m at the Tashi Lapcha (Parchamo 6318m ?)	HC-Newsletter 19; HJ, XXIII (1961), 195

Date	Expedition Leader	Region or Massif	Principal Results	Source
IV–V	A. Takahashi (Japanese Exp.)	Nepal E Jugal Himal	Lönpo Gang (7083m) = "Big White Peak"	HC–Newsletter 19; BK, 1962/63, 473
	Glentworth	Nepal E	Reconnaissance of Langtrang Himal: Pass N of Hagen's Col; P. ca. 20000' = 6100m	HC–Newsletter 19
IX–XI	K. G. Egeler & Lionel Terray	Nepal C Annapurna–Himal	Nilgiri N Peak (7032m); geological research in the Annapurna region	AJ, May 1963, 139; Montagne 1962, 340; BK, 1962/63, 474
IX–X	J. O. M. Roberts	Nepal W Dhaulagiri–Himal	Dhaulagiri IV (7640m), reconnaissance to 6100m; "Sharksfin" (ca. 6400m)	HC–Newsletter 19 & 20
IX–X	South Korean Expedition	Nepal W Dhaulagiri–Himal	Attempt on Dhaulagiri II (7750m)	HC–Newsletter 19 & 20
IV–V	S. Ishizaka (Nihon University Exp.)	Nepal W Makut Himal	Hongde (6956m); reconnaissance of Churen (7364m) in the Dhaulagiri Himal; Khaniokhal (? m)	HC–Newsletter 19
IV–VI	D. Gravina (British Women's Jagdula Exp.)	Nepal W Kanjiroba Himal	"Pinnacle Peak" (ca. 6550m; poss. = P.6867m ?): Kagmara I, II & III (ca. 6100m)	AJ, May 1963, 65–77
VI	Jagjit Singh (Indian Exp.)	Garhwal E	Nilgiri Parbat (6474m) & Mana (7273m)—attempt; P.6062m (S mana Peak);	HC–Newsletter 20
X	Amulya Sen (Himalayan Ass. of Calcutta Exp.)	Garhwal E	Nilgiri Parbat (6474m), 2nd ascent	HC–Newsletter 20

237

Date	Expedition Leader	Region or Massif	Principal Results	Source
VI	P. S. Bakshi † (Indian Army Mount. Ass. Exp.)	Punjab	Leo Pargiyal (6790m), Reconnaissance to 6460m	HC–Newsletter 19
IX–X	K. Onodera (Kyoto University Exp.)	Punjab (Kulu)	*Indrasan* (6221m); Deo Tibba (6001m), 6th ascent	AJ, May 1963, 123; Bergsteiger 1962/63, 456
V–VI	Herrligkoffer	Kashmir	Nanga Parbat (8125m), 2nd ascent: *1st time via Diamir Flank* (!)	BK, 1961/62, 722–32; Montagne 1962, 308; Mitt. DAV, 1962, 110
VI–VII	T. Shidei (Pakistan–Japan Joint KK Exp.)	Karakorum (Siachen)	*Saltoro Kangri (7742m) = K-36*	AJ, May 1963, 122–23; HC–Newsletter 19
IX/61– IV	K. Hewitt (International Biafo–Gyang Exp.)	Karakorum (Biafo)	Scientific research (climatology, etc.)	HC–Newsletter 18
IV– VIII	G. Furrer (Swiss Biafo–Gyang– Exp.)	Karakorum (Biafo)	Scientific research (botany, morphology, etc.)	HC–Newsletter 19
VII– VIII	A. Desio	Karakorum	Scientific research (geology, etc.) in the Skardu–Gilgit–Hunza region. *Tehri Sar (5050m)*	HC–Newsletter 19; AJ, May 1963, 123
VI–VII	E. J. E. Mills † (British Pakistan Forces KK Exp.)	Karakorum (Hispar)	Khinyang Chish (7852m), *reconnaissance and attempt S-ridge— 6300m*	AJ, May 1963, 100–107; HC–Newsletter 19
VII– VIII	John Hunt (British–Soviet Pamirs Exp.)	Pamir NW	*Peak Cooperation (5640m)*; Peak Patriot (6100m): *1st ascent via the west ridge*; Peak Garmo (6595m), 2nd ascent (?): *1st ascent via W-ridge*; Peak Communism (7495m)	AJ, Nov 1962, 342, 348; AJ, May 1963, 90–99